About the Author

Jonathan Tepperman is the managing editor of *Foreign Affairs*. After growing up in Canada, he studied English at Yale and law at Oxford and New York University. He is a frequent contributor to *The New York Times*, *The Wall Street Journal*, *The Washington Post*, and *The Atlantic*. He lives in Brooklyn with his family.

THE FIX

HOW NATIONS SURVIVE AND THRIVE IN A
WORLD IN DECLINE

JONATHAN TEPPERMAN

BLOOMSBURY

LONDON · OXFORD · NEW YORK · NEW DELHI · SYDNEY

Bloomsbury Paperbacks
An imprint of Bloomsbury Publishing Plc

50 Bedford Square   1385 Broadway
London   New York
WC1B 3DP   NY 10018
UK   USA

www.bloomsbury.com

BLOOMSBURY and the Diana logo are trademarks of Bloomsbury Publishing Plc

First published in Great Britain 2016
This paperback edition first published in 2017

British Library Cataloguing-in-Publication Data
A catalogue record for this book is available from the British Library.

ISBN: HB: 978-1-4088-6653-5
TPB: 978-1-4088-6654-2
PB: 978-1-4088-6655-9
ePub: 978-1-4088-6656-6

2 4 6 8 10 9 7 5 3 1

Text design by Lauren Dong
Printed and bound in Great Britain by CPI Group (UK) Ltd, Croydon CR0 4YY

To find out more about our authors and books visit www.bloomsbury.com.
Here you will find extracts, author interviews, details of forthcoming
events and the option to sign up for our newsletters.

To Alexis, Gerome, and Novi, who were with me from the start.
And to Leo, who joined us by the end.

Politics is the art of looking for trouble, finding it, misdiagnosing it, and then misapplying the wrong remedies.

—GROUCHO MARX

Contents

INTRODUCTION

LEGENDS OF THE FALL

THIS IS A GOOD NEWS BOOK. WHAT FOLLOWS IS A COLLECtion of success stories gathered over several years I spent traveling around the world in search of solutions to the great problems of our day—and the leaders who figured them out. In the ten chapters ahead, I'm going to introduce them to you and take you on a tour of their laboratories, which also happen to be some of the most successful (or at least most interesting) countries on the planet. Along the way, I'll weave in leadership lessons and practical advice on problem solving distilled from their experiences. And I'll make an argument for hope in this time of overpowering gloom. More than anything else, this book is meant as a testament to the power of people to get things done. At a time when most of us have glumly concluded that our governments are broken and our domestic and international problems are insurmountable, I aim to show how the right individuals can overcome the most intimidating obstacles—if they follow the right strategies. This book makes a data-driven case for optimism at a moment of gathering darkness.

Before we can get to the good news, however, we need to start with the bad—as so many other conversations do these days.

We're living, after all, in an era of unprecedented decline—or so, at least, we're constantly being told. Open a newspaper or a magazine, browse the nonfiction titles at your bookstore, or click on cable news, and the black tide can easily overwhelm you.

Welcome, as *The New Yorker*'s George Packer has put it, to the great "unwinding."

Of course, most of us don't need anyone to tell us that things are falling apart; we feel it every day. We hear about terrorists murdering innocents and fear for our own families. We sense the trouble in our gut when we tear open our stubbornly flat paychecks. If you live in a big city like New York, as I do, you feel the dysfunction in the soles of your feet as you rumble homeward, bouncing along pitted roads or jostling for space on overcrowded subways. Once you do make it home, you confront more ill omens when your bills and bank statements arrive; according to a recent study by the Federal Reserve, 47 percent of Americans now have so little in savings that they couldn't cover an emergency outlay of just $400. You're reminded of the problems yet again when your kids walk in the door, having valiantly navigated their underresourced schools. And if they're lucky enough to get into college, you'll confront the troubles one more time when their sky-rocketing tuition comes due. (Don't count on them being able to pay you back, either; unlike previous generations, few young Americans today can reasonably expect to make more money in their lifetimes than their parents did.)

Feeling anxious? If so, you're not alone: 72 percent of Americans still think we are in a recession, and according to a poll taken in December 2016, less than a third of US citizens think their country is headed in the right direction. Such pessimism is not just an American phenomenon either; another recent survey found that only 47 percent of Israelis, 38 percent of Russians, 35 percent of Turks, and 20 percent of Frenchmen expect their economic outlook to improve in the next year. People everywhere are afraid—one reason so many of them, in countries ranging from the United States to Poland to the Philippines, are embracing semi-authoritarian outsiders, populists, and demagogues.

The irony is that not so long ago, the world seemed to be improving at a blistering pace, and experts and politicians were assuring us that the good times were here to stay. Remember the Aughts, that golden age of progress, progress, and more progress? Fueled by innovation, higher education, and a red-hot real-estate market, America's economic engine—the world's mightiest—roared ahead. So did the economies of virtually every other country; during the 1999–2008 boom years, it seemed like your economy was guaranteed to thrive so long as your president or prime minister had a pulse. By the middle of the last decade, emerging markets were growing by an average of more than 7 percent a year, and the developing world had begun to enjoy undreamt-of prosperity. Some 440 million people were lifted out of poverty in just ten years. By 2007, as the emerging-market growth rate hit a scorching 8.7 percent, the global middle class topped 1.8 billion people, and even normally staid economists began declaring that we'd entered an era of "convergence"—a long-prophesied moment when the rest would finally catch up with the wealthy West.

And then came the crash. In September 2008, Lehman Brothers vaporized and the US economy staggered. Soon Europe also caught the bug. Then, like a scene from a zombie movie, the pandemic spread to the developing world. As cash-strapped Westerners stopped buying so many foreign-made smartphones and shoes, factories from Shenzhen to Saigon to San Salvador began shuttering their doors. These closures diminished demand for raw materials—and so the world's commodity superstores also began to sicken. With fewer goods to transport and cost-conscious drivers cutting back on fuel, the hydrocarbon giants started ailing: Russia's economic growth rate, for example, fell from 4.5 percent in 2010 to negative territory in 2015.

As the storm spread throughout the global economy, the geopolitical forecast also darkened. The 2011 Arab Spring was soon snuffed out by icy winds as autocrats reasserted control in Egypt, Bahrain, and elsewhere. Vicious civil wars flared up from one end of the Middle East (Libya) to the other (Yemen). And none burned hotter than the one at its core, in Syria.

Then came the terrible spring and summer of 2014. Beijing stepped up its bullying in the South and East China Seas, positioning oil rigs, building airfields, and stationing troops on disputed coral reefs and narrow strips of sand. Russia surreptitiously sent commandos to join the civil war in eastern Ukraine, and then formally annexed Crimea: Europe's first such brazen land grab since World War II. A formerly obscure offshoot of al-Qaeda known as Daesh or ISIS stormed out of the Syrian badlands and into Iraq. Its fighters erased the 1918 border, seized a third of the country—including Mosul, Iraq's second-biggest city (along with oil fields and hundreds of millions of dollars' worth of US-supplied military equipment)—declared themselves the Islamic

State, and then began beating and beheading Iraqi and Syrian civilians into submission. In West Africa, meanwhile, Boko Haram—another Islamist death cult—slaughtered some ten thousand victims. And a virulent strain of Ebola began to spread through the region, claiming thousands of victims in Liberia, Sierra Leone, Guinea, and elsewhere.

Things were supposed to get better in 2015 and 2016, if only because it was hard to imagine them getting worse. But with very few exceptions they have gotten worse. In January 2015, Islamist terrorists shot up a satirical Paris magazine, *Charlie Hebdo*. Seven years after the Great Recession, economic growth remained lower than the precrisis average in every major region of the world. Greece teetered on the edge of bankruptcy and, by revealing deep schisms within the European Union, threatened to bring down the whole European project. Confronting pollsters, British voters decided to abandon the flailing EU entirely. Populists and right-wing nationalists surged ahead in Italy, France, and Germany—Europe's core.

Meanwhile, IS tightened its grip on its new domain, escalating its atrocities, and then, when it began to lose ground, started lashing out abroad: downing a civilian jet over Sinai in October, hitting Paris again in November, inspiring two Californians to commit mass murder in December, and killing more than thirty innocents in Brussels in March 2016. Iran and Russia increased their meddling in Syria, intensifying the savagery. Saudi Arabia and its Gulf allies blundered into Yemen's civil war, killing thousands of innocents and allowing the local Qaeda franchise to flourish. Millions of desperate refugees fled the region—many headed for Europe, where they produced panic, nativist backlashes, and still more squabbling within the EU. And China's worsening economic woes, along with the worldwide slump in commodity prices, took whatever shine remained off most emerging markets. Apart from India and a few other bright spots, the world seemed to be entering a dismal new era of slow growth. Between 2010 and 2015, the average emerging-market growth rate fell from 7.4 to 3.8 percent. And the whole planet seemed to be sliding toward another crisis.

All these events, in isolation, would have been frightening enough; General Martin Dempsey, a former chairman of the Joint Chiefs of

Staff, captured the prevailing mood well when he called it "the most dangerous time" in his life. Yet what made these episodes even scarier was the way they seemed to expose two more alarming trends. The first was the slow-motion disintegration of Westphalian nation-states in multiple areas of the globe, including the Middle East, the Sahel, and Russia's periphery. Second, many of these incidents seemed to underscore a growing weakness at the heart of the liberal, rules-based global order. That order was established by Washington and its allies after World War II, and was then reinforced and extended at the end of the Cold War. It has brought unparalleled prosperity and peace to the world in the years since. And yet it now seems to face more threats on more fronts than ever before.

I KNOW I told you that this would be a good news book, and I know it doesn't seem like that so far. But bear with me—we'll get to the good news soon. Before we do, however, I need to say a few more things about the unhappy narrative I've just recounted.

One of the basic premises of this book is that while the details of all the troubles currently wracking the world vary, they share an underlying cause: the failure of politicians to do their jobs. More specifically, most of them stem from the failure of our leaders to adequately address ten big problems—roughly half of which are political and half of which are economic—that together represent some of the toughest and most persistent challenges states have faced in the modern era. The inability of most governments to resolve them goes a long way toward explaining the mess we're in today.

These persistent failures have also convinced many analysts that the problems themselves are unsolvable. Voters, in disgust, have turned to radicals and rogues who promise to upend the entire system.

But I think both the fear and the pessimism are misplaced, and in the ten chapters that follow, I'm going to try to prove it to you.

Before I do, however, we should delve a bit deeper into the problems themselves. Doing so will underscore the stakes, which are very high indeed—so high, in fact, that if our leaders keep failing to surmount the challenges I'm about to describe, they'll condemn us all to even more of the hardship and tumult we've experienced lately. They'll also smother the still-fragile economic recovery that the United States and a few other countries are starting to enjoy.

Understanding the problems in depth is also the first step toward understanding their solutions. For this book's second basic premise is that, contrary to what the pessimists argue, all these problems are actually fixable. And not just in theory. The answers are already out there; as the ten following chapters will show, a tiny band of freethinking, often underrated leaders has already managed to defy all odds and expectations and figure them out. I'm going to show you how they did it—each chapter will tell the story of one government and one solution.

But before we get to them, let's look more closely at the problems themselves.

THE TERRIBLE TEN

I. INEQUALITY

Inequality is not a new phenomenon. It is an inevitable by-product of capitalism, one that modern nations have been struggling with for about as long as there have *been* modern nations. But inequality is a good place to start our tour of dysfunction because of the way it has come to define our age, perhaps more than any other challenge discussed in this book—preoccupying politicians, protesters, and ordinary people alike.

Inequality is also a two-headed problem, which makes it doubly difficult to deal with. What I mean is that inequality is both a *consequence* of some of the other challenges on this list and a *cause* of or contributor to many of them. Inequality promotes corruption, perpetuates poverty, sparks popular unrest, heightens xenophobia, deepens personal despondency, and undermines public faith in democracy and free markets. New research suggests that it's even harmful to your health: residents of unequal communities tend to have lower life expectancies than people who live in more equitable ones.

And inequality keeps getting worse. The Organization for Economic Cooperation and Development (OECD) recently predicted that if current trends continue, the global wealth gap will widen by 30 percent over the next five decades. Already the problem is provoking intense anxiety. Even before the French economist Thomas Piketty became a publishing phenomenon in 2014 (it takes a hell of a lot of public concern to turn a dense, seven-hundred-page tome on economics into a bestseller), the unease was rising fast. In the early part of this decade, protesters in New York's Zuccotti Park and at more than nine hundred other Occupy demonstrations around the world underscored the breadth and depth of the discontent. More recently, the unrest has fueled the rise of unconventional politicians ranging from Beppe Grillo to Marine Le Pen, from Bernie Sanders to Donald Trump.

The agitation isn't hard to understand. In the United States, the richest 20 percent of the population now take home half of all annual earnings, and the most affluent 10 percent own more than three-quarters of the nation's wealth. To put it in less abstract terms, America's 25 top hedge-fund managers collectively now earn more than the country's 158,000 kindergarten teachers combined. And the number of Americans living in abject poverty—on $2 or less a day—has doubled in the last two decades. Globally, meanwhile, the fabled 1 percent now control more assets than the rest of the world's population put together.

The answer to all this injustice might seem obvious: we just need to increase economic growth. This strategy worked well in the past; when countries expanded the size of their overall pie, everyone got a bigger slice. That's what happened in the United States in the immediate postwar years, and that's what happened in China after it embraced capitalism in the late 1970s and then pulled more than a quarter of a billion people out of poverty.

More recently, however, the formula has broken down; growth alone no longer seems to work its salubrious magic. During the height of China's 1999–2010 boom, for example, inequality hit unprecedented levels. And something similar has happened in the United States, where precious few Americans have benefited from the country's recent recovery. (Indeed, as noted earlier, three-quarters of Americans don't even know we're in a recovery.) Unemployment may have fallen dramatically, but so have many salaries, especially in service sectors like retail, restaurants, and home health care. Incredible as it sounds, the average American wage (adjusted for inflation) peaked more than four decades ago, in 1973. It's been falling ever since.

According to the economist Robert Reich, the decline in wages has occurred because most of the recent gains in the US economy have been funneled into executive pay, corporate earnings, and the stock market. The US tax system, which heavily favors the rich through its many deductions and loopholes, also hasn't helped.

But there are deeper explanations for the breakdown in the link between growth and equality. These range from globalization to automation to corruption to a shift in developed countries from manufacturing to financial services, an industry that disproportionately benefits the few at the top. (Finance now accounts for 41 percent of all corporate profits in America, but employs only 6 percent of the workforce.) Recent studies have also linked high inequality with low social mobility, which helps explain why the problem is proving so persistent. According to Alan Krueger, a former chairman of the US Council of Economic Advisers, the best predictor today of how much money young people will earn in their lifetime is what their parents made. That's not the way America is supposed to work. But that's the way it now does.

You'd think that all these worrisome trends would have inspired a serious global effort to address them by this point. But for various reasons, there's been little progress. Despite all the evidence to the contrary, most Americans remain convinced that anyone can make it here if he or she works hard enough—and so they resist openly redistributive policies. (The financial services industry also works diligently to block tax reform and other changes.) Europeans, for their part, have traditionally been more open to social engineering—but the austerity forced by the ongoing economic crisis has made it hard for most governments in Europe to maintain their existing safety nets, let alone expand them. As for the developing world, many of the biggest attempts to attack the problem have backfired, resulting in costly boondoggles that only set back the cause even further.

In the absence of progress, the divide between rich and poor keeps growing. And people around the world keep getting angrier.

INTRODUCTION 9

2. IMMIGRATION

In the summer of 2015, the miserable stream of refugees fleeing poverty and chaos in the Middle East and Africa suddenly became a flood—the largest such human exodus since World War II. Most of the migrants headed toward Europe—more than one million entered Germany alone—triggering ugly spasms of nativism and fierce fighting among the continent's leaders that further frayed the EU's already tattered fabric.

Even as this crisis was dominating the conversation, however, a related but much larger and older problem was continuing to fester: the refusal of governments throughout the developed world to deal rationally with the ordinary immigration of people who aren't fleeing war or persecution (as refugees do) but merely want to create better lives for themselves and their children in new homelands.

The failure to deal with this sort of immigration has been highlighted most dramatically in the United States (though it is by no means the worst offender). Almost from the start, the 2016 Republican presidential primary was dominated by an extraordinary contest to see which candidate could denounce immigration, and immigrants, in the harshest terms. Long before Donald Trump began using the 2015 terror attacks in the West as a pretext to scapegoat all Muslims, he set the tone for the race by throwing casual barbs at blacks, Jews, Mexicans, and Asians; by promising to build a wall along America's southern border; by pledging to deport all undocumented migrants; and by vowing to revoke the Constitution's birthright provision (which grants citizenship to anyone born in the United States). Desperate to tap the same rich vein of white male anxiety and bigotry, many of his supposedly more mature adversaries soon followed suit. While none quite matched his rhetorical extremes, most were all too ready to echo his xenophobia in more polite language.

Not only was this spectacle dispiriting, craven, and utterly un-American; it was also bizarre. Notwithstanding the fears caused by economic turmoil and terrorism, attacking immigrants and immigration is a strange strategy in a country where you soon won't be able to win the Oval Office without minority support. It's also hard to find another issue where the need for reform is so pressing—and where the benefits of change would be so profound.

That's because, for starters, the current American system is already cruel: under President Obama, the federal government deported almost three million undocumented immigrants—or about eleven hundred people a day.*

It's also irrational. Today American universities educate many of the globe's best young students, yet the US government then sends them home to start businesses and create jobs elsewhere. As a policy, that's simply nuts, given that 60 percent of the top tech companies in Silicon Valley are run by first- or second-generation immigrants. America's top CEOs understand the problem; led by Facebook's Mark Zuckerberg, a number of them have formed a super PAC to fight for reform. Ordinary Americans also get it: according to recent polls, more than 70 percent of them (including lots of Trump voters) support liberalizing the nation's immigration laws.

Changing the system would have an enormous material payoff. Most immigrants are ambitious and hardworking—you'd have to be to uproot yourself and your family and transport them halfway around the world. Contrary to conventional wisdom, immigrants don't steal jobs or depress wages, either. Nor do they increase lawlessness; a September 2015 report by the National Academies of Sciences, Engineering, and Medicine found that in the United States immigrant men between the ages of eighteen and thirty-nine are incarcerated at a rate one-fourth that of native-born citizens, and research conducted in numerous other countries has found similar results. Immigrants are also more likely to start new businesses. Were the United States to merely formalize the status of the undocumented workers already in the country, another recent study calculated, their higher earning power would increase net personal income by $30 billion to $36 billion in just three years. All that cash would also generate up to $5.4 billion in new tax revenues, and enough new consumer spending to support 750,000 to 900,000 new jobs.

---

* In 2014 and 2015, the Obama administartion tried to bring these numbers down somewhat, but with limited success.

In case these economic and humanitarian arguments somehow fail to convince you, one other growing problem should make the case for change a no-brainer, and not just in the United States. Most advanced industrialized democracies are aging fast, and few are producing enough children to support their rapidly graying populations. Unless they find an effective way to admit large numbers of outsiders, countries ranging from France to Japan (where the population is already shrinking) will face economic collapse. And I mean *really* large numbers; the OECD estimates that to maintain a fairly modest 3 percent growth rate over the next fifty years, the United States and Europe will need to absorb fifty million immigrants—each.

It's true that a few rich countries already have relatively permissive entry policies. But because of the way most of these are structured, they create as many problems as they solve. Germany, for example, has been extraordinarily generous when it comes to accepting refugees (unlike the United States). But for many years, Germany also made it almost impossible for its legal immigrants to obtain citizenship. This created a large, resentful minority underclass. The failure to properly integrate these residents—a mistake made by many other northern European countries and the United Kingdom as well—has led to their radicalization and produced ugly backlashes among the rest of the populace. Germany alone suffered more than two hundred attacks on immigrants and migration facilities in the first half of 2015. Arsonists burned down three mosques in Sweden around the same time, and an anti-immigrant party shot to the top of the polls. (Something similar has happened in Denmark.)

Yet rather than fight such bigotry, most of Europe's politicians have pandered to it. In May 2015, then–Prime Minister David Cameron, despite having just won reelection, promised to tighten Britain's already stingy entry quotas. And the rhetoric in the United States keeps getting more absurd. If it weren't so tragic and self-defeating, the Republican Party's terror of even mentioning the words "immigration reform" would be funny. In 2014, for example, conservative members of Congress rejected a bill that would have let Canadian retirees spend a little more time in Florida each winter.

Forget about Trump and his race-baiting for a second. You know you're in trouble when the specter of a few white-haired and wealthy snowbirds sunning themselves on the Sarasota sand is enough to send your political leaders scurrying for cover.

3. ISLAMIC EXTREMISM

When the fighting in Syria started in 2011, a lot of foreign policy analysts (myself among them) argued that one important reason the United States and its allies should intervene was to prevent the radicalization of what had long been one of the Middle East's most secular populations. If the West didn't help the rebels, we argued, those rebels would soon find help elsewhere—and we wouldn't like the consequences.

That, of course, is exactly what happened. While the West dithered, Qatar, Saudi Arabia, and Turkey stepped in and provided the more extreme Islamist insurgents with billions of dollars in aid, arms, and training. Forced to fend more or less for themselves, the moderate rebels were soon crushed between Assad's army and the radicals. At the same time, many Sunni Muslims from outside the region began flocking into Syria to enlist in the jihad. By December 2015 an estimated thirty thousand of them from eighty-six countries—more foreigners than had fought with the Afghans during their nine-year war against the Soviets—had joined the struggle.

The Islamic State—which offered recruits high wages, sex slaves, and the prospect of helping to create a new caliphate—proved the most powerful draw for these aspiring holy warriors. Though on the retreat, the group is still plenty lethal. IS affiliates downed a Russian jet over the Sinai in October 2015, killing 224 people, murdered another 130 in Paris in November, and killed 35 more in Brussels in March 2016. The group claims to have franchises in Afghanistan, Algeria, Libya, Nigeria, Saudi Arabia, Somalia, and Yemen. And it has become a powerful source of inspiration for disturbed lone wolves, as the tragic events in San Bernardino on December 2, 2015, showed. Meanwhile al-Qaeda is also down but not out, fully capable of carrying out and inspiring attacks of its own. And according to Seth Jones of the Rand Corporation, the number of jihadi groups worldwide has exploded in recent years, growing by 58 percent between 2010 and 2013 (and increasing still more since then). In 2014 (the last year for which figures are available) the world suffered 39 percent more terrorist attacks than in the previous year, and 83 percent more fatalities. Countries as far afield as Bangladesh and Thailand have also been targeted.

What's happening? Weren't the killing of Osama bin Laden and Washington's drone campaign supposed to have decimated the global jihadist movement?

Three factors explain its resurgence. First, as mentioned earlier, Syria and northern Iraq have become powerful incubators for would-be terrorists from around the world. Second, although al-Qaeda Central has indeed been grievously weakened by the sustained American assault, the group has splintered, allowing autonomous cadres fueled by local grievances to take up the cause. (Remember that this is how IS got its start.) Finally, though radical Islam as an ideology suffered a setback during the early months of the Arab Spring—when peaceful, popular revolutions seemed to offer a bloodless alternative both to extremist groups and to the Muslim world's repressive regimes—the ironfisted authoritarian backlashes that followed (which the West either tacitly supported or just ignored) inspired a whole new generation of violent jihadists.

4. Civil War

The author Steven Pinker has famously argued that despite the bloody images we see on the news every day, the world has actually been growing steadily more peaceful ever since 1945. Among other evidence, he cites the fact that western Europe—which started two wars a year during most of the last six centuries—hasn't fought a single one in seven decades now, and he points out that the number of people killed in armed conflicts each year has declined.

At least, it *was* declining. While Pinker's claim may have been supportable a few years ago, it's recently become much harder to believe. Wars *between* states may still be exceedingly rare, but wars *within* them are proliferating.

Unlikely as it may sometimes seem, however, even these new wars will eventually end. In fact, as the scholar Kristian Skrede Gleditsch has shown, civil conflicts now burn out faster than ever before; since 1991, he's found, the average length of such wars has dropped by 20 percent. That means that for every ongoing war, like those in Libya, Syria, and Ukraine, there will be a Sri Lanka, which finally stopped fighting in 2009. And it means that even Libya, Syria, and Ukraine will eventually achieve some sort of peace.

The problem is that for all of humankind's experience with conflict, we're still not good at making sure that the cease-fires hold and the fractures heal once the fighters lower their guns.

No current crisis makes that clearer than the one in Iraq, which US combat troops left in 2011. Despite Washington's gargantuan investment, Iraq today is a basket case. Nuri al-Maliki—who served, with US support, as prime minister from 2006 to 2014—thoroughly trashed the place, reinforcing sectarian divisions, encouraging corruption, and gutting the Iraqi state and its army (as IS's 2014 blitzkrieg made plain). He left his successor, Haider al-Abadi, a government that controls a mere fraction of Iraq's territory and is utterly dependent on outside help—including from Iran and from the American forces that have recently returned to the country. All that makes it very difficult to imagine how Abadi or anyone else will ever put the country back together.

These events have Washington worried, and rightly so. The mayhem in Iraq not only directly threatens a critical region but also has alarming implications for Afghanistan, which US troops are also supposed to exit sometime soon (although the date keeps getting pushed back). Afghanistan has been in a state of constant war since 1979. Its ethnic and sectarian divisions are just as bitter as Iraq's, and even more numerous and complicated. Absent a credible mechanism for reconstituting the nation, what chance does it have of surviving on its own?

And what about Syria, whose civil war has split it into at least three fortified ministates? Or the Central African Republic, the Democratic Republic of the Congo, Côte d'Ivoire, Mali, or South Sudan—barely functional countries that recently emerged from civil wars of their own? Without some sort of system or formula for healing these places, it's unlikely they'll manage to stay peaceful for long. Especially since help from the divided, cash-strapped, and war-weary West is getting harder and harder to come by.

5. CORRUPTION

Like inequality, corruption is a two-headed challenge, both a cause and a consequence of many other problems on this list.

Westerners often think of corruption—at least the large-scale variety—as a poor-country pathology, the product of desperation, unscrupulous rulers, rudimentary education, and a lack of shared values. Few rich-country dwellers are surprised when they read stories like the one about Otto Pérez Molina, the former president of Guatemala (per capita GDP: $3,667), who was forced out of office by a corruption scandal in the summer of 2015. Or of Zine el-Abidine Ben Ali, the last dictator of Tunisia (per capita GDP: $4,316), who was recently discovered to have stolen up to $2.6 billion from the state before his ouster. Or that the family of Wen Jiabao, the former premier of China (per capita GDP: $7,594), amassed close to $2.7 billion in assets during his tenure.

The truth, however, is that corruption is an equal-opportunity illness, one that infects rich and poor nations alike (although the scale may differ). In May 2015, for example, Ehud Olmert, a former prime minister of Israel (per capita GDP: $37,032), was sentenced to eight months in prison for taking bribes—making him the latest in a long string of Israeli leaders to face similar charges. Around the same time, prosecutors in the United States (per capita GDP: $54,629) accused New Jersey senator Robert Menendez of influence-peddling, and a grand jury indicted Sheldon Silver, the former speaker of the New York State Assembly, on similar charges. No nation is immune: a few years ago, even squeaky-clean Canada (per capita GDP: $50,271) was rocked by scandal after a number of its senators were caught fiddling with their expense accounts—in an uncanny echo of a similar episode in Britain's House of Lords several years before that.

Watching powerful men and women brought down can be entertaining (in a guilty sort of way, like eating junk food). But such episodes aren't so amusing when you happen to live in the neighborhood. For corruption in all its forms wreaks terrible damage, impoverishing individuals and societies alike. Worldwide, ordinary people are forced to pay an estimated $1 trillion in bribes each year, and corruption is thought to leach about 5 percent out of the global GDP. Corruption can even kill: child-mortality rates in highly corrupt states are a third higher than in less crooked places.

Corruption also corrodes the machinery of government and undermines citizens' confidence in their leaders and systems of rule. It's hard to have faith in your politicians when you have to grease some official's palm to get anything done, or when you realize the reason you still lack running water or dependable electricity is that your leaders have lined their pockets with your tax contributions. Corruption means your roads are broken, your bridges fall down, and your teachers are lousy. It makes your life more difficult in countless ways. Like a fast-acting toxin, it poisons everything it touches.

And all the evidence shows that it keeps getting worse.

6. THE RESOURCE CURSE

In the next few years, large swaths of the developing world are set to experience an economic shift on a seismic scale. The epicenter of this upheaval will be Africa. And the change will be driven by massive new discoveries of underground oil and gas.

Africa is no stranger to resource wealth; parts of the continent, such as Sudan and Nigeria, have enjoyed big petroleum profits for years. But the recently discovered hydrocarbon deposits dwarf anything the region has ever seen. The resulting windfalls could total trillions of dollars, even if energy prices stay low for some time. And a long list of countries stands to benefit, including Ethiopia, Kenya, Liberia, Malawi, Mauritius, Niger, Sierra Leone, Tanzania, and Uganda—some of the world's poorest nations.

While the changes there will be the most widespread, several other underdeveloped regions farther afield are also about to experience similar resource bonanzas. Experts predict that Papua New Guinea could soon increase its natural gas sales sixfold. Vast, scantly populated Mongolia has discovered new mineral reserves that could earn it more than $1 trillion. And war-racked Afghanistan has found underground stores of gold and other minerals that experts value at three times that amount.

It all sounds like wonderful news for a group of countries that could badly use some happy tidings. And it's true that resources on this scale could indeed transform all these places. The McKinsey Global Institute has calculated that the extra cash—if used wisely—could lift half the world's poor out of poverty.

Unfortunately, such riches almost never are used wisely.

Instead, due to a counterintuitive phenomenon economists call the Resource Curse, sudden mineral windfalls usually further immiserate already poor countries. The number of states that have managed such earnings well—or even adequately—is tiny. (Places like Canada and Norway have but don't count because they started out with so many other advantages.)

The reason is that resource wealth almost invariably produces a witches' brew of pathologies. First among them is corruption. It's not hard to see why: when money starts gushing into poor, fragile states, the temptation to skim some of it can feel irresistible. The theft usually starts at the top, which then signals to the rest of the population that they might as well grab what they can. During the mid-1990s, for example, when Nigeria's then dictator, Sani Abacha, and his cronies started socking away about $3 billion in stolen oil revenues, it didn't take long for lower-ranked officials to get in on the game.

What they don't steal outright, resource-rich governments tend to blow on expensive and unnecessary trophy projects: airports, stadiums, or shiny new capitals in the middle of nowhere. At the same time, they rarely invest in things that actually matter, like education. Why bother with school when you can get rich by digging in the dirt?

The problems don't end there. Resource wealth also drives up the value of local currencies, which makes imports cheaper but exports less competitive. Commodity-rich countries thus generally neglect the nonextractive sectors of their economies, such as agriculture and manufacturing. Once these industries die off, the states in question are left reliant on resource sales to sustain themselves—a dangerous proposition, given how volatile commodity prices can be.

As always, the least powerful citizens suffer the most. In the years since Zambia and Nigeria became major resource exporters, for example, poverty has increased significantly in both places. Things are even worse in oil-rich Equatorial Guinea. In 2014 this tiny country had a per capita GDP higher than Poland's. Yet more than three-quarters of its eight hundred thousand citizens live in bitter poverty, scraping by on less than $2 a day. Now, Equatorial Guinea may be an extreme case, but slightly less dramatic versions of its story are common. As the economists Jeffrey Sachs and Andrew Warner first documented, the economies of major resource-exporting nations tend to grow significantly slower than those of ordinary countries. Indeed, in the last several decades, 80 percent of resource-rich states have underperformed the global average.

The challenges aren't just economic: mineral wealth also undermines good government. Diamonds have underwritten Robert Mugabe's vicious mismanagement of Zimbabwe, just as oil sales enabled Muammar Gadhafi's bizarre and brutal reign in Libya. And these aren't exceptions: according to the academic Michael Ross, resource-rich countries are 50 percent more likely to be led by dictators than are regular states. The reason for this is simple: it's all too easy to ignore your citizens' desires when you can buy their acquiescence with cash. It's no coincidence that of all the governments hit by protests during the Arab Spring, only one of those that subsequently fell (Libya) had much resource wealth. Saudi Arabia and its fellow Gulf monarchies staved off that fate the same way they've avoided unrest in the past: by lavishing handouts and other perks on their citizens.

Finally, much like the golden apple that kicked off the Trojan War, the sudden appearance of underground riches often induces bloody battles for control. Numerous studies have found that countries rich in commodities are twice as likely to suffer civil wars as those lacking such wealth. Think of Angola and Sierra Leone and their blood diamonds and you'll get the picture.

Mineral booms and busts have been wreaking havoc ever since Australia's gold rush in the 1850s. But the sheer size of the new discoveries in Africa, Afghanistan, and elsewhere suggests that the fallout is about to get exponentially worse—making the search for a solution more pressing than ever before.

7. ENERGY

Natural resources don't just start fights within states—they also seed conflicts between them. That doesn't mean that resources are always a curse, however. Far from it. Just look at the United States.

Despite the intense political paralysis that's gripped Washington in the last few years, the US economy has refused to stagnate, as one might expect it to. Instead, it's enjoyed a steady recovery, averaging more than 2 percent growth each year since 2010. Of all the forces that have powered this revival, one of the biggest was also the most unexpected: the shale revolution.

The size of this boom has exceeded almost everyone's imagining and will benefit Americans for years to come. Yet it will still fall short in one sense: massive as it is, even it won't be enough to slake the rest of the world's growing thirst for fuel. In the coming decades, energy consumption in India alone will grow by 132 percent. Despite its slowdown, China, already the world's largest fossil fuel user, will see its appetite grow by 71 percent. No matter how many new wells it drills, the United States just won't be able to fill those needs.

But it shouldn't have to. The real potential for shale to transform the world lies not in North America's legendary Bakken Formation or the other giant US fields. For the United States sits on only about 15 percent of the world's total recoverable shale reserves. The rest lurks far afield in places such as Argentina, China, France, and Poland. Unlocking those reservoirs would have enormous benefits: doing so could reinvigorate the global economy, slow climate change (since gas burns much cleaner than coal), and even reduce international conflict.

Yet none of the countries I've just mentioned are likely to tap their riches anytime soon. Thanks to the dominance of slow-moving state-owned energy companies, various structural problems, misguided policies, unfriendly legal regimes, the absence of the right kind of capital markets, and popular opposition to drilling, no other nation is likely to replicate America's energy revolution, or even come close, in the foreseeable future. And that's even if energy prices do start climbing again soon. Too many problems stand in the way.

The great irony is that all of them are man-made and have nothing to do with actual resources or raw materials. Yet that may make them even harder to deal with.

8. THE MIDDLE-INCOME TRAP

Otto von Bismarck is said to have remarked that God has a "special providence for drunkards, fools, and the United States of America." The sudden US energy revolution suggests that the old Prussian knew what he was talking about.

Few other countries can rely on natural resources—or divine providence—to drive their economies, however. They need to find other ways to generate growth and to keep it going.

Unhappily for them, sustaining growth over long periods turns out to be fiendishly difficult. If you were to do a quick survey of the last century, you'd find that while many states managed to make it into the middle-income bracket—defined by a per capita GDP of about $10,000 in current US dollars—the vast majority then got stuck in what economists call the Middle-Income Trap.

The odds of escaping that trap are long. Of the dozens of states that made it into the middle tier in the last one hundred years, most then slowed down dramatically in the subsequent decade; one economic historian has pegged the average decline at 2.8 percent, and others think the drop-off is even sharper. Whatever the exact number, the consequences are stark. Only thirteen states that qualified as middle income in 1960 have since made it into the ranks of rich countries and stayed there. Only thirty-four countries—representing just 18 percent of the world's population—belong to that exclusive club today.

The reason, as the rest have discovered, is that while climbing up through the early stages of development is fairly straightforward—you just need to establish basic infrastructure, shift your workers into low-cost manufacturing, and then start selling their products overseas—the path then suddenly gets a lot steeper. Pools of underemployed rural workers dry up, which causes wages and other costs to rise. That makes your exports more expensive and hence less competitive. To surmount those challenges, countries must adopt a whole new strategy. Ruchir Sharma, who runs Morgan Stanley's emerging-markets portfolio, argues that this formula must include measures to boost productivity, to increase human capital through education, and to move up the value chain. Countries also need to cut red tape and regulations to promote competition, build reliable courts to protect physical and intellectual property rights, and help direct investment toward start-ups and other creative ventures.

None of those steps may sound especially difficult. But most governments find it impossible to take enough of them—and to keep taking them year after year. Vested interests oppose disruptive changes, and politicians quickly lose their stomach for the fight. Thus most leaders start to ease off the gas pedal as soon as their countries achieve a modicum of growth.

That's despite the fact that the middle tier is not such a great place for countries to linger. Sure, it beats dollar-a-day poverty. But don't be fooled by the name: it's not like middle-income countries are filled with middle-class citizens (at least not in the Western sense). Take China. In 2012 its per capita GDP was about $6,000. While that may sound pretty good, it doesn't mean that most Chinese actually earned that much, for the figure was calculated by taking China's total economic output and dividing it by the number of its citizens. The actual income that an average Chinese family earned that year (the last for which statistics are available) was just $2,100. Translation: being a middle-income country means that most of your citizens remain hard up, and that your government lacks the resources for a lot of important priorities.

So escaping the trap is critical for developing nations everywhere. All of them know what's required to do so—in theory. But putting that knowledge into practice is a whole different story.

9. Gridlock I

All of the problems we've looked at so far are hard enough for countries to deal with when their governments work the way they're supposed to: when their leaders lead, their legislators legislate, and their judges judge. When governments get jammed up by partisanship, personal rivalries, and special interests and stop performing those functions, the challenges become insurmountable.

Consider the case of Mexico, a country that features prominently in this book (see chapter 9). For most of the years following its transition to democracy in 2000, legislative warfare between its three major parties kept Mexico from deregulating its economy, breaking up its smothering monopolies, or forcing open its inefficient state-dominated oil sector. In Italy, meanwhile, infighting has produced forty-two prime ministers and sixty-four governments in seventy years, allowing problems like corruption, inefficiency, and excessive debt to molder. In Lebanon, the decay has been literal: political rivalries kept Parliament from agreeing on a new president for more than a year, which (among other things) prevented trash from being collected in Beirut in the hot summer of 2015. Things are almost as bad (if less malodorous) next door in Israel, where fractious coalition politics and razor-thin parliamentary majorities have kept the country from advancing the peace process or from making much-needed social reforms.

Gridlock isn't limited to the West. Japan still boasts the world's third-largest economy, and since the 2012 election of Shinzo Abe, that economy has started to rouse itself from its decades-long slumber. But Japan's recovery remains uneven—in large part because Abe hasn't yet pushed through the toughest but most needed reforms on his agenda. And that's because of bitter splits in Japan's National Diet and within Abe's Liberal Democratic Party.

Things may be even worse, finally, in the world's largest democracy. During much of the previous decade, India's economy grew so fast that many analysts started predicting it would soon overtake its giant northeastern neighbor and become a more congenial superpower that could balance Beijing. Instead of locking in growth by extending Prime Minister Manmohan Singh's reforms, however, petty power brokers within the ruling Congress Party and its small-minded coalition partners spent most of Singh's second term fighting with him and one another. The results were predictable: India's boom deflated, with its growth rate falling by half between 2010 and 2012. Things got so bad that in May 2014 angry voters threw Singh out and replaced him with Narendra Modi, who had overseen the economic revitalization of the state of Gujarat and was known as a man who could get things done.

Since Modi's election, India's growth has started edging up again. But the prime minister is finding it exponentially harder to do business in New Delhi than it was in Gandhinagar (Gujarat's capital). Having captured a mere 31 percent of the popular vote, he hasn't ruled like a strongman, as many feared he would. Instead, he's seemed surprisingly timid, talking big but doing little. He needs to restructure India's banks and its bloated state-owned enterprises; so far, he's barely touched them. Meanwhile, the Congress Party—which, with its allies, still controls the upper house of Parliament—has managed to block his vital tax and land reforms. Like Singh before him, Modi is rapidly learning a frustrating lesson: gridlock means ineffective leadership. Gridlock means no problem solving. Gridlock means no progress.

10. Gridlock II

Partisan paralysis is so hard to deal with, and amplifies so many other problems, that it gets two chapters in this book: one focused on gridlock abroad, and one that grapples with the challenge in the United States. The stalemate here has grown so profound that a whole chapter is needed to encompass it.

Now, American gridlock is nothing new. But virtually from the moment Barack Obama was first elected president in 2008 on promises that he'd bring the country back together (remember those inspiring words about there not being "a liberal America and a conservative America" but a "United States of America"?), the divisions began to grow even bitterer, and the business of American government ground to a virtual halt.

Neither party was guiltless. Obama showed too little interest in reaching out to members of Congress (of either party). And Ray La-Hood, a GOP congressman who served in his cabinet, complained that "the White House [never] committed fully to a genuine bipartisan approach to policy making, despite the president's words to the contrary."

While that may be true, the Republicans still bear more of the blame. In 2010, Mitch McConnell, the Senate majority leader, declared that "the single most important thing we want to achieve is for President Obama to be a one-term president"—a startlingly honest, if dispiriting, admission. McConnell failed to accomplish his goal, but the GOP did block government action on a huge range of issues. (The diehards also toppled one House Speaker and scared away most of his potential replacements.) Despite the near-constant obstruction, Obama nonetheless managed to forge ahead on health care, the Iran deal, and climate change. But these cases only illuminate the depths of the problem—for the first two measures were passed with no Republican votes, and the last required executive action. Apart from these and a few other accomplishments (like the passage of fast-track trade authority), the last several years have been among the least productive in Washington's history.

Just consider some of the things the US government didn't address under Obama. Immigration reform foundered. Congress blocked the appropriation of money to rebuild the nation's crumbling infrastructure. Congressional Republicans also repeatedly refused to pass a budget, shut down the entire government over minor disputes, and repeatedly balked at extending the debt ceiling—nearly ruining the country's credit rating in the process. They let desperately needed long-term unemployment benefits expire, declined to pass housing finance reform, stalled the passage of agriculture bills (in the hope of eliminating food stamps), and refused to even consider most new gun limits, despite the ongoing epidemic of firearm deaths. Ben Bernanke, a former chairman of the US Federal Reserve, has complained that "far from helping the economy," Congress often "appeared to be actively working to hinder it." And when I asked then–Secretary of Defense Ashton Carter about the problem in 2015, he said that partisan warfare "gives a misleadingly diminished picture of America around the world, suggesting that we can't get our act together."

But the problems don't end there. Not only did Congress refuse to legislate, tax, or spend; it even abandoned its constitutional duty to approve the president's appointees. For ten months, Congress stonewalled Obama's nominee to the Supreme Court, Merrick Garland.

Outrageous as it was, this tactic shouldn't have been surprising. Senate Republicans filibustered more executive branch nominees during Obama's tenure than under all other presidents combined. Congress took almost six months to confirm Loretta Lynch as attorney general, and it confirmed fewer federal judges in the first half of 2015 than in any year since 1969. There are now so many vacancies on the federal bench that more than twenty-four US courts have declared "judicial emergencies."

Make no mistake: Americans noticed this dereliction of duty. Surveys show that trust in the federal government has reached its lowest level on record, and the two parties are as unpopular as they've ever been. Congress's approval rating now hovers in the single digits—hitting figures so low that, as John McCain likes to joke, the only people still supporting the institution are blood relatives and paid staffers.

The only mystery is why they too haven't given up on it.

In November 2016, all that frustration vaulted Donald Trump—the least popular presidential candidate in US history—into office. Republicans now control all three branches of the US federal government, giving them a big chance to finally end the infighting and get the government working again. But I wouldn't get your hopes up. Thanks to its inexperience and its incompetence, the Trump administration has proved incapable of actually delivering on its promises. But many of those pledges directly constrict those of Congressional Republicans—especially the deficit hawks among them, who will resist his free-spending, debt-friendly policies. The stage is set for even more conflict ahead.

ABANDONING HOPE certainly is tempting—especially at a moment when so many things seem to be going wrong with the world.

The problem with despair, however, is that it's unproductive. And that makes it a dangerous indulgence at times like these.

Fortunately for us, it's also unnecessary. As the following chapters will show, none of these challenges (bad as they look) are actually insurmountable. The solution to gridlock—and to all the other problems we've just reviewed—is already out there.

You just have to know where to look for the answers.

PROFITS TO THE PEOPLE

How Brazil Spreads Its Wealth

L OOK." LULA LEANED HIS STOCKY FRAME OVER THE ARM
of his chair and pushed his face close to mine, locking eyes. "It
sometimes bothers my educated friends when I say this. But the
number one teacher in my life was a woman who was born and died
illiterate: my mother," he said. "With all due respect to experts and
academics, they know very little about the poor. They know a lot about
statistics, but that's different, *sabe?* To an intellectual, putting fifty dollars in the hands of a poor person is charity; an academic has no idea
what a poor person can do with it. But that's because at university, they
don't teach you how to care for the poor. And it's because most experts
have never experienced what the poor go through every day. They've
never had to go to work without breakfast. They've never lived in a
flooded house, or had to wait three hours at a bus stop. To experts, a
social problem like inequality is only numbers. But I took that social
problem and made it into a political one, a practical one. And then I
tried to solve it."

It was December 2014—summer in Brazil—and Lula and I were
sitting in his map-lined private office in Ipiranga, a slightly scruffy
middle-class neighborhood of São Paulo. I'd traveled there to ask Brazil's former president—formally known as Luiz Inácio Lula da Silva,
though nobody calls him that—just how he'd done it. How had Lula
turned inequality into what he'd just described as a politically manageable problem—and then tackled it with such stunning success?

Finding the answer felt urgent. After all, income inequality has exploded around the world in recent years, becoming a source of intense
global anxiety. The gulf between the ultrarich and the rest seems to be

growing inexorably just about everywhere. And no one seems to know what to do about it.

One reason for this helplessness is that economic growth—long seen as the key to improving general welfare—is no longer working the way it's supposed to. Though politicians often blame the current inequality crisis on the Great Recession and its aftershocks, that hypothesis doesn't hold up. For if you look at many of the countries whose income gaps have grown the widest in the past few years, you'll make a counterintuitive discovery: the list includes some of the world's fastest-growing economies, like China's.

What this means is that merely getting the world's struggling economies back on track isn't going to do much to close the yawning income gaps. It might just produce more Chinas. Truly solving our inequality problem is going to take a much more creative and comprehensive approach.

The hunt for that strategy is already well under way, with pundits and increasingly desperate national leaders racking their brains for an answer. Of the serious proposals (let's stipulate that "Make America Great Again" is a little vague), the best known is probably that of Thomas Piketty, the superstar French economist who, in his 2014 bestseller, called for the imposition of a global wealth tax.

It's not hard to see why so many people have fallen for this scheme. It's appealingly simple, and packs a gratifying soak-the-rich punch. But there are two big problems with Piketty's plan, as well as other similarly extreme approaches to inequality. First, they'd never work, for both political and technical reasons; the global elite are too good at protecting their interests and avoiding the taxes they're already supposed to pay.

And second, such controversial strategies are unnecessary.

Over the last dozen years or so, one country—Brazil—has shown that there's a far better, less radical, and more market-friendly way to fight inequality. This approach has been tested, and it works.

The man sitting across from me on that hot day in Ipiranga was the one who'd made it happen, presiding over one of the most successful, least disruptive social transformations the world has ever seen.

———

IN REAL LIFE, even more than in fiction, stories generally follow predictable paths. The good-looking woman gets the guy. The better-funded politician with the thicker head of hair wins the race. The rich get richer, and everyone else gets screwed. Improbable and unexpected victories are exceedingly rare.

Yet every once in a while they do occur, and this is one of those cases. So before explaining just how it happened—how Brazil pulled it off—it's worth considering just what made the happy ending so implausible and, as a consequence, so inspiring.

First there's the story's setting. It's hard to imagine that Brazil today could be a model for anything. The country is a shambles, crashing from one crisis to the next. As things fall apart, Congress has gridlocked and the political establishment is being wrenched apart by high-level corruption scandals. Lula's chosen successor, Dilma Rousseff, has been impeached and replaced by the venal old guard. Even Lula himself now faces trial.

Until very recently, moreover, the idea that Brazil might have something to teach the world about inequality would've sounded like a joke. For decades, the country didn't just have a problem with inequality—it *was* the problem. Latin America's largest nation was among the most unequal places on earth, a state synonymous with savage social injustice. Sure, it was blessed with a big, youthful population and abundant natural resources (including an eighth of the world's freshwater and among its largest offshore oil and gas reserves). But when it came to spreading the wealth, Brazil did as bad a job as you could imagine; even tiny, benighted Haiti was more equitable. Throughout the 1980s and 1990s, although Brazil moved from dictatorship to democracy and bold reforms by President Fernando Henrique Cardoso finally brought hyperinflation under control, its miserable masses remained trapped in rural penury or urban favelas while the fortunate few soared over the country's ungovernable megacities in helicopters. As the new century dawned, about a third of Brazil's population languished beneath the international poverty line (generally defined as living on less than $2 day), and about 15 percent of the country was indigent (living on less than $1.25 a day).

But that was the moment Brazil finally started changing, first slowly and then, beginning in 2003, with tremendous speed. By 2011 its economy, thanks to Cardoso's reforms and Lula's subsequent encouragement, was growing by a respectable 4 percent a year and unemployment had hit a record low. And for once, the benefits were actually being widely shared. During this same period, close to forty million Brazilians moved from poverty into the middle class. Average household income shot up by 27 percent. And, perhaps most impressive, inequality fell dramatically—at the same time it was growing almost everywhere else.

JUST AS SURPRISING as the speed of this metamorphosis was the identity of the man most responsible for it.

Before the recent scandals hit, Lula had become such an iconic figure—in 2012 he left office with an 87 percent approval rating, shortly after President Obama had called him "the most popular politician on earth"—that it can be hard to remember just how polarizing he was back in 2002, when the campaign that would carry him into office caught fire. Shaggy and wild-eyed, with a low-slung stevedore's body, the candidate scared the pants off Brazil's elites, its corporations, its investors, and many of its foreign partners—especially the United States.

The problem was personal. Whereas Lula's predecessor, Cardoso, was a centrist and an urbane academic, Lula was about as rough-hewn and unpolished as one could get, something he made no attempt to hide. Indeed, he was a proud child of the country's destitute northeast. Born in 1945 in the hardscrabble state of Pernambuco, Lula was the seventh of eight children. His family had started out poor and found itself even worse off when, shortly after Lula's birth, his father slunk away and drank himself to death. That had left the rest of the clan so hard up that the future president was forced to drop out of school after the second grade in order to make money shining shoes. At ten he taught himself to read, and at fourteen Lula somehow worked his way into a factory, where he lost his left pinkie finger to a machine press a few years later. Not long after that, he got involved in Brazil's powerful labor movement and discovered his calling. Rising rapidly through the ranks of the São Bernardo Metalworkers Union, Lula became the organization's leader at age thirty. And in 1980—at a time when Brazil was still ruled by a military junta—he helped found the leftist Workers' Party (known by its Portuguese acronym, PT) in the hopes of giving the downtrodden a louder voice on the national stage.

By the time of the 2002 election, Lula had already run for president—and lost—three times. While he'd never been a Marxist (unlike many of his PT comrades), his earlier campaigns had featured calls to nationalize industry and default on the country's debt. Such talk, along with his rough roots and his campaign promise to eradicate poverty within a generation, thoroughly spooked Brazil's moneyed classes and foreign capitalists when he finally started climbing in the polls. As Mac Margolis, a longtime Rio-based correspondent, recalls, Lula's rise sent many Brazilians—who feared "the hirsute lefty union man would win the presidential election and turn Brazil into an oversize Cuba"—into a lather.

Though Lula himself protested that "Brazil has changed, the Workers' Party has changed, and I have changed," few bought it. In the United States, Henry Hyde, the Republican chairman of the House International Relations Committee, denounced him as a "pro-Castro radical." Goldman Sachs began publishing a "Lulameter" that purported to track the risks to investors should the PT win. Even George Soros reportedly warned that Lula's election would bring chaos. Nervous foreign banks started cutting off credit. And Brazil's fragile economy, which was just starting to pick up, went into a dive. The main stock index fell by 30 percent. Investors started dumping their Brazilian holdings, yanking more than $12 billion in capital out of the country within a few months. And the value of the real, Brazil's currency, fell 40 percent against the dollar, hitting an all-time low toward the end of 2002.

Yet enough Brazilians were sick of the country's feudal social structure and the pain caused by Cardoso's necessary but unpopular structural reforms and austerity measures that Lula won anyway. As the unkempt union man prepared to take office and the economy continued to crater, the country braced for the epic confrontation that was sure to come.

BUT A FUNNY thing happened: the cataclysm never arrived.

Lula did indeed assume office with revolution on his mind. But it turned out to be a very different sort of transformation than his conservative critics feared. Neither his earlier defeats nor the nasty reaction to his eventual victory had weakened Lula's commitment to social change. But—and this would prove key to the rest of this story—they had profoundly altered *how* he planned to make that change happen. All the setbacks and the controversy surrounding him had driven Lula to do some serious soul-searching. Between 1993 and 2001, he and José Graziano da Silva, a balding and bearded American-born agronomist who was one of his closest advisers (despite sharing a name, the two are not related), had traveled some ninety thousand kilometers throughout Brazil on listening tours they called *caravanas da cidadania* (citizenship caravans). And the politician who emerged was far more moderate, conciliatory, and politically canny than most people yet recognized.

Of all the lessons that failure had taught the new president, the most important was that he'd never get far if he tried to govern on behalf of just part of Brazil. If he was going to use his new mandate to really change things, he'd first have to win over his many powerful skeptics. And that meant finding a way to make sure that the transformation benefited everyone.

And so the rabble-rouser metamorphosed into the Great Conciliator. Lula banished all talk of debt defaults and wealth redistribution from his lexicon. He tamed his hair and started wearing suits. And he recast himself as what Margolis calls the "CEO-whisperer, amigo to the middle class, [and] champion of a rules-based market democracy." Though this move to the middle caused a lot of grumbling within the PT—"many members of my party, and people from the trade unions, did not like the idea at all," Lula recalls—he held firm. On taking office, Lula pledged to preserve Cardoso's tight fiscal and monetary policies. And shortly after his inauguration in January 2003, he put his money where his mouth was, picking Henrique Meirelles—a well-regarded former BankBoston executive and member of Cardoso's party, the PSDB—to run Brazil's central bank. He also named Antonio Palocci, another sober centrist, as finance minister. And Lula then started hacking away at Brazil's bloated national budget, cutting spending by about $4 billion in his first year and imposing an even stricter budget-surplus target than the International Monetary Fund recommended.

The payoff was immediate. Many of the same antagonists who'd attacked him throughout the previous year's campaign fell into a swoon. In March 2003 Mohamed El-Erian, then managing director of the bond giant PIMCO, declared that the president's initial moves—"from policy announcements, to appointments, to implementation"—had been "very good." The markets agreed; within six months of Lula's inauguration, the value of Brazil's bonds had risen by 20 percent. Even Goldman Sachs sheepishly admitted that its earlier warnings had been wrong.

At the same time that Lula was wooing the moneymen, however, he was hard at work on another front, preparing to use his growing political capital to launch a wildly ambitious new social welfare campaign. Rolled out a few months after his election, Fome Zero (Zero Hunger) would feature more than forty different programs run by close to twenty government ministries. But one initiative stood at the campaign's core: Bolsa Família (Family Grant), a poverty-fighting effort that was groundbreaking in its size, ambition, and design.

BOLSA FAMÍLIA INCORPORATED several innovations that would prove critical to the program's eventual success—both as policy and as politics.

First, rather than provide the poor with goods or services, as most development programs did at the time, Bolsa Família would attempt something much more audacious: simply hand out money instead. Brazil had actually started experimenting with this approach a few years earlier. In 1995 two cities—Campinas and Brasília—had launched small cash-giveaway programs on a trial basis. These had proved so effective at ameliorating poverty that they were soon copied by more than one hundred other local governments. And President Cardoso had begun testing a similar scheme on the national level in 2001, though the payments were tiny and the execution was flawed. Still, the results were promising enough that Lula, acting on Graziano's advice, decided to roll all these various programs into a single new streamlined national initiative—and to expand it to a scale far larger than even most experts had imagined possible.

Despite the success of the Campinas and Brasília experiments, Bolsa Família was extremely controversial when Lula first launched it in October 2003. At the time, most experts and international organizations still considered the idea of simply handing money straight to the poor to be dangerously wrongheaded. It just *felt* wrong, on an intuitive level. It also flew in the face of decades of social science research and what the World Bank had long considered best practice. "Experts did not accept the idea," Lula recalled. "They preferred to give the poor dietary staples, or to do things for them." As Lena Lavinas, a welfare economist at the Federal University of Rio de Janeiro, told me, that was because the prevailing wisdom then held that "the poor didn't know how to allocate resources correctly." Translation: it was assumed that they'd just blow the money on booze, cigarettes, or shiny baubles. Policymakers, not the people, knew best, so they should be the ones making the decisions.

Yet three insights had convinced Lula and his advisers to reject that notion. First, Brazil's own experience had shown that large-scale attempts to alleviate poverty by distributing goods, like a massive food program Cardoso launched in the late 1990s, tended to flop in embarrassing and expensive fashion. Providing the poor with physical stuff is extremely complicated, costly, and inefficient. It also requires a large bureaucracy, which creates endless opportunities for corruption—a perennial problem in Brazil.

Second, a few groundbreaking academic studies (which would later be confirmed by a slew of follow-on research) had started to reinforce what Lula, with his disdain for experts, already knew: that the people who best understood what the poor *really* needed were people like his mother—namely, the poor themselves. The new research also showed that, when given the chance, destitute families generally didn't squander their money. Most spent it quite rationally—especially when the cash went to mothers, not fathers, as it would under Bolsa Família.

Finally, Lula had realized that the wave of privatizations that had swept Latin America in the eighties and nineties—as governments sold off everything from airlines and energy producers to utility providers—had left hundreds of millions of citizens stranded, too poor to participate in the expanding market economies. Lula and his advisers reckoned that rather than go through the nightmare of renationalizing big businesses, the best and simplest way to reverse the poor's exclusion was to put a little cash in their pockets.

So that's what they set out to do.

As the president and his aides devised it, qualifying for assistance under Bolsa Família would be simple. Any family that could prove it lived in extreme poverty—then defined as less than 50 reais (about $42) per person per month—would be eligible for payments, as would moderately poor families that earned less than 100 reais a head.

But Lula also decided that Bolsa Família wouldn't just hand out money for nothing. Getting into the program would be easy, but staying in it would take work. Participants would have to meet several conditions, or *contrapartidas* (counterpart responsibilities): ensure that all their children between six and fifteen years old attended school at least 85 percent of the time; make sure any children under seven got immunized; and guarantee that both moms and their kids got regular medical checkups. (Pregnant women would also be required to get prenatal care and to breast-feed their infants.)

Lula had two very shrewd reasons for imposing such rules. First, while he himself might have managed to claw his way out of poverty by the tips of his nine fingers, he knew that he'd been exceptionally lucky to do so. For most Brazilians, demographics were destiny: if you were born poor, you would die that way too. Indeed, contemporaneous academic research showed that the correlation between what parents earned and what their children eventually would make was higher in Brazil than in almost any other country. The reason for this lack of mobility was that many impoverished Brazilian parents felt compelled to send their kids to work instead of to school, even though doing so deprived them of the tools that could someday help them improve their lives. Lula was determined to break this intergenerational trap by fighting poverty today *and* tomorrow at the same time. In practical terms, that meant enabling—and requiring—parents to give their children greater advantages, in the forms of education, health care, and nutrition, than they themselves had enjoyed.

But Lula's motivation in designing Bolsa Família the way he did was only partly about policy. The Great Conciliator, newly devoted to the Middle Path, was also thinking strategically: he knew that attaching strict conditions to his aid program would also make it much easier to sell to the rest of society. And he knew he'd need all the help he could get. Prior to Lula, most social assistance programs in Brazil had taken the form of insurance schemes that disproportionately benefited the middle and upper classes (it's tough to qualify for a government pension if you don't work in the formal economy). Bolsa Família was the first time a Brazilian president had really put combating poverty and inequality at the center of his agenda (though earlier politicians had gestured at it). That all but guaranteed a fight.

Sure enough, the pushback started as soon as the program was introduced in October 2003. Not only did Bolsa Família fly in the face of established practice, but some economists also argued that the government should be investing in infrastructure like schools rather than paying people to attend them. Others said that parents shouldn't be told what to do with or for their children. And conservative pundits warned that the cash transfers would create welfare dependency, known in Portuguese as *assistencialismo*. (Never mind the fact that the idea for cash transfers was originally hatched by an icon of the right, the American economist Milton Friedman.) As Tereza Campello, the country's social development minister, recalls, in Bolsa Família's early days critics would constantly confront her with the tired old Confucian aphorism about how it's better to teach people how to fish than to feed them seafood. "The opposition said we were going to create an army of lazy people," Lula told me.

Brazil's constitution gave the president the ability to launch Bolsa Família on his own executive authority. But the law also stipulated that he'd need congressional approval to renew the program within a year. That meant Lula would have to secure broad-based support if his signature program was going to survive—and the *contrapartidas*

were his key to getting it. "The idea was to show that we are not giving out money for free," Lula explained to me. "We had to build trust,
even among those who were skeptical about this kind of a program."
As Ariel Fiszbein and Norbert Schady, two World Bank economists,
have documented, the conditions helped Lula do that by creating the
popular impression that Bolsa Família was not some sop to the poor,
but rather represented a new sort of social contract with them under
which recipients had to do their part. Making beneficiaries show "clear
evidence of commitment" to the "positive behaviors" required by the
program made those beneficiaries seem more deserving, giving the
public the sense that they had earned the cash.

Of course, simply announcing formal conditions wasn't enough;
there also had to be consequences for noncompliance. To that end,
Bolsa Família's architects designed a system of graduated penalties for
those who failed to do their part. Rule breakers would get a warning;
if they still didn't comply, their benefits would be suspended, and if the
trouble continued, they'd eventually get bounced out of the program
altogether.

While such sanctions looked good on paper, Lula soon discovered
that getting the public to take them seriously would require still stronger medicine: hard proof that the rules were actually being enforced.
In 2004 Lula's administration became so preoccupied with expanding
the program's reach (the number of recipients would go from 3.8 million families, or almost 16 million individuals, in late 2003 to nearly
triple that in 2006) that it stopped paying much attention to whether
or not those new recipients were holding up their end of the bargain.
When, partway through the year, the government discovered that only
55 percent of Brazil's public schools were even bothering to report on
whether Bolsa Família recipients were meeting their attendance quotas, the administration decided to temporarily suspend its monitoring
efforts altogether.

That choice might have made sense bureaucratically; the government was just trying to buy itself time to get its house in order. But
it proved a PR disaster. On October 17, just a few days before nationwide municipal elections, *Fantástico*, a popular Sunday-evening
news program, broadcast an investigative report alleging widespread

abuse of Lula's flagship program by undeserving recipients. (Think of Reagan-era complaints about welfare queens driving Cadillacs and you'll get a sense of the broadcast's tone.) The rest of Brazil's media quickly jumped on the story, blasting the government from all sides. The public was incensed; in just one week after *Fantástico*'s broadcast, the government received several thousand angry complaints.

Sensing the danger, Lula decided to face his critics head-on. "What is the lesson we learned from this moment? Humility," he told me. "You have to recognize that a very big program will have mistakes. You have to admit them. And then you have to fix them." To that end, Lula set up a new Ministry of Social Development (known by its Portuguese acronym, MDS) to centralize oversight of Bolsa Família. Departing from Brazil's long tradition of patronage politics, he staffed the new body with highly trained technocrats (including many members of the opposition PSDB party) rather than partisan hacks. And in January 2005 he personally presided over the public launch of a sweeping new multiagency strategy for improving Bolsa Família's implementation; among other measures, he established a unified national registry to keep track of everyone who got any form of government assistance, centralized Bolsa Família's eligibility criteria, implemented formal audits and spot checks, set up citizen oversight committees and complaint hotlines, and required that Bolsa participants get recertified every two years.

By mid-2006, monitoring and enforcement had improved dramatically: in June of that year, the MDS cut some half a million ineligible recipients off its rolls. Brazilians noticed, and were impressed. The surge of criticism of Bolsa Família quickly ebbed, and public support for the program began to climb. Indeed, a 2010 analysis of polling data and the media's treatment of Bolsa Família by Kathy Lindert and Vanina Vincensini, two World Bank experts, found that by imposing rigorous conditions for assistance, Lula's government legitimized Bolsa Família with Brazilian voters, generating widespread enthusiasm for it on both ends of the political spectrum.

As useful as Lula's *contrapartidas* were in boosting Bolsa Família's popularity, two other innovations would prove almost as important.

First, for all its ambitions, Bolsa Família was, and remains, cheap—radically so, compared with most other social welfare programs in Brazil and elsewhere. Today, more than a decade after its launch, Bolsa Família reaches about fourteen million families, which translates to about fifty-five million Brazilians—an enormous number. Yet because Lula and his advisers recognized that it only takes a very small sum of money to make a very big difference in a poor family's life, the individual payments (which vary according to income and family size) are tiny: the average recipient gets just $65 a month, and benefits top out at $200. As a result, "the amount spent on Bolsa Família"—despite its scope—"is nothing," says Yoshiaki Nakano, director of the School of Economics at the Getúlio Vargas Foundation in São Paulo. That's an exaggeration, of course, but not a big one. The fact is that one of the world's most ambitious antipoverty programs currently costs Brazilian taxpayers less than half a percent of the country's $2.2 trillion GDP—far less than the 12 percent the government spends on pensions, for example (a much more regressive support mechanism). Though precise international comparisons are hard to make, the evidence suggests that Bolsa Família is one of the cheapest antipoverty programs anywhere. Indeed, a 2011 study by the British government found that cash transfer programs like Bolsa Família cost 30 percent less per person than more traditional aid programs, thanks in part to their minimal administrative expenses.

One final aspect of Bolsa Família's design also helped Lula win broad backing for it: the program was structured in such a way that it would ultimately benefit *all* Brazilians, not just those at the bottom. As Lula explained when he first introduced Bolsa Família, "When millions can go to the supermarket to buy milk, to buy bread, the economy will work better. The miserable will become consumers." By giving people money that they could spend however they want, Lula created what Lavinas, the Rio-based welfare economist, calls "a pro-market approach to combating poverty." Indeed, no less an authority than Jorge Castañeda, a former conservative foreign minister of Mexico turned columnist and self-appointed scourge of the Latin American left, has called Bolsa Família an "innovative welfare program" that is as "neoliberal . . . as one can get."

This aspect of Lula's huge new antipoverty campaign initially bemused his critics on the right, who still suspected him of being a Castro clone in CEO's clothing. But Bolsa Família's market-friendly features were just one expression of the happily heterodox path Lula would follow throughout his presidency. As Bernardo Sorj, a sociologist at the University of São Paulo, put it to me one afternoon in Rio, Lula's genius as a politician—and the secret of his success—was the president's blithe disregard for traditional pieties. Lula's biggest gift, Sorj said, is his ability to be "neither left-wing nor right-wing, but a walking metamorphosis, and a completely pragmatic one." Eschewing ideology, President Lula's basic approach was "to make everybody happy."

A close student of Lyndon Johnson, Lula—who even perfected LBJ's knack for physically discomfiting and seducing his interlocutors at the same time (during our interview, the president repeatedly touched my forearm for emphasis, then started squeezing my bicep, and then, toward the end of our meeting, held my hand for minutes at a stretch)—was also a master triangulator who even managed to win over international antagonists like President George W. Bush. Throughout his tenure, Lula found ways to remain true to his base, which he catered to through progressive social policies, while (especially during his first term) also taking pains to "respect the basic rules of a modern liberal economy," as Sorj put it. Having first "domesticated" the radicals within his own party, Lula then repeatedly sought to reassure key economic constituents—investors and foreign governments—through conservative macroeconomic policies. He also cozied up to big business by, for example, offering large firms cut-rate loans from Brazil's state-financed National Development Bank.

The result was a unique brand of what PIMCO's El-Erian has called "financially principled populism." Lula made no bones about what he was doing. "I feel no shame when I tell you that under my government, everybody won, from the poorest to the wealthiest," he told me. Refusing to be bound by party or class, the president consistently sought to achieve the greatest gains for the greatest number. He knew this could be disorienting at times. "Sometimes former comrades would come to me and say, 'Come on, Lula! You used to be a steelworker! Aren't you disturbed that bankers are making such high profits?'" he recounted. "I would say, 'No—what would concern me is if they were *losing* money.' If there's one thing I'm not ashamed of, it's profit. But I want people to know that my philosophy, at heart, is that of a mother. No one is fairer than a mother. Even if she has three hundred kids, she will treat them all equally. That's what I used to say to the Brazilian people: that I govern for all. And I feel very proud that I maintained good relations with everyone: the biggest farmers and the landless; the greatest bankers and their employees."

The strategy worked brilliantly. Ruthless pragmatism and a lift-all-boats approach would, within a few years, turn Lula into "an icon for everyone," Sorj said. "He managed to become a hero at Davos *and* at the World Social Forum"—a populist alternative to the elite Swiss conference. "And that was no easy feat."

WHILE LULA'S RELENTLESSLY inclusive rhetoric was politically ex-pedient, Brazilians (like everyone else) know that talk is cheap. It was by delivering results that Lula ultimately won his country over. For those results—from an average GDP growth rate of close to 4 percent throughout his tenure to his dramatic success fighting poverty and inequality—were extremely impressive. Though the price tag for Bolsa Família may have been small, its impact proved enormous. Not only would it eventually reach more than a quarter of the overall population (and 85 percent of the poor), but the payments, tiny though they are, have doubled the income of Brazil's most destitute families. In Bolsa Família's first three years, it cut extreme poverty by 15 percent, and by 2014 the percentage of Brazilians living in indigence had been slashed from 9 percent to less than 3—a level the World Bank considers equiva-lent to eradication. At the same time, Bolsa Família helped lift a total of thirty-six million people out of general poverty, producing what Matias Spektor, a political scientist and a columnist for Brazil's biggest news-paper, *Folha de São Paulo,* described to me as "the single largest ten-year change to a country's class structure since Japan after World War II."

As for inequality, recent studies credit Bolsa Família with having helped reduce the country's overall income gap by a third and rank the program as the second most important contributor to this change after general economic growth. According to Tereza Campello, the head of the MDS, the income of the poorest 20 percent of Brazilians rose by 6.2 percent between 2002 and 2013, while that of the country's richest fifth grew by only 2.6 percent. (That stands in sharp contrast to the United States, where, during the same period, the incomes of the richest 10 percent rose by 2.6 percent while those of the poorest 10 percent shrank by 8.6 percent.) Though the Brazilian government has also implemented a number of other important social support programs, including big hikes to the minimum wage, and though a growing economy also helped matters, most experts agree that Bolsa Família deserves a huge amount of credit for the overall improvement in the lives of the country's poor. Bolsa Família has also proved an important cushion as Brazil's growth has slowed in recent years. The country's overall economy may be hurting today, but thanks to the buffer provided by Bolsa Família, the masses are not—or at least not suffering as much as they did during the country's many past crises.

Bolsa Família has also made great strides toward Lula's goal of breaking the transmission of poverty between generations: by helping increase vaccination rates to 99 percent of the population, by decreasing malnutrition among children in Brazil's poorest regions by 16 percent, and by increasing their chances of having a healthy weight-to-age ratio by 26 percent. Infant mortality has dropped by 40 percent in the last decade, with deaths from malnutrition specifically down by 58 percent—one of the sharpest reductions ever seen anywhere. Meanwhile, the number of children forced to work instead of attending school has fallen by 14 percent. Bolsa Família recipients now boast a graduation rate double that of poor Brazilian children outside the program, and the initiative is credited with improving school attendance in the country's poorest regions by 14 percent. One happy consequence: the national literacy rate has already risen.

The program has also produced some less tangible and less predictable—though just as important—changes in the lives and attitudes of Brazil's poorest citizens. Research has shown that Bolsa

Família has empowered Brazilian women by giving them authority over their families' bank accounts; for example, female Bolsa Família participants are 10 percent more likely to say they have exclusive authority over contraception in their marriages. And the program seems to have had a dramatic impact on poor Brazilians' sense of agency. A recent survey of fourteen hundred Bolsa Família beneficiaries in three different cities found that rather than feeling stigmatized by their dependence on the government program, three-quarters of respondents said they were proud to be enrolled and that, by allowing them to properly feed and clothe their families without having to beg, Bolsa Família has helped them "lead more autonomous and dignified lives."

Brazilians enrolled in the program even express increased faith in their country's democracy. That might seem an odd outcome for a welfare program, but Spektor explained that Bolsa Família—which, thanks to its strict monitoring and the use of electronic bank cards to transfer funds, has remained remarkably corruption-free*—"broke the political mechanisms that had kept Brazil's poor poor for such a long time: the system of patronage whereby social policy was made by the local bosses in cahoots with the local government. Bolsa killed these guys because suddenly you had a very small group of people in far-off Brasília—all of them with PhDs from Western universities—giving money directly to the poor." In our conversation, Lula put things more bluntly: "Part of the reason Bolsa Família was so successful is because the money is paid directly, with no intermediary. It is the beneficiary who goes to the bank with a plastic card to withdraw the money. So this person doesn't owe any favors to the president, to their governor, to their congressman, or to their mayor."

Finally, just as Lula promised, Bolsa Família has provided a significant boost to the overall economy. By giving the poor more money to spend, the program has increased domestic consumption, an especially important economic driver in a country like Brazil, which shuns most imports. While most of the money is spent on food, Lula said that "of

---

* It's worth noting that although Lula's overall reputation has been hurt by the recent corruption probe, no one has questioned the success or integrity of Bolsa Família.

the people that received benefits under the Bolsa, 80 percent of them bought a television set, 79 percent of them bought a refrigerator, and 50 percent of them bought a washing machine. So what had seemed like a program just for people who were living in eighteenth-century conditions helped meet the needs of modern manufacturers, generating millions of jobs. Everyone won." That may sound like boasting, but the numbers bear it out: economists calculate that, since its launch, Bolsa Família has increased Brazil's GDP growth by 1.78 reais for every 1 real disbursed.

THIS LONG LIST of accomplishments has combined to make Bolsa Família incredibly popular in Brazil; polls put its approval rating around 75 percent. Everyone is happy with it, Lavinas told me. "The poor because they are less poor, and the rich because the program is so cheap that they don't care." Even the middle class, traditionally the most conservative segment of Brazil's electorate, has embraced Bolsa Família. As Spektor explained, this group "grew up in a country that was always getting worse. As Brazil democratized [in the mid-1980s], violence went up, inequality went up, inflation went up. We were geared toward thinking things were awful. If you hoped for a future, you wanted to learn English and get the hell out of here. Now, suddenly, I'd rather be here than anywhere else. And that's thanks to Bolsa."

Such across-the-board enthusiasm was first demonstrated during Lula's reelection campaign in 2006. Despite strong economic growth figures and his assiduous outreach to the right as well as the left, Lula faced a fierce headwind going into the race. An embarrassing chain of corruption scandals had erupted in 2005 and 2006, leading to the forced resignation of many of his top advisers. (Unrelated to the current allegations swirling around the state oil company, Petrobras, the largest of these earlier scandals, known as the *mensalão*, involved revelations that the government had been paying its congressional allies monthly bonuses to buy their support.) The allegations dealt a serious blow to Lula's poll numbers, and many analysts began predicting that he'd lose in the first round (Brazil holds two-stage elections). Yet when Brazilians finally voted, Lula didn't just survive the first round; he crushed his opponent, the PSDB's Geraldo Alckmin, by twenty-two points in the runoff.

The explanation? Despite all their anger and embarrassment over Lula's apparent indifference to graft (an indifference that would later get him into more trouble), most Brazilians ultimately decided to vote with their wallets. That was especially so among the country's poorest and least educated citizens, the very group that had profited most from Bolsa Família. According to an election analysis performed by two US academics, Wendy Hunter and Timothy J. Power, 60 percent of those earning less than five times the minimum wage embraced the incumbent that year, and Lula swept the underdeveloped northeast by 85 percent.

That Brazilians whose lives had been transformed by government spending would reward their benefactor might not seem surprising. But despite his roots, Lula's strong showing among the poor in 2006 actually broke previous voting patterns. Before that year, most impoverished voters had shunned him and the PT, which they saw as an elitist party of intellectuals. In fact, despite Lula's origins on the left, most of his support during his four previous campaigns had come from the country's richer provinces. The poor had always seen him, in Spektor's words, as "a guy with a funny beard, hair all over the place, promising revolution. And because they had been screwed by Brazil's political system for so long," those promises "seemed crazy to them." So they'd rejected Lula—until 2006, that is, when Bolsa Família redrew the electoral map.

This swing wasn't lost on Brazil's other politicians, and in the years since, virtually all of them have enthusiastically embraced Lula's brain-child. President Rousseff, Lula's handpicked heir, expanded the program's reach and upped its benefits several times. She even launched a program called Busca Ativa (Active Search) that sends intrepid social workers fanning out to the country's most remote corners—sometimes by jungle boat—in search of more needy Brazilians to enroll. Both of her opponents during the 2014 election promised to extend Bolsa Família still further. And Michel Temer, a conservative who replaced her as president in August 2016, hasn't dared touch it. To do otherwise would have been "political suicide," says Thiago de Aragão, a political consultant in Brasília.

None of this enthusiasm means that Bolsa Família is perfect. While the program has helped Brazil make historic progress, the country still remains far too inequitable. Under Lula's maladroit successor, economic growth has ground to a halt and the country's debt has soared. And despite Bolsa Família's massive reach, about twenty-eight million Brazilians still live in poverty. Some experts worry that by focusing so intensely on the needs of Brazilian children the program neglects their impoverished parents (whose benefits drop precipitously when their kids reach seventeen). Feminist scholars like Maxine Molyneux of University College London caution that "by making transfers conditional on 'good motherhood'" initiatives like Bolsa Família reinforce traditional gender roles. Lavinas, among others, points out that while the Brazilian government has done a good job getting children into schools, it's done far less to actually improve the education they get there—one of many reasons massive numbers of Brazilians took to the streets to protest poor government services in 2013.

Bolsa Família's positive impact is also significantly undermined by Brazil's regressive tax system, which relies excessively on consumption tariffs; these fees, which cover virtually every imaginable good and many services, eat up a huge share—as much as 55 percent, by some estimates—of Bolsa Família stipends. Finally, financial analysts attack Bolsa Família for reducing inequality at the expense of overall growth, while some Brazilians still insist the cash transfers only make people more dependent on the dole.

Bolsa Família, in other words, certainly can and should be improved. The country also desperately needs tax, health care, and education reform, as well as much more investment in infrastructure. But a wealth of evidence contradicts at least the last two of the charges listed above. Government statistics show that 75 percent of adult Bolsa Família recipients do work, and those who don't generally can't—they live in areas with too few job opportunities. This finding isn't so surprising when you consider that, as Wendy Hunter points out, Bolsa Família payments are so low that "no one in their right mind would take them instead of having a decent job."

It should come as no surprise, then, that despite its imperfections the program's fans have come to wildly outnumber its critics. Nancy Birdsall, the president of the Center for Global Development (a Washington think tank), has called Bolsa Família "as close as you can come to a magic bullet in development." Other boosters range from the *New York Times*, which has dubbed Bolsa Família "likely the most important government anti-poverty program the world has ever seen," to *The Economist*, which has declared it "a stunning success."

Perhaps the best testament to the brilliance of Bolsa Família's design, however—as well as to the defiantly unorthodox, something-for-everyone approach Lula used to formulate and then sell it—is the fact that since the program's creation more than sixty-three countries have sent experts to Brazil to copy its model. Within just a few years of Bolsa Família's inception, in fact, the MDS was so swamped by all the foreign requests for advice that it began holding twice-yearly seminars on how to launch similar programs elsewhere. As of this writing, at least forty other countries have taken that step, including most of Latin America as well as Bangladesh, Indonesia, Morocco, South Africa, and Turkey (to name just a few others).

Bolsa Família's appeal has even stretched to the rich world. In April 2007 Mayor Michael Bloomberg—another politician famous for ignoring orthodoxy and grabbing the best ideas from wherever he could find them—launched Opportunity NYC, the developed world's first Bolsa Família–style conditional cash transfer program, on a trial basis. Programs like Bolsa Família are more complicated and expensive to run in wealthier countries, for obvious reasons, and New York's pilot program was predictably criticized by both conservatives (who grumbled about its cost and the fact that it paid people to do what they should do anyway) and liberals (who called it condescending). Yet a review by the University of Michigan's National Poverty Center found that while it had some flaws, the program did significant good for participating families. Which is why both New York and Memphis recently launched a trial of yet another Bolsa Família–inspired program, called Family Rewards 2.0, that builds on Bloomberg's first effort, and Lula's before him—more proof, if it's needed, of the global appeal of Brazil's great experiment.

2

LET THE RIGHT ONES IN

CANADA'S IMMIGRATION REVOLUTION

THE MIDDLE OF THE LAST CENTURY WAS A TIME OF EPIC turmoil around the globe. The devastation of World War II and the chaos of decolonization set millions upon millions of people in motion in search of safer and more prosperous homelands. No matter how desperate you were to leave your old life in the Old World for a better one in the New, however, odds were you didn't consider Canada—especially if you had a little pigment in your skin. For most of the war years, Canada admitted few immigrants of any kind (just 7,500 in 1942), and while the numbers increased in the next decade, those it did take in were conspicuously pale. Under the "White Canada" policy, Europeans and Americans were virtually the only people allowed to settle there; everyone else was considered too scary. As Prime Minister William Lyon Mackenzie King bluntly told Parliament in 1947, there was "general agreement" among Canadians that unfettered migration would "make a fundamental alteration in the character"—read: lily-white Anglo-Saxon purity—of the country. And surely no one wanted that.

These days things are a little different, a change that was on vivid display one recent winter morning. It was December 10, 2015. At the time, populism and xenophobia were on the rise around the globe, politicians in the United States and Europe were fighting bitterly over whether to admit any of the refugees then fleeing Syria, and many countries were erecting new barriers at their borders. But in Toronto, Justin Trudeau, Canada's young new prime minister, stood in an airport arrivals hall handing winter coats to the first of the twenty-five thousand Syrian asylum seekers Canada would admit over the next few months (more than twice the number the United States would accept all year). "You're safe at home now," he told them.

Dramatic as it was, Trudeau's gesture was far from exceptional for contemporary Canada. Today aspiring immigrants barely need to seek Canada out. Canada is already looking for them, especially if they're young, skilled, and educated. The country's immigration minister tours the world touting the benefits of living and working in his homeland. The government even advertises abroad; in 2013, for example, it sponsored a billboard in Silicon Valley that targeted foreign-born computer geeks having trouble getting US work visas with the slogan "H-1B Problems? Pivot to Canada." Wherever you come from, in other words, the government of Canada probably wants you.

And so do its citizens. Canada today has one of the highest per capita immigration rates in the world—more than double that of the United States. For the last two decades, it has admitted about 250,000 newcomers a year, close to 1 percent of the population, and the government has projected that the annual total will hit 337,000 in 2018. Already, more than 20 percent of Canada's inhabitants are foreign-born—again almost twice the US total, even if you lump in undocumented migrants—and the proportion is expected to rise to more than a quarter of the population by 2031. And in recent years the top three countries of origin for new Canadians were the Philippines, China, and India. So much for Anglo purity.

Yet ordinary Canadians couldn't be happier about it all. Polls have shown that two-thirds of them feel that immigration is one of Canada's key positive features, and the same proportion favors keeping it at its current level—or even increasing it. Despite the global recession and the specter of terrorism, public support for immigration in Canada recently hit at an all-time high. Only a quarter of Canadians see immigration as a problem, by far the lowest figure in the industrialized world. Twice as many Canadians approve of the way their government is handling the issue than do Americans or Brits. Meanwhile, only 20 percent of the Canadian public wants to reduce the number of newcomers. As Jeffrey Reitz, a sociologist at the University of Toronto, has pointed out, Canadians love immigration so much that even the country's immigration *critics* favor higher levels than do *advocates* in other wealthy states. And while virtually every other advanced industrialized democracy has suffered spasms of nativist anger in recent years, a lone holdout has escaped the backlash. You can probably guess which one. (For the record, Canada hasn't had a single anti-immigrant riot in half a century.)

What's going on in the Great White North? Why are modern Canadians—unlike their predecessors a few short decades ago and virtually everyone else today—so content to hold open their nation's doors? How has Canada inoculated itself against the ugly populism infecting the rest of the planet? It's not enough to say that Canada has always been a country of immigrants; although that happens to be true, so has the much more xenophobic United States. Nor are Canada's current attitudes the expression of some weird genetic predisposition. True, Canadians are often praised (or mocked) for being excruciatingly polite do-gooders. (They'll say sorry after bumping into inanimate objects.) But they are not, despite what my Canadian mother will tell you, simply more generous than Americans or anyone else. Their striking openness and resistance to nativist demogoguery are not innate. They are, rather, the product of extremely deft leadership: the same basic formula behind every other success story discussed in this book. In Canada's case, that leadership produced government policies brilliantly designed to convince the country's citizens that immigration is both a necessity and a good. Ottawa has taught Canadians that immigration is not a bug in their country's political and social system, but a central feature: an essential source of the nation's identity and its remarkable success.

Yet the Canadian government didn't craft this policy out of selflessness or principle. The country embraced immigration because it had to. Canadian virtue was born of necessity.

No INDIVIDUAL DEMONSTRATES that fact and epitomizes Canada's evolution better than the father of Canada's current leader, who served as prime minister from 1968 to 1984 (with one brief interruption): Pierre Elliott Trudeau.

These days the elder Trudeau is usually remembered as the epitome of the highly evolved intellectual turned statesman: a dashing, cosmopolitan philosopher-king who quoted Plato, wore his sideburns long, grooved with the Beatles, practiced yoga, and showed the world that you actually can combine "sexy" and "Canadian" in a single sentence without a punch line. (Despite being hollow-cheeked, pockmarked, and balding, Trudeau was irresistibly charming. He entered politics in 1965 as Canada's most eligible bachelor, and would date a string of celebrities, including Barbra Streisand, before ultimately marrying a beautiful, dark-haired hippie twenty-nine years his junior.)

But—and this is key to the story, as it helps explain both his and Canada's subsequent evolution on immigration—Trudeau didn't start out so enlightened. Born in Montreal to a wealthy family—his father, Charles-Émile, was a farmer's son who liked to drink and gamble and made a fortune in the gas station business—Trudeau began his public life the same way many other members of Canada's traditionally oppressed francophone minority did at the time: as a reactionary Catholic, a French nationalist, and an ethnic chauvinist. Although he was the product of a mixed marriage—his mother, Grace Elliott, came from French and Scottish stock, and the family spoke both French and English in the home—as a teen, the young Trudeau had joined a revolutionary separatist secret society (the Frères Chasseurs), written racist plays, participated in at least one anti-Semitic riot, and during World War II (a war he thought Canada should stay out of) told a crowd that he "feared the peaceful invasion of immigrants more than the armed invasion of the enemy."

But after earning a law degree from the University of Montreal, Trudeau left the cloistered world of Quebec. In 1944 he headed first to Harvard, where he tacked a sign declaring "Pierre Trudeau, Citizen of the World" to his dorm-room door while working toward a master's degree in political economy. He moved on to France and then England, where he studied at the London School of Economics with the renowned political scientist Harold Laski—who also happened to be a socialist and a Jew. That education, plus a subsequent year spent backpacking around the world, thoroughly cured the young French Canadian of his nativism; Trudeau came home in 1949 sporting a beatnik beard and a very different philosophy. He spent several years working as a journalist, civil rights advocate, and law professor, and by the time he entered politics in 1965, he had transformed into a bona fide leftist and a committed Canadian federalist. Still rich, aristocratic, and patrician—he drove a Mercedes convertible and wore a gold Rolex—Trudeau had also become hip and impishly unconventional (at least for a politician). He started sporting a red rose in his lapel, and was once mocked for wearing an ascot in Parliament—only to undercut the image by then showing up in sandals. By the time he was elected Canada's leader in 1968, he'd also developed into a shrewd pragmatist who made "Reason Over Passion" his personal motto and hung a quilt embroidered with the slogan in his official residence, at Ottawa's 24 Sussex Drive.

While Trudeau may have evolved, however, most of his compatriots had yet to catch up. This scion of French Canada ascended to power at precisely the moment when unrest among his francophone constituents, who then made up about a third of the country's population, was reaching a fever pitch.

Quebecers in those days had plenty of reasons to feel disgruntled. In the decades following Canada's independence in 1867, they'd been subjected to forced assimilation, official discrimination, and casual bias. Canada's British-affiliated elites tended to view francophones as a base and subject people; in 1889 a Toronto newspaper encapsulated this view when it referred to French Canadians as "dirty, grimy, rheumy-eyed . . . specimens" who no more resembled the average anglophone "than South-African Hottentots resemble educated and civilized Europeans." Such prejudice lasted well into the 1900s; in the early part of the century, many Canadian provinces banned French-language education in their schools and required teachers to pass English-language competency exams. Things were so bad that between 1840 and 1930, close to a million French Canadians fled the country for the United States—an exodus historians attribute to the particularly unpleasant conditions they faced at home.

The nastiest forms of oppression were slowly rolled back in the decades that followed, but by the time Trudeau took power, average per capita income in Quebec was still just two-thirds that of the country's as a whole, and French speakers remained underrepresented in the upper levels of the federal bureaucracy and in the corporate world.

Following World War II, resentment over such injustices and the smothering influence of the Catholic Church had produced what came to be known as the Quiet Revolution, an attempt by the Quebecois to finally equalize their status in Canada. But by the late 1960s, that revolution had erupted into a furiously loud one. Support for Quebec's secession was growing in the province—spurred on by no less a figure than the French president Charles de Gaulle, who had visited in 1967 and shouted *"Vive le Québec libre!"* from a Montreal balcony. (He was promptly sent packing.) Things were so bad that a militant group, the Front de libération du Québec (FLQ), had sprung up and begun plotting an armed war of independence. Throughout the 1960s, the FLQ was involved in more than two hundred bombings, the worst of which was a February 1969 explosion in the Montreal stock exchange that injured twenty-seven people. The wave of violence would culminate the following year, when the FLQ kidnapped Britain's trade commissioner, James Cross, as well as the province's labor minister, Pierre Laporte, who was ultimately found strangled to death—with his own gold necklace—in the trunk of a green Chevrolet. (Cross was recovered unharmed.)

ALL THIS MEANT that when Trudeau took power in 1968, he faced two daunting and interlocking problems, which would soon lead him to revolutionize Canada's immigration policies.

The first was how to address the rage of his Quebecois constituents while keeping the country, a loose and often fractious federation, together.

It was a challenge that Trudeau, as Canada's third-ever francophone leader, took very personally. And it was one that, given his bicultural background and his own early flirtation with militant separatism, he seemed perfectly positioned to address. Yet Trudeau's first attempt to do so was hardly a triumph. After decades of ignoring the problem, Ottawa, worried about what a government report called "the greatest crisis in [Canada's] history," had five years earlier finally appointed a Royal Commission on Bilingualism and Biculturalism to propose solutions. In 1969, in one of his first major initiatives, Trudeau seized on the recommendations of the B & B Commission to push through the Official Languages Act (OLA). The bill formally gave French equal status alongside English for the first time in Canada's history, requiring the government to do business in both and guaranteeing bilingual education throughout the country.

Rather than assuage tensions, however, the OLA only further inflamed them. The legislation was predictably popular with francophones. But it certainly wasn't with the anglophone elite. And it met with even more intense opposition from Canada's *other* minorities, especially in the country's distant western provinces. Championed by Senator Paul Yuzyk—a square-jawed son of Ukrainian immigrants who had worked as a Slavic studies professor in Manitoba before entering politics—these often-overlooked groups, which began calling themselves the "Third Force," were mostly made up of eastern Europeans but also included Italians, Armenians, Portuguese, Greeks, and Jews. They represented about 26 percent of Canada's population at the time and were a key part of Trudeau's Liberal Party support base. But they didn't consider either English *or* French their native language, and definitely didn't want either to become dominant. Led by Yuzyk, they denounced the OLA and its sponsor for overlooking the very fact of their existence.

That forced Trudeau to adopt a broader strategy. Rather than make another incremental move, this time he decided to try something breathtakingly audacious: to transform Canada's fundamental identity from a binary nation into a multicultural one. On October 8, 1971, Trudeau strode into Canada's neo-Gothic Parliament building and, in a bombshell speech, announced that "cultural pluralism is the very essence of Canadian identity"—and that the government's two-language policy wasn't doing enough to nourish it. "There cannot be one cultural policy for Canadians of British and French origin, another for the original peoples, and yet a third for all others," he declared. "Although there are two official languages, there is no official culture, nor does any ethnic group take precedence over any other. No citizen or group of citizens is other than Canadian, and all should be treated fairly."

To make sure they were, the prime minister proceeded to create a new Ministry of Multiculturalism—the first of its kind anywhere in the world—as well as a Canadian Consultative Council on Multiculturalism. Trudeau steadily increased support for these bodies throughout his tenure, from an initial funding of $3 million a year up to a total of $23 million in 1984, the year he left office. And he set up the Canadian Human Rights Commission in 1978 to lead federal education campaigns aimed at fighting discrimination and to hear complaints of unequal treatment in the private sector.

Trudeau's motivation for doing all this was at least partly idealistic, as he liked to emphasize with the public. ("If Canada is to survive, it can only survive in mutual respect and in love for one another," he later said.) All evidence suggests that the self-declared Citizen of the World truly wanted to create a new multihued but distinctly *Canadian* identity that everyone—francophones, anglophones, and Canada's other minorities—could buy into. (Though briefly mentioned in Trudeau's 1971 speech, Canada's native peoples were, as usual, largely left out of the conversation.)

There's also no question that his attempt to reshape Canada's ethnic self-image was politically perilous. Conservatives mocked it as a feel-good exercise that would amount to nothing more than government funding for "folk dances, festivals . . . and songfests." (This wasn't quite fair; while the government did increase funding for celebrations of ethnic heritage, it also promoted integration by financing ethnic advocacy groups and other initiatives.) Many Quebecers, meanwhile, feared that multiculturalism meant that "French culture was being downgraded to one among many," in the phrase of Jeffrey Reitz, the University of Toronto sociologist.

Multiculturalism, moreover, would soon earn a bad reputation in other parts of the globe—a taint that has only grown over the decades. In recent years, politicians ranging from the former British prime minister David Cameron to the German chancellor Angela Merkel have denounced multicultural policies; Cameron, summing up the standard critique, blamed them for discouraging a common sense of national identity and promoting cultural balkanization. Even in 1971, Trudeau's new approach produced anxiety; the *Toronto Star* worried that it might encourage immigrants to think of Canada as an unconnected "chain of ethnic enclaves."

But Trudeau anticipated such dangers, and was very deliberate both in how he crafted his new initiative—and how he sold it. As John English, the prime minister's leading biographer, told me, Trudeau knew that he risked creating "ethnic ghettos," which he staunchly opposed. So when he declared in his October speech that his government would begin supporting all of the country's cultures—"the small and weak groups no less than the strong and highly organized"—he also announced that this support would come with a condition: such groups had to first demonstrate "a desire and effort to . . . contribute to Canada." His underlying message was clear: social integration remained a key goal. The only difference was that Trudeau was now insisting that integration and the retention of one's native culture need not be mutually exclusive.

Although Trudeau's move may have looked like the height of utopian policymaking, it was also coldly pragmatic. Despite what he publicly announced at the time, and though he'd avoid mentioning it in subsequent speeches, one of Trudeau's main priorities in crafting multiculturalism was practical and political: to preserve Canada's newly mandated bilingualism in order to reduce the threat of Quebecois separatism and keep Canada together.

But defending federalism was only part of the story. Remember that when Trudeau took office, he faced *two* big problems. Canada's cultural divide was just the first of them. The second was every bit as pressing: how to assimilate the tidal wave of immigrants who had just then started pouring into the country.

What made this second challenge even more urgent was the fact that, for the first time in Canada's history, a great many of these newcomers weren't white.

TO UNDERSTAND HOW this sudden and momentous change had come about, you first have to understand that Canada, back in the 1950s and 1960s, was a strange sort of country—one "built against any common, geographic, historic or cultural sense," as Trudeau himself once put it.

On the one hand, it was physically immense, the world's second-largest state by landmass. On the other, its population was tiny: less than 18 million in 1960 (or about a tenth that of the United States at the time).

Those two facts had long provoked intense anxiety in Ottawa. In 1966 a report by the Department of Manpower and Immigration had fretted that Canada was "an underpopulated country by most standards of measurement" and had urged the government to "fill up our empty spaces as rapidly as possible." A few years earlier, the Conservative prime minister John Diefenbaker had warned that "Canada must populate or perish."

There were two reasons for this urgency. First, the paucity of Canadians made it hard for the federal government to control its vast territory. That was especially the case because then as now the bulk of the country's residents inhabited a narrow band that stretched alongside the four-thousand-mile southern border with the United States. And they affiliated almost as strongly with their neighbors immediately to their south—Nova Scotians with New Englanders, Manitobans with Minnesotans, Alberta cowboys with Montana ranchers, and rain-soaked British Columbians with Washingtonians—as they did with their compatriots living on the other side of their gigantic continent.

Second, Canada's economy was starting to boom—between 1939 and 1962, the country's GDP rocketed from $5.7 billion to $36 billion—and unless it got more workers, it risked stalling out and falling into a tailspin. Yet getting those workers was proving difficult because the United States was also booming at the time. In fact, the US appetite for laborers, especially skilled ones, had grown so ravenous in the postwar years that the few such workers Canada possessed were starting to get sucked south (between 1953 and 1963 Canada lost more than forty thousand professionals and another forty thousand trained workers to the US market). As a consequence, Ottawa desperately needed to produce more Canadians. The question was how.

For many years, there had been no question. Back in 1947, when Mackenzie King gave that infamous speech justifying the "White Canada" policy, he wasn't announcing a new direction but defending what had been Ottawa's practice for decades. Ever since Confederation in 1867, the Canadian government had followed an explicitly discriminatory immigration policy. (To be fair, so had most other states.) To ensure that Canada was settled by the right sort of people, Ottawa had distinguished between three types of foreigners: "preferred," "non-preferred," and "excluded." The first group came from the British Isles or northern Europe and were actively recruited. The second hailed from southern or eastern Europe and were only admitted—reluctantly—during particularly intense manpower shortages. As for the third, they included everybody else, and as the name suggests they were to be barred at all times. (As in the western United States in the 1800s and early 1900s, Asian immigrants were particularly feared and detested.)

Such racism was rationalized through all kinds of pseudoscientific studies; as the academic Elspeth Cameron has documented, Canadian "doctors, journalists, philosophers, politicians, and poets alike" all argued during this period that "Canada's northern environment was only suited to . . . white northern races." In 1952, according to Valerie Knowles, the author of a history of immigration to Canada, legislation had been passed that gave the federal cabinet the unlimited discretion "to prohibit or limit the admission of persons by reason of such factors as nationality, ethnic group, occupation, lifestyle, unsuitability with regard to Canada's climate"—whatever that actually meant—"and perceived inability to become readily assimilated into Canadian society." Such policies were widely popular; in 1954—the same year the US Supreme Court struck down official segregation in *Brown v. Board of Education*—Canada's most liberal newspaper had declared that racial discrimination was "an established (and most would say sensible) feature of our immigration policy."

But World War II, the Holocaust, decolonization, and Canada's enthusiastic participation in the rise of the global human rights movement had started making such explicitly discriminatory policies awkward to sustain. Beginning in the 1950s, Canada's nonwhite friends in the British Commonwealth, as well as domestic advocacy groups like the Canadian Congress of Labour, had begun quietly pointing out the conflict between Ottawa's progressive rhetoric at the UN and other international bodies and its racist policies at home. Such pressure had set the Canadian government to worrying about its image; an internal working paper from 1957 recommended "revising our immigration legislation so as to avoid the charge of racial discrimination" while continuing to limit nonwhite immigration "to prevent aggravation of the Asiatic minority problem."

The trouble with maintaining such limits—even in secret—was that starting in the early 1960s Canada was confronted by an even bigger problem than international opprobrium. Just when its labor shortage was growing most acute, immigration from its preferred source, Europe, began drying up, as the Continent finally rebounded from the wreckage of World War II. Skilled workers in particular became harder and harder to find.

So Ottawa—again, more from necessity than principle—needed to switch course. In 1962 Canada formally abandoned ethnicity as a basis for evaluating immigrants, becoming the first country in the world to do so. And in a move that would prove critical to the success of Canadian immigration in later years, it decided to start judging applicants on their educational, professional, and technical qualifications instead. As Ellen Fairclough, then Canada's immigration minister, explained the new rules, "any suitably qualified person, from any part of the world," would henceforth be eligible for entry, and the government would look solely at "his own merit, without regard to his race, color, [or] national origin."

That sure sounded good. But as Richard J. F. Day, a sociologist at Queen's University in Kingston, Ontario, has revealed, Fairclough "was simply not telling the whole truth." The new color-blind approach turned out not to be as impartial as it pretended: over the next five years, Ottawa maintained strict limits on the numbers of non-European immigrants who could be sponsored by relatives already in Canada, and only actively recruited from the United States, the United Kingdom, and northern Europe. Such hypocrisy probably shouldn't have come as a surprise: just a year before Fairclough's declaration, a district superintendent of immigration, W. R. Baskerville, had said that while the aim of the reform was to officially "abolish racial discrimination," Ottawa would "still give preference . . . to those countries which have traditionally supplied [its] immigrants."

The persistence of such preferences, however, meant that the new policy didn't achieve either of its goals: attracting enough new workers or protecting the government from domestic and international condemnation. So five years later, Prime Minister Lester Pearson's Liberal government finally dropped all remaining ethnic criteria from Canada's immigration system. In its place, Pearson adopted an innovative new policy, the basic contours of which remain in place today. Henceforth, all independent applicants for residency—regardless of birthplace or race—would be assessed by assigning them points on the basis of nine criteria, such as education, age, fluency in English or French, and whether or not their skills fit Canada's economic needs. Those who scored above a certain number would get in, period. Nothing else would matter.

The effects of this policy shift were immediate and dramatic. Between 1946 and 1953, 96 percent of immigrants to Canada had come from Europe. Between 1968 and 1988, that figure dropped to 38 percent. By 1977 Asians, Caribbeans, Latin Americans, and Africans, who had been effectively banned until 1962, came to constitute more than half of all immigrants admitted each year.

As might be expected given Canada's less-than-noble history, as well as its ethnic makeup at the time, these changes initially provoked intense opposition, especially in Quebec. Although much of the political establishment had been forced to come around to the idea of race-blind immigration, most Canadians had not. In 1960 the public opposed *any* increase in immigration by a whopping 67 percent, and a poll taken a year later found that a majority of Canadians wanted the government to continue restricting the entry of nonwhites. Five years later, on the eve of Trudeau's ascent to power, more than half of Canadians surveyed still opposed the government's color-blind immigration system.

THIS, THEN, WAS the second problem that Trudeau inherited. And according to English, his biographer, it was the prime minister's other big reason for launching his new multiculturalism policy in 1971.

The truth is that Trudeau was no immigration zealot; in the later years of his tenure, when Canada was hit by a sharp recession, he actually lowered admissions quotas. But that only emphasizes the fact that here again Trudeau's decision to bet everything on multiculturalism owed more to necessity than it did to principle; he was putting reason over passion, as his motto dictated.

And whatever his true motivation, Trudeau's new emphasis on pluralism, coupled with Canada's shift to a color-blind and economic-focused immigration system, quickly began to change the way Canadians thought about the issues. Indeed, the two policies soon proved mutually reinforcing. By selecting immigrants primarily based on what they could contribute in material terms, instead of what they looked like—or whether they already had family in the country—the new system promptly began producing financial dividends that helped convince still-wary Canadians that opening their doors would benefit everyone, especially themselves. (This is a critical difference between Canada and the United States, which still uses family reunification as its primary entrance criterion today: a well-intentioned but extremely irrational approach that, in effect, lets an arbitrary factor—whether or not an applicant's relatives had the cunning or dumb luck to get into the country before them—shape the nation's immigrant population.)

Meanwhile, generous government support for multiculturalism and the integration of newcomers has gradually persuaded native-born Canadians that the broadening of their country's ethnic makeup makes their nation *more* Canadian, not less.

In the years since Trudeau left office, successive governments have tinkered with both policies, but almost always in ways that have enhanced their positive impact. In recent years, for example, Ottawa has put greater stress on formal education, and has made it easier for businesspeople likely to create new jobs to settle in the country; in 2013 it even created a Start-up Visa Program, which aims to attract entrepreneurs by granting them immediate permanent residency if they can secure venture capital from Canadian investors. To enhance local buy-in (especially in Quebec), the federal government has given provinces greater input into the selection process so they can ensure that it meets their particular economic needs. And Ottawa is developing a web portal that will function like an online dating site, matching applicants to specific unfilled jobs.

Throughout this period, the government also steadily increased its support for multiculturalism. In 1982 Trudeau oversaw the passage of the Charter of Rights and Freedoms: a sweeping and progressive constitutional document that formally bans discrimination, mandates equality in hiring, and instructs judges to keep Canada's multicultural heritage in mind when interpreting the country's laws. And the government has increased spending to promote pluralism, such that it now dishes out more than $1 billion a year on a wide variety of related programs. These range from pro-immigration TV documentaries to teaching aids for primary and secondary schools to support for community-based immigrant integration efforts.

Taken together, all these policies help explain what scholars call "the Canadian Exception": the fact that the country has managed to avoid the anti-immigrant backlashes that have rocked virtually every other industrialized state in recent years. They help explain why the Migrant Integration Policy Index (a global survey) ranks Canada's immigration system among the best on the planet. And they help explain why Canadians themselves would probably rank it even higher. It's not an accident that as immigration levels have steadily risen over the last two decades—remaining high even in the face of several economic downturns—Canadians' support for the country's generous immigration policies has also gone up.

After all, Ottawa's stress on economic admissions criteria—65 percent of newcomers to Canada in 2015 were admitted under that program—has created one of the world's most successful immigrant populations. Today Canada's foreign-born citizenry is more educated than any other nation's: about half of new Canadians enter the country with college degrees, compared with 27 percent in the United States, and second-generation Canadians are more likely to attend university than peers with native-born parents. While immigrants represent about 21 percent of Canada's population, they occupy 35 percent of all university chairs, and two of the last three governors-general (the country's symbolic head of state) were nonwhites born overseas; in fact, both came to Canada as refugees. Canadian immigrants work hard and don't suck in many benefits; indeed, economic-class migrants consume less in welfare spending than do native-born Canadians. Their employment rate is among the highest in the OECD, and without them, Canada's workforce would be shrinking and aging. Little wonder, then, that 70 percent of Canadians view immigration as a key way to strengthen the economy. Even a large majority of Canada's unemployed feel the same way.

And thanks to multiculturalism, Canadians also see immigration as a key way to strengthen the nation's identity. Such sentiment has grown steadily since Trudeau first launched the policy. When a polling firm asked Canadians in 1985 what made them proudest of their country, multiculturalism came in tenth. By 2006, however, it had climbed into second place. And in a similar survey, Canadians listed multiculturalism ahead of hockey—*hockey!*—bilingualism, and the queen. (Yes, Canada has a queen; Google it.) Polls show that, all told, 85 percent of Canadians now see multiculturalism as very or somewhat important to the national identity. That explains why the most patriotic among them also tend to be the most pro-immigration—unlike Americans, for whom the opposite is true. It's not that Canadians don't expect immigrants to blend in. Rather, as Reitz argues, Trudeau's initiative has fostered "a more open or tolerant"—and, one could argue, patient—view of how integration is supposed to work and what it's supposed to look like.

Multiculturalism has also provided Canadians, who have always been slightly uncertain about what being Canadian actually means, a convenient way to distinguish themselves from their giant neighbor to the south. As Reitz explains, pluralism has come to join the list of peculiarly Canadian policies, such as generous state-run health care, strict gun control, and an embrace of gay rights, that help Canadians feel proud of who they are—and who they are not. Today multiculturalism even sells beer: in the summer of 2015, Molson ran a TV commercial featuring a computerized fridge placed on sidewalks that would unlock and dispense free suds once passersby said the magic words—"I am a Canadian"—in six foreign languages.

Scholars think a couple of other factors have probably also contributed to Canada's extraordinary openness. One is the fact that, unlike the United States, Germany, Japan, and many other industrialized countries, Canada has never had sizable temporary worker programs; indeed, according to government statistics, Canada has the highest naturalization rate in the world, with 85 percent of eligible permanent residents becoming citizens. That's important because citizens are more likely than guests to invest in their new homeland and be welcomed for doing so. (Recent Conservative governments have experimented with guest worker programs in a way that makes immigration experts nervous, but so far such policies haven't had much impact.)

It's probably even more significant that Canada has never had much of a problem with illegal immigration. Thanks to its geographic isolation—Canada is sheltered by vast oceans to its east and west, a frozen wasteland to its north and the American border to its south—illegal migration only "laps gently onto Canadian shores, it does not come in large waves," in the words of one academic. As a result, whereas almost a third of the United States' current foreign-born population is undocumented, the figure is much smaller in Canada—somewhere between 3 and 6 percent. While these small numbers probably play a role in explaining Canadians' remarkable openness, however, they hardly tell the whole story; after all, the United Kingdom is also isolated geographically, and has close to the same percentage of undocumented workers as Canada does. Yet Brits are twice as hostile to immigration as are their former colonial subjects.

AS I MENTIONED earlier, the story of Canada's astonishing evolution on immigration had a lot more to do with pragmatism and necessity than idealism. It's a story of a country doing the right thing because it had to, not because it necessarily wanted to. After all, a flow chart of the development of Canada's key reforms would look like this:

white Canada policy + economic boom + European labor shortage

↓

international condemnation + Canadian labor shortage

↓

adoption of race-blind system

And the evolution of multiculturalism would look like this:

oppression of francophones
↓
separatist threat
↓
passage of OLA
↓
rise of the "Third Force"
↓
creation of Trudeau's multiculturalism policy

One other, more recent coda to the story therefore bears mentioning, both because it reinforces my point (and suggests that Canada is likely to preserve its pragmatic approach in the future) and because it highlights what makes Canada such a good model for other countries struggling to get their own immigration systems right.

The hero of this part of the tale is an unlikely one. Immigration in Canada has long been something of a bipartisan cause. It was a Conservative prime minister, Diefenbaker, who first moved the country toward a color-blind system. And it was another Conservative—Brian Mulroney—who enshrined Trudeau's multiculturalism policy into law in 1988, and who, in a dramatic break with tradition, maintained high immigration levels despite a sharp recession in the early 1990s—a step that contributed to Canadians' growing conviction that immigration strengthens rather than weakens the economy.

But both Diefenbaker and Mulroney were centrists, leaders of what was then known as the Progressive Conservative Party (a very Canadian oxymoron). In 2006 Canadians elected a man cut from a very different Conservative cloth. Prime Minister Stephen Harper was much more right-wing and far closer in style to an American Republican than to the Canadian Tories of old. Ruthless and high-handed, Harper had made his name in the short-lived Reform Party, a populist protest movement that arose in Canada's oil-rich libertarian west. Reform was highly skeptical of both multiculturalism and immigration; its 1988 platform declared that immigration should not be "designed to radically or suddenly alter the ethnic makeup of Canada, as it increasingly seems to be," and a 1991 revision to the party's manifesto called for opposition to "the current concept of . . . hyphenated Canadianism" and proposed abolishing the Ministry of Multiculturalism altogether.

Many Canadians feared that Harper would act on such sentiments when he took office in 2006. Yet for the most part his government confounded such assumptions. True, Harper made some tweaks to the system (by canceling backlogs, for example, and putting still more emphasis on aspiring immigrants' economic potential), but he was generally careful not to upset the basic structure. And although he was justly criticized in 2015 for trying to curry nationalist support by banning Muslim women from wearing the *niqab* during citizenship ceremonies (a ban the courts promptly overruled), his government also took a long list of surprisingly progressive steps on immigration and multiculturalism, such as reducing immigration fees; organizing commemoration days for the Armenian and Ukrainian genocides; and creating a Community Historical Recognition Program, with a $13.5 million budget devoted to memorializing the struggles of ethnic Canadians in the country's past. Harper even apologized to and compensated victims of the notorious "head tax" that the Canadian government used between 1885 and 1923 to discourage Chinese immigration.

Given Harper's style and background, there's good reason to believe that these moves stemmed more from cold political calculations than some Damascene conversion. It turns out that a few years before his election, Jason Kenney—a young Conservative activist who went on to serve as Harper's minister for immigration and multiculturalism—had quietly convinced his boss that if it ever hoped to achieve majority status, their party needed to boost its popularity among Canada's immigrants. But that wouldn't be hard, Kenney argued, since most newcomers hail from traditional cultures, which could make them natural Conservative voters. Harper bought the argument, and with his blessing, Kenney spent the years between 2006 and 2011 endlessly visiting mosques, Sikh temples, and immigrant centers (sometimes hitting twenty-five venues in a single day), where he would greet crowds in Punjabi or Mandarin. He even organized several "friendship days" each year, during which ethnic leaders could visit Parliament Hill and meet with government ministers.

These efforts paid off handsomely. During the 2011 election campaign, the Conservatives fielded more minority candidates than the Liberals or even the far-left New Democratic Party. They ran ads in a host of foreign languages. And when the ballots were counted, the Conservatives had outpolled Trudeau's old party among foreign-born Canadians for the first time ever—a historic breakthrough.

Was the strategy a cynical ploy? Maybe; but it doesn't really matter. For if it was, Harper and Kenney were only following what has become a Canadian tradition: embracing effective, progressive policies for unsentimental and hardheaded reasons. As Trudeau showed more than forty years ago, virtue in government is no less valuable when born of necessity. The results are what matter. And the results in Canada have been spectacular: they turned a small, closed, ethnically homogeneous state into a vibrant global powerhouse and one of the most open and successful multicultural nations in the world.*

That's a record politicians everywhere, especially in the United States, would be wise to study carefully.

---

* Indeed, Canadians would punish Harper when he ultimately strayed from this path; his Islamophobic gestures during the 2015 race, mild as they were by US or European standards, helped doom his reelection bid. And it is highly revealing about Canadians' true preferences that the man who replaced him, Justin Trudeau, brought with him the most diverse cabinet in history, featuring four Sikhs—double the number then serving in India's cabinet—as well as a former Afghan refugee.

3

KILL THEM WITH KINDNESS

How Indonesia Crushed and Co-opted
Its Islamic Extremists

I N THE SPRING OF 1998, THE CITIZENS OF INDONESIA TOOK TO
the streets and, in one of history's most electrifying displays of people power, tossed their long-serving dictator out of office.

Happy though that moment was, almost everyone expected the country to quickly fall apart. Enormous and wildly diverse—Indonesia is made up of 17,500 islands scattered over three thousand miles of ocean, and is home to some 250 million citizens speaking more than seven hundred languages—the nation barely seemed to make sense in the first place.

Suharto* may have been a tyrant, but at least he'd been a competent one. That was especially true when it came to the economy, which he'd kept growing by an average of 7 percent a year for his thirty-year tenure. And it was true when it came to the management of religious tensions. For all his faults, Suharto had been a reliably *secular* tyrant. Though almost 90 percent of Indonesians are Muslim, and the country never separated church (or mosque) and state the way many Western nations do, Suharto had ruthlessly crushed or co-opted any attempt to make the place more Islamic.

With the strongman suddenly gone, the economy in free fall, and the lid of repression removed, the country seemed headed for a cataclysm. In December 1998 the *New York Times* warned that Indonesia was "facing one of the most dangerous years in its history," and *Time* predicted that the nation would burn. Even sober academics warned that this massive, impoverished archipelago could explode and disinte-

---

* Like many Indonesians, Suharto generally used only one name.

grate Balkan-style. Or the still-powerful army would reassert itself. Or the world's largest Muslim-majority country would adopt a tyrannical form of Islamic rule, becoming an Asian Iran on the Andaman Sea.

In the months that followed, Indonesia seemed headed in just those directions. As the state faltered, riots rocked Jakarta. Nationalist thugs targeted Indonesia's wealthy and much-resented ethnic-Chinese minority, looting their stores and killing over a thousand. Separatists relaunched insurgencies in outlying provinces. Mulyanto Utomo, the editor of a local newspaper, captured the exhilaration and terror of the moment well when he told a reporter, "Indonesian people have been in chains for 30 years, and now everyone wants to shout. Nobody is in control."

Islamist militias soon jumped into the fray, unleashing a nationwide bombing campaign that racked up hundreds of casualties and sparking a virtual Muslim-Christian holy war in several regions. Theocratic political parties began to rebuild themselves, training cadres and setting up ultraconservative *pesantrens* (religious boarding schools) in areas underserved by the rudderless central government. When, in 1999, Indonesia held its first free legislative elections in forty-four years, Islamic parties scored an alarming 36 percent of the vote.

Now fast-forward to today: against all odds, not one of the worst predictions about Indonesia's future has actually materialized. Instead of descending into dysfunction or repression, the world's fourth-most-populous country has become one of its more successful (if messy) democracies; in the 2014 presidential elections, for example, some 135 million ballots were peacefully cast at 480,000 polling stations, and power changed hands in a fairly orderly fashion for the fourth time in sixteen years. Civilian control over this former military dictatorship has been so thoroughly consolidated that nowadays the generals wouldn't dream of challenging their elected bosses. All but a few corners of the country are at peace: terrorist attacks, which once claimed hundreds of lives and kept most Western tourists and businesspeople away, have become rare, and most of the long-burning insurgencies have been peacefully resolved. At the same time, what was once one of the world's most unified states has undertaken an extraordinarily far-reaching experiment in decentralization, doling out most political power to its regions (the only briefs Jakarta retains are defense, justice, religious affairs, and foreign, economic, and fiscal policy). Indonesia has become a rare thing in the Muslim world—indeed, in the developing world at large—a safe and stable beacon of open, decent, and tolerant rule.

That last adjective—"tolerant"—bears underscoring, since it represents contemporary Indonesia's greatest accomplishment. Even as its citizens have raucously embraced their new freedoms, including the right to practice Islam far more openly and devoutly than before, the vast majority have stopped their ears to the siren song of extremism. Today fewer Indonesian Muslims think their state should adopt sharia (Islamic law) than do the citizens of Afghanistan, Egypt, Iraq, Malaysia, or Pakistan. While Indonesia's Islamic parties can still mount big street protests from time to time, they have consistently underperformed at the polls. Since hitting a high point in the 2004 legislative elections, with a combined 38 percent, their popularity has dwindled: they managed just a quarter of the vote in 2009, and though their tally improved slightly in 2014, more than half that share went to the moderates among them, while support for ultraconservative parties fell.

As for terrorism, Indonesia's success there has been even more dramatic. True, militants still manage to pull off the occasional attack, but these are generally small. The big truth is that Indonesia has come close to effectively eliminating the threat of extremist violence. Hillary Clinton, during a 2009 visit to the country as secretary of state, was moved to declare: "If you want to know whether Islam, democracy, modernity and women's rights can coexist, go to Indonesia."

She was right: Indonesia has solved the puzzle and figured out how to put all these pieces together. That makes its story an invaluable object lesson for the world's forty-eight other Muslim-majority states, most of which are still desperately trying—often in vain—to beat back radicalism in its many ugly forms.

To UNDERSTAND HOW exactly Indonesia managed all this, it's important to start by acknowledging that, as scary as things looked in 1998, the country did have a few things going for it.

First, while its population has long been overwhelmingly Muslim,

Islam had traditionally looked different there than it did closer to the Arabian heartland. The religion, which is thought to have arrived in the islands around the thirteenth century, was never imposed by the sword, as it was by the princes and sheikhs of the Near East. Instead, locals picked it up piecemeal from visiting Arab and Indian traders. That slow process of accretion produced an extremely diverse set of practices and beliefs, which incorporated preexisting animist and tribal traditions and tolerant Sufi teachings. This blending of faiths, which academics call "syncretism," made Indonesians unusually open-minded and resistant to centrally imposed doctrine. And its legacy can still be felt today: as Elizabeth Pisani, author of *Indonesia, Etc.*, documents, despite an influx of more orthodox influences from the Middle East, some Indonesians still get their spiritual guidance from reading bird entrails. Every year, the Muslim sultan of Yogyakarta commemorates his romantic ties to the goddess of the South Sea. And many ordinary Indonesian Muslims regularly visit the tombs of holy saints or attend performances of *wayang*: Java's famous indigenous form of theater, in which baroquely filigreed shadow puppets act out tales inspired by Hindu epics like the *Ramayana*.

Indonesia's second advantage had to do with its Islamist political parties. While these groups have become a significant force in the country since Suharto's overthrow, they've turned out to be a reliably incompetent one—consistently failing to present a coherent economic agenda or live up to the more ethical, less corrupt standards they claim to represent. In 2013, for example, Luthfi Hasan Ishaaq, the head of one major Islamist party, was busted for taking a billion-rupiah (about $100,000) payoff to help secure a government contract—after investigators discovered his bagman holed up in a hotel room with a naked nineteen-year-old girl. And just a few years earlier, another of Luthfi's lieutenants was captured on camera watching porn on his iPad—during a session of the legislature, no less. So much for Islamic values.

So Indonesia got lucky in at least a couple of ways. But it would be a big mistake to chalk up its success to fortune or history alone. By the time Indonesia became a democracy, its blended approach to Islam was actually on the wane, as many locals turned to more conventional Sunni practices. In fact, Indonesia's population has actually been growing steadily more religiously conservative (at least in a personal sense) for some time now, as is illustrated by the growing popularity of headscarves and of fasting during Ramadan.

Indeed, what makes Indonesia such a striking case is that its moderation has little to do with secularism. Paradoxically, the nation has been moving further and further away from Islamic extremism at precisely the same time that its population has been growing more devout. This apparent contradiction can confuse visitors. On the surface, the increasingly visible displays of faith can look like signs of trouble. So do public opinion surveys like the 2012 poll in which some 70 percent of Indonesian Muslims said they favored the idea of living under Islamic law. But dig a little deeper, and you'll find that picture is more complex. So, for example, while many Indonesians do indeed now tell pollsters they're interested in sharia, most of them shudder at the harsh way it's enforced in places like Saudi Arabia. And very few of them stand up for Islamic law where it could actually make a difference: in the polling booth.

What explains these seemingly contrary trends: growing personal piety on the one hand and increasing antipathy toward political and militant Islam on the other? Apart from what I've already mentioned, the lion's share of credit goes to the top: to Indonesia's first three democratic leaders. This trio—Abdurrahman Wahid, Megawati Sukarnoputri, and Susilo Bambang Yudhoyono—was a highly diverse and often-underwhelming bunch. The truth is that they could be downright incompetent at times. But they got things right where it counted most, managing to steer their nation toward the moderate middle and outmaneuver Indonesia's Islamists at almost every turn.

THEIR STRATEGY FOR doing so involved five basic parts—though calling their approach to extremism a "strategy" may be a bit of a stretch. Much of it was improvised, and in some cases the three leaders stumbled backward or had to be pushed into the right policies. Nonetheless, it's worth considering their various efforts as a whole, since it's in aggregate that they proved so effective and offer a template that can be used elsewhere.

The first major prong of their approach actually had nothing to do with Islam per se. Different as Indonesia's first three democratic rulers were from one another, they shared one key trait: a dogged determination to consolidate their country's still-fragile freedoms. And that determination would reap major rewards. If not for their efforts to stabilize and strengthen Indonesia's fledgling democracy, the country could easily have gone in the other direction—which would have made subsequent reforms impossible. By making pluralistic politics more effective, these three leaders also made them seem more attractive to ordinary Indonesians. And that helped make the alternatives—like Islamic rule—seem less so.

To see what I mean, I need to take you back to October 1999, when Indonesia's freshly elected legislature, the People's Consultative Assembly (known by its Bahasa Indonesia acronym, MPR), chose Wahid to become the country's first democratic president.* Gus Dur, as everyone called him, was only fifty-nine at the time of his inauguration, but he was already virtually blind and recovering from a stroke. He seemed like a tired old man—and that impression never improved once he took office. He was a highly respected intellectual and a beloved religious leader (Wahid was a cleric and a former head of Nahdlatul Ulama, the country's biggest Islamic social welfare organization, which has some thirty to forty million members). But he turned out to be a clumsy, erratic politician, and his presidency is better remembered for his habit of nodding off in public—including, at least once, during one of his own speeches—than for any major legislation or reforms. That said, Wahid was a steadfast progressive and a pluralist, and he consistently stood up for the rights of ethnic and religious minorities during his tenure—stands that, given his Islamic credentials, made a lasting impression on ordinary Indonesians. Wahid was also a longtime critic of military rule, and he used his office to challenge and cashier a number of powerful generals when they tried to interfere in politics.

Yet Wahid's conduct proved so ineffectual in most other respects that just nineteen months after it made him president the MPR decided to replace him with his vice president, Megawati. Unlike Wahid,

---

* Indonesia didn't start holding direct elections for president until 2004.

who had cut his teeth opposing the country's old regime, Megawati was a product of it: her father, Sukarno, was independent Indonesia's first ruler, and she had always viewed the presidency as her birthright. Helmet-coiffed and imperious, Megawati rarely deigned to speak in public and was widely derided for her limitations; *The Economist* once scoffed that she "makes George Bush seem like an intellectual." Joshua Kurlantzick, a Southeast Asia expert at the Council on Foreign Relations, recalls that after taking office Megawati never showed much interest in the tedious work of actually running the country. She allowed Indonesia's economy to languish, and she was far too slow to acknowledge the growing terrorist threat.

Megawati thus accomplished little more in office than her predecessor had, and she didn't manage to hold on to her job for much longer either. She does, however, deserve great credit for building on Wahid's efforts to ease the army out of politics. When she first became president, the country had only been a democracy for two tumultuous years. The generals who had served as Suharto's praetorians still held considerable sway, were very leery of Indonesia's new freedoms, and were determined to retain the wealth and perks their old boss had used to buy their loyalty. Reasoning that, at the end of the day, they probably cared more about money than power, Megawati offered them a deal: she would let them keep their ill-gotten riches if they, in return, retreated to their barracks and abandoned their remaining roles in Indonesia's government.

The generals accepted. But because Megawati only lasted a few years in office, it fell to the man who replaced her—Yudhoyono—to consolidate and extend these gains.

Unlike his predecessors, SBY (as everyone calls him) managed to serve two full terms, holding power until October 2014. That can make it hard today to remember the somewhat ominous figure he cut when he first arrived on Indonesia's political scene. Back then he hardly looked likely to become a champion of civilian rule; if anything, Yudhoyono's ascent seemed to augur a return to the country's dark old days. The man was a recently retired and much-decorated four-star general who had staffed his campaign with many former military men. He'd also been a reliable Suharto stalwart back when he was still in uniform—even serving in East Timor during its bloody war for independence.

Underneath SBY's medals, however, beat the heart of a democrat. Despite his many years in the army, Yudhoyono—unlike a lot of his former brothers-in-arms—was never credibly accused of human rights abuses. He'd also, critically, spent several stretches of his military service in the United States, studying at Webster University in St. Louis, where he got a master's degree in management, and then at Fort Benning, Georgia, and the US Army Command and General Staff College at Fort Leavenworth, Kansas. These experiences had imbued SBY with a deep love for America, which he liked to call his "second country." And they seem to have left him with some American ideals as well.

That would become clear during a dramatic episode early in SBY's political career. In 2001 Yudhoyono, newly out of uniform, was serving as Gus Dur's senior security minister. In late May, his boss, facing impeachment at the hands of a hostile legislature, panicked and made an uncharacteristically illiberal move: he ordered SBY to declare a state of emergency in the hope that it would intimidate the president's enemies. Yudhoyono refused, and was immediately sacked for his defiance. The standoff temporarily ended his time in government (though Megawati soon reinstated him). But it helped establish his democratic bona fides and reputation for integrity.

Once he did become president, SBY used his military background to push the army even further to the political sidelines. As Robert Hefner, an anthropologist who has long studied Indonesia, explains, the president's rank and connections allowed him to persuade the still-anxious officer corps that "a détente with democracy was possible." (Yudhoyono's efforts to reform the once-notorious army were so effective that in 2005 Washington normalized military relations with the country.)

Even as he reassured his fellow officers, however, SBY also sought to reassure Indonesia's public that he'd put his old life firmly behind him. As president, he carefully avoided stiff-backed military mannerisms, adopting a mild-mannered, technocratic style instead. According to General Agus Widjojo, who'd served as SBY's commanding officer, this move was deliberate; his former protégé consciously eschewed the "charismatic, hero styles of leadership." SBY's placid, even plodding, demeanor, coupled with his portly and sleepy-eyed affect, would earn him the scorn of his opponents, who liked to compare him to a water buffalo. But it endeared him to a public that, after five decades of dictatorship, was sick of being ruled by domineering strongmen.

ALL THESE EFFORTS proved essential to Indonesia's democratic development. But they were only the first part of its leaders' campaign against extremism. The other four components, which were mostly developed and deployed by SBY, involved appropriating key chunks of the Islamists' agenda in order to steal their thunder—and much of their electoral support; inviting Islamist parties into the governing coalition, thereby giving them just enough rope to hang themselves, which they proceeded to do; relentlessly pursuing Islamist terrorists; and doing so in an extremely nimble way, avoiding many of the repressive tactics that would let the Islamists marshal public outrage to their cause.

Step one—depriving Muslim parties of their value proposition—involved something of a double game. On the one hand, Yudhoyono, like Gus Dur and Megawati, was always careful to publicly denounce the idea of Islamic government. While the Indonesian state had never been fully secular in the Western sense—the national ideology, *pancasila*, is premised on belief in "the one and only God," and all citizens are required to subscribe to one of six officially recognized faiths—that was as far as things went, and SBY insisted on keeping them there. He frequently criticized the idea of greater government involvement in religion; in 2010, for example, he blasted the notion of a sharia-based constitution as "unacceptable to Indonesians." And he often preached the virtues of tolerance, especially when talking to foreign audiences. The president told Charlie Rose in 2011 that his government took religious diversity very seriously and understood that it required steadfast support. And speaking at an award ceremony hosted by an American interfaith organization two years later, Yudhoyono promised to "always protect our minorities and ensure that no one suffers from discrimination."

Yet even as he was making such pledges, Yudhoyono also began to skillfully steal key parts of the fundamentalists' agenda for himself.

In the legislative contest held a few months before his election in 2004, the Islamist Prosperous Justice Party (PKS) had exploded onto the political scene, winning 7.2 percent of the popular vote (up from 1.4 percent in 1999) and forty-five seats in the lower house of the MPR. The PKS, which calls for the imposition of sharia and which analysts often compare to Egypt's Muslim Brotherhood, had campaigned on promises to be more *peduli* (caring) and *bersih* (clean) than Indonesia's secular parties—specifically, by fighting poverty and government graft. This second pledge, in particular, was especially appealing in a state long bedeviled by epic levels of what locals call "KKN": *korupsi, kolusi,* and *nepotisme.* It's estimated that during his decades in power, Suharto and his family had embezzled $15 billion to $35 billion from the state—a world record. And things hadn't gotten much better since the dictator's fall; in 2004 Transparency International ranked the country 133rd in its global Corruption Perceptions Index.

Seeing the opportunity this tradition gave him, SBY cast himself as a clean-government zealot. Shortly after his inauguration, he declared that the country would be "destroyed" if it didn't finally tackle corruption and he pledged to make its eradication his top priority. Launching what he called a "shock therapy" campaign, he directed his attorney general to target any banks suspected of dirty dealings—"regardless of who is behind them," he told an interviewer—and threw his weight behind the country's Corruption Eradication Commission, which he encouraged to go after high-profile targets. Over the next ten years, the KPK, as it is known in Indonesian, managed to convict and jail some 160 senior officials, including, in 2009, the former governor of Indonesia's central bank—who also happened to be the father-in-law of Yudhoyono's son. In 2013 the KPK even nailed the head of the constitutional court.

To undermine the Islamists' promise to improve living standards, meanwhile—an attractive idea at a time when more than half of Indonesians still lived on less than $2 a day—SBY launched a major antipoverty campaign, featuring direct cash transfers and increased food subsidies. He also focused hard on boosting the economy by pushing through a series of banking and other macroeconomic reforms, slashing government debt, and insisting that the country's educational system place greater emphasis on job skills. These moves, combined with a ravenous global appetite for commodities, helped turn Indonesia's moribund market into one of the world's hottest for most of the decade. Between 2006 and 2011, the country more than doubled its exports and slashed poverty and unemployment; in early 2012 it even regained investment-grade ratings for the first time since the 1998 Asian Financial Crisis.

SBY obviously had plenty of reasons to take on both these issues. But commandeering the Islamists' main campaign themes appears to have been at least part of his calculus. Greater uncertainty surrounds what would become the most controversial part of his legacy: his refusal to condemn vigilante groups, such as the Islamic Defenders Front, which would harass Christians and smash up bars and nightclubs in the name of religious purity. SBY was also accused of turning a blind eye to attacks on members of Indonesia's tiny Ahmadiyah sect, whom Sunni fundamentalists view as heretics.

Figuring out why SBY tolerated such behavior is tricky; indeed, the question continues to puzzle experts today. It's not as if the president, who is personally secular, ever subscribed to the vigilantes' worldview himself. Some analysts have therefore interpreted his refusal to intervene as a sign of simple weakness. But given that Yudhoyono showed plenty of mettle in other contexts and stared down even more daunting enemies, there's good reason to believe his passivity here was deliberate—another instance of his double game in action. This theory—that here too the president was working to steal the Islamists' thunder—is given further credence by the way his administration, on at least two occasions, acceded to those parties' demands that the government play a greater role in promoting Islam. The first of these instances occurred two years after SBY's election, when he issued a "religious harmony" decree that ostensibly applied to all the country's faiths, but in practice was used exclusively to keep minority sects from building new houses of worship. And the second came in 2008, when

SBY's Democratic Party backed a loosely worded antipornography law that bans any images or sounds "that violate the morals of society."

Scholars and human rights groups have angrily criticized the president's conduct in these areas; R. William Liddle, an Indonesia expert at Ohio State University, calls SBY's acquiescence to the persecution of the Ahmadis the greatest stain on his record. That judgment has merit—but it also lacks nuance. Liddle is certainly right that, whatever SBY's motivation, the president made some unpleasant compromises during his ten years in office. Yet such unpleasantness effectively kept Indonesia's true radicals weak and off guard—and so in a cold, utilitarian sense may have benefited the country as a whole.

THE THIRD STAGE of Indonesia's fight against extremism was premised on the recognition that attempts by secular governments elsewhere—think Egypt under Mubarak—to exclude Islamist parties from power have tended to backfire, only enhancing their appeal and radicalizing their members. To avoid this outcome, SBY did the opposite. Not only did he refrain from restricting the rights of Islamist parties, but he even brought four of them, including the sharia-based PKS, into his coalition and cabinet.

Once again, parsing SBY's motivation with perfect clarity is impossible. The president himself was far too smart to ever openly declare his intent to co-opt the Islamists, since saying so out loud would, obviously, have been self-defeating. And SBY's strategy seems to have been at least partially determined by political mathematics, given that his Democratic Party controlled only 7.5 percent of the legislature during his first term (its share grew to 21 percent in his second). SBY's big-tent approach was also very much in keeping with local culture. As one US diplomat with experience in the region told me (asking not to be named since he still works for the government), Yudhoyono's inclusiveness "was very Indonesian: rather than draw sharply opposing positions, you work toward the middle."

Whatever his exact thinking, however, SBY's close embrace of his opponents proved extremely effective in diminishing their appeal.

"Keeping the Islamists in the circle was useful," the US official explained. Just as involvement in the messy world of elections and governance, with its inevitable missteps, disappointments, and failures, dramatically reduced the popularity of the Muslim Brotherhood in Egypt and Hamas in Gaza, bringing Indonesia's Islamic parties into the political mainstream—and forcing them to try to accomplish something—demystified their allure, as their falling poll numbers and the long list of scandals suggest.

YET POLITICAL ISLAM, remember, was only part of Indonesia's problem. The new democracy faced an even deadlier threat during its early years: Islamist terrorism. Between 1999 and 2002, fighting in just one province—Maluku—killed more than five thousand people and displaced another five hundred thousand, while in 2001 alone extremists successfully staged more than one hundred attacks nationwide.

The bloodshed reached a terrible peak on the night of October 12, 2002. At 11:05 that evening, Jemaah Islamiyah (JI), a terrorist group linked to al-Qaeda, set off a small bomb inside Paddy's Bar, a tourist restaurant on the easygoing, mostly Hindu island of Bali. Seconds later, as panicked vacationers flooded the streets, the terrorists detonated a second, much larger explosive outside the packed Sari Club. The carnage was horrifying: by the time the smoke had cleared and the dismembered bodies had been counted, 202 people were dead, including 88 Australians and 7 Americans, and more than 500 had been injured. (A smaller bomb was also set off outside a nearby US consulate that night, but it did little damage.)

Megawati, who was president at the time, had initially ignored the growing terrorist threat. She had rejected offers of assistance from Washington and other allies and had refused to even acknowledge that Indonesia had a problem, at one point insisting that JI did in fact not exist. But the Bali bombings, as well as a number of subsequent grisly attacks—especially the beheading of three Christian schoolgirls on the island of Sulawesi—horrified and galvanized the public, forcing them to accept that they were all at risk. Under intense pressure at home and from outside partners—President George W. Bush sent a high-level envoy to demand that Megawati get serious, while Australia threatened to use its own forces to start arresting suspects—Jakarta finally reversed course.

Megawati's first step, less than a week after the Bali attacks, was to support the passage of a broad new antiterrorism law that made it easier to try militants in court. About eight months later, her government set up an elite new counterterrorism unit known as Densus 88 (Detachment 88). And Megawati finally agreed to start accepting outside aid—albeit quietly, so as to avoid provoking a nationalist backlash. With US diplomatic and financial support, Australia embedded a number of police officers with Indonesian units, where they joined in the hunt for suspects and started training local cops in state-of-the-art scientific crime-scene investigation. Indonesia's allies also flew Detachment 88 members around the world for intelligence training and supplied the unit with high-tech surveillance and military gear. This equipment included, most critically, devices for monitoring cell phone conversations, which Sidney Jones, head of the Institute for Policy Analysis of Conflict (IPAC) in Jakarta, says were responsible for about 90 percent of subsequent arrests. Finally, Western states also provided generous counterterrorism funding and education to Indonesia's courts and criminal prosecutors; at one point, Washington even arranged to fly in judges and lawyers to conduct training courses.

With the encouragement of Yudhoyono, who took office two years later, the country proceeded to mount what *Time* magazine has called "one of the world's most determined campaigns against terrorism." Detachment 88 quickly grew into a force of over four hundred agents, and soon after it reached full strength the number of successful terrorist attacks in Indonesia began to plummet, becoming so rare that in 2008 the US government lifted its travel warning for the country. There have been few major incidents in recent years. And the death toll has been tiny compared to the early 2000s. Tellingly, almost all of the victims have been police officers. In 2014 the Institute for Economics and Peace ranked Indonesia thirty-first in its Global Terrorism Index (a better score than it gave the United States or Great Britain). While the government continues to uncover the occasional plot, hardly any of them succeed; Jones describes the current threat as "low-tech, low-competence, [and] low-casualty."

The reason? Indonesia's terrorist groups have been all but eviscerated, and foreign groups like ISIS haven't found much of a foothold. The men who planned and carried out the Bali attack, as well as most of JI's leaders, have been captured or killed. Facing extermination, the group has officially renounced violence in Indonesia. A few of its diehards have formed new splinter cells, but Detachment 88 has pursued them just as relentlessly. In 2010, for example, it swooped in on a training base in Aceh run by a coalition of JI successors known as Jamaah Anshorut Tauhid. During the raid, counterterrorism officers apprehended a number of senior leaders and recovered a treasure trove of information that has led to the trial and imprisonment of two hundred more militants. (The government is thought to have jailed a total of about nine hundred terrorists since 2002.)

As such operations show, Detachment 88 can function with devastating force. But—and this represents the final part of the government's larger strategy to counter extremism—it's not just a hammer. Indonesia's unhappy history with dictatorship taught its democratic leaders that too punitive an approach only fuels the resentment that feeds extremism in the first place. So Indonesia's war on terror has been waged with uncommon precision, even delicacy.

Indeed, "war" is probably the wrong word to use; Jakarta has treated terrorism more like a law-enforcement problem than a military one. Instead of relying on the army, which had enthusiastically enabled Suharto's repression, the government turned to the national police force, forming Detachment 88 from its ranks. And Jakarta has tried to avoid any other moves that might create more sympathy for the Islamists. It has generally only detained terrorism suspects when it has had enough hard evidence to do so. And it's held public trials for those it seeks to imprison. Taking this approach has involved some painful compromises—for example, to the dismay of investigators, numerous suspects widely thought guilty have been released by the courts or given sentences lighter than counterterrorism officials would have liked.

But Indonesia's emphasis on law enforcement has also proved highly advantageous. Trying suspects in open court instead of leaving them to rot in secret cells has produced a wealth of evidence that cops and prosecutors have been able to use in subsequent investigations, and provided them with a more sophisticated understanding of how ordinary Indonesians become militants in the first place. Even more important, this approach has also reinforced the rule of law and public trust in government. And, adds Solahudin, a terrorism investigator with IPAC, Jakarta's use of public hearings has forced ordinary Indonesians—many of whom had grown conspiracy-minded during the Suharto era, when their government often used trumped-up charges to prosecute peaceful political opponents—to accept that Indonesia's terrorism problem wasn't the invention of the security services or a CIA-Mossad plot, but rather a genuine, homegrown threat.

The government's efforts to win the war of ideas haven't stopped here; in another powerful innovation, it has worked hard to rehabilitate as well as incarcerate. Rather than treat captured terrorists as unredeemable criminals—"evil incarnate," in Jones's terms—Detachment 88 has handled them as what she describes as "good men gone astray." In practice, this has meant offering suspects a range of inducements to try to turn them into informants and get them to renounce violence. Guards allow their prisoners to worship freely, and to build trust and establish their own Islamic credentials, they and Detachment 88 interrogators often share meals with the militants and join them in prayer. Prisoners who agree to cooperate are generously rewarded: the government pays for their weddings, for family visits, and even for their children's school fees and medical expenses.

To supplement this charm offensive, SBY's administration mounted a very public campaign to undermine the root causes of terrorism. Spearheaded by the National Counter-Terrorism Agency (BNPT), which Yudhoyono created in 2010, and backed by various civic organizations, the campaign has involved setting up moderate *pesantrens;* getting prominent local and Middle Eastern imams to denounce violence on Islamic grounds; trotting former terrorists out on TV to graphically describe their crimes and express remorse; and enlisting everyone from comic-book artists to pop stars to promote tolerance

and moderation among the public at large (some of the resulting al-
bums have even topped the charts on MTV Asia). Lumped together,
these programs constitute what Magnus Ranstorp of the Center for
Asymmetric Threat Studies has called one of the most systematic and
successful antiextremism initiatives anywhere. One payoff: according
to Pew Research polls, between 2002 and 2013 the number of Indonesians opposed to terrorist attacks against civilians rose from 66 to 81
percent.

AFTER ALMOST A decade of steady progress in its complex campaign
against radicalism, Indonesia's efforts began to flag toward the end of
the Yudhoyono administration. Whether it was out of complacency,
indolence, or exhaustion—or, most likely, a combination of the three—
SBY began to ease up on many of his most effective policies.

For instance, he allowed Indonesia's economic revival to falter. In
2012 the country's current account and trade balance went into deficit, GDP growth began to slow, and the rupiah became one of Asia's
worst-performing currencies. In short order, Indonesia went from being
touted as a new economic superstar—the next India—to being called
one of the world's "fragile five" economies by Morgan Stanley. Apart
from the hardship it's caused, what makes this ongoing slowdown worrisome is the fact that poverty has been a potent source of extremism
in Indonesia—or at least a potent propaganda tool that Islamist parties
have exploited. While SBY made a dent in the problem, by the end of
his tenure some 43 percent of the population (about one hundred million people) still lived on less than $2 a day.

As he prepared to leave office, SBY's commitment to fighting corruption also seemed to flag, especially as the investigators he had once
empowered drew closer and closer to his own inner circle. In 2012 both
the chairman and the treasurer of Yudhoyono's Democratic Party were
implicated in a scandal linked to the rigging of construction tenders—
yet the president stood behind both men. Around that time, the KPK
(Indonesia's anticorruption agency) also began to encounter increasing
pushback from the MPR and the police, only to discover that it could

no longer count on public or bureaucratic backing from its erstwhile patron.

Allegations of torture, unlawful detention, and "encounter killings" (the unprovoked shooting of suspects during their capture) by Detachment 88 and the national police also began to rise, threatening to undo the government's careful PR campaign. More recently, an unknown number of Indonesians (experts put the figure at several hundred) have joined up with ISIS in Syria and Iraq—raising fears that they could return home and unleash a new wave of terrorism, just as veterans of Afghanistan did a dozen years before. Already these militants have managed to claim several new victims.

Despite these fears and Yudhoyono's disappointing turn, however, the greatest validation of his general approach to extremism—and confirmation of its moderating effect on ordinary Indonesians—came in July 2014, when those same Indonesians elected fifty-three-year-old Joko Widodo (universally known as Jokowi) to be their next president.

Jokowi's election was an electrifying event for a number of reasons. For starters, his opponent, Prabowo Subianto, had represented all the worst aspects of Indonesia's past. A former son-in-law of Suharto and an ex–special forces general with a shady human rights record, Prabowo is an angry nationalist who openly advocated a return to "guided democracy"—the soft authoritarianism practiced by Sukarno, the country's first dictator.

Jokowi, by contrast, represents the best hopes for Indonesia's future, and seems even more committed to promoting democracy and fighting extremism than was SBY. Unlike Indonesia's previous three presidents—all of whom came from elite backgrounds and had ties to the old regime—he is a true man of the people. A former two-term mayor of the central Java city of Solo who then spent two years as governor of Jakarta before unexpectedly vaulting to the presidency, Jokowi is the son of a carpenter and ran a small furniture business before entering politics. He has an extraordinary public touch; as mayor and governor, he spent hours every day walking the streets and listening to his constituents' concerns. He is also a technocratic reformer who promotes transparency and the use of new technologies to fight corruption: when I interviewed him in Jakarta a few months after his election, he spent most of the time talking about the virtues of e-government and the benefits of using smart cards to deliver government services. Jokowi is known to be fiercely principled—as mayor he declined to draw a salary—and is an unapologetic champion of tolerance. When he first took charge of Solo in 2005, it had a reputation for Islamic radicalism. Yet rather than bow to local extremists, Jokowi made merit, not religion, the core principle of his administration—a tradition he continued in Jakarta, where his deputy was an ethnic Chinese who liked to call himself a "pork-eating infidel."

Like Barack Obama, to whom he's often compared, Jokowi had little national or international experience before taking high office, and like Obama, he made some predictable stumbles (low commodity prices, the lousy international economic climate, and meddling by Megawati, who leads his political party, also haven't helped). He soon found his footing, however. By December 2016, his approval rating had climbed to 66.5 percent and the economy was starting to recover. And apart from his specific policies, Jokowi himself is a potent symbol of Indonesia's great progress. Such a principled politician could never have become Indonesia's leader without the shrewd, messy, and often baldly cynical strategies his predecessors used to such great effect in all but defeating the Islamist threat to their country. The fact that their approach combined both flashes of idealism and some less-than-attractive compromises should not diminish its appeal—either for Jokowi himself or for other states still struggling to outflank their own extremists. Indonesia shows that the fight against radical Islam is actually winnable—provided that leaders have the courage, cunning, and flexibility to do what's necessary.

4

LEARN TO LIVE WITH IT

RWANDA'S WRENCHING RECONCILIATION

N THE SPRING OF THE YEAR 2000, PAUL KAGAME FOUND HIM-self facing an impossible test.

Just six years earlier, his country had come close to hacking itself out of existence. In one of modern history's grisliest atrocities, members of Rwanda's Hutu majority had tried to exterminate the country's Tutsi minority, and had almost succeeded. Between April and July of 1994, the Interahamwe (as the Hutu Power militias were known) had butchered up to a million people, including almost three-quarters of Rwanda's Tutsi population.

Kagame—who was then the leader of the Rwandan Patriotic Front (RPF), a rebel army that had been fighting the Hutu-led government since 1990—had finally managed to stop the slaughter when his troops seized Kigali. It was an impressive victory in military terms. The Tutsis had only ever made up about 15 percent of Rwanda's population, and their numbers had been thinned by earlier pogroms and decades of discrimination that had driven many of them into exile. The RPF also had few allies, apart from the government of neighboring Uganda. Rwanda's Hutu army, by contrast, had been trained and amply equipped by its great-power patron, France.

Yet the Inkotanyi, as the Tutsi insurgents came to be known (the word means "the Invincibles"), had managed to prevail. They'd had little time or occasion to celebrate their victory, however. And six years later, Kagame—then forty-two and newly installed as Rwanda's president—was still struggling to reassemble a nation that the World Bank had deemed "nonviable."

The job seemed utterly overwhelming. More than 40 percent of

Rwanda's total population had been killed or displaced during the war. Skeletons and mass graves still littered the countryside. Armed remnants of the Hutu army and the Interahamwe, itching for revenge, lurked just over the border in the Democratic Republic of the Congo (DRC), less than one hundred miles away. As for Rwanda's institutions, they scarcely existed. The war had obliterated virtually everything: most competent bureaucrats had been killed or fled, and looters had stripped government offices down to the last piece of paper. When the postwar Government of National Unity had taken charge in July 1994, the country had no running water and little electricity. Nor did Kagame and his colleagues have much expertise or institutional knowledge to draw on. Before the killing started, Rwanda had had close to eight hundred judges, for example. Fewer than fifty had survived the slaughter.

Conditions among the general population were similarly desperate. Rwanda had always been poor. Although it is a strikingly beautiful place—known as the land of a thousand hills, it boasts jade-green forests, rich red earth, and a forgiving highland climate—it is also tiny (with a landmass the size of Maryland), crowded, and landlocked, and has few natural resources. Long before the genocide, Rwanda's child mortality, literacy, and per capita income rates had all languished well below the sub-Saharan average. But the war had made things exponentially worse. Six years later, in 2000, Rwanda was one of the poorest countries on the planet, with a per capita GDP of just $217. Sixty percent of its population was mired in extreme poverty, and life expectancy was a medieval forty-six years. Malaria, HIV, tuberculosis, and other infectious diseases were ravaging the populace, killing one in four children before their fifth birthday. And more than a million refugees had recently returned home, adding to the government's burden.

They were the lucky ones—the survivors.

But luck, in this case, was a highly relative term. According to a UN report, 99.9 percent of surviving Rwandan children had witnessed at least one act of brutality during the spring of 1994. Four-fifths of them had lost at least one relative, and a third had seen some form of sexual assault firsthand. Close to one hundred thousand minors had been orphaned. A postwar study published in *World Psychiatry* had found that a quarter of all Rwandans were suffering from some form of post-traumatic stress disorder. The country, as Kagame put it to me during one of several conversations, was a land of "confusion, death, and despair."

Knowing that the first step in rebuilding was simply to keep the survivors alive, his government was struggling to feed, employ, house, and otherwise support its battered constituents.

But the new president faced an even more complicated problem. It was one that has confronted former conflict zones from Bangladesh to Bosnia, and will someday face places like Syria and Ukraine too. And that was how to stitch the nation's social fabric back together and to heal the wounds of war—or at least cauterize them well enough that the country could avoid still more bloodletting.

Key to that process was figuring out what to do with those responsible for all the killing. But that task was made especially formidable by the unusually low-tech and intimate nature of the Rwandan genocide. Neighbors had killed their neighbors, teachers their students, all hand-to-hand and face-to-face; most of the slaughter had been conducted using clubs and machetes. This meant that the number of suspected *génocidaires* was enormous: up to a million people by some counts, or a full third of the adult population at the time. What could the government possibly do with them all?

WITH MUCH FANFARE, the UN had stepped in to help in 1995, setting up the International Criminal Tribunal for Rwanda (ICTR) in Arusha, Tanzania. Despite the ICTR's historic significance—it was just the third such multilateral war-crimes court ever created—the tribunal was plagued by problems from the start. Soon after its founding, numerous ICTR administrators were accused of sexual harassment, nepotism, and corruption, forcing the UN to fire two of the court's most senior staffers and its chief prosecutor. To Rwanda's frustration, meanwhile, the court was designed to deal only with the highest-level perpetrators. And it moved at a glacial pace: by 2000, despite a staff of more than a thousand people and an annual budget of $140 million, it had tried just a handful of cases. (By the time it concluded its work in 2015, the total would reach fifty-five.)

Kagame's government had originally dealt with the rest of the genocide suspects in a vengeful fashion. According to several accounts, RPF troops had killed tens of thousands of Hutu soldiers, militia members, and civilians during the war and subsequent mopping-up operations in Rwanda and in the DRC. It had also rounded up huge numbers of suspected *génocidaires*—by 2000 the number would exceed 130,000—and thrown them into jail to await trial by Rwanda's own decrepit court system. But postwar Rwanda had just thirteen dilapidated detention facilities, and these had been built to hold no more than fifteen thousand people. Conditions within thus quickly reached a hellish state; according to one account the detainees were "underfed, drinking dirty water, and crammed into tiny rooms where they were often made to sleep in latticework formations for lack of space." They soon began to sicken and die. Rwanda's courts did manage to try to convict a few of them, and the state publicly executed twenty-two perpetrators in 1998. But given their almost nonexistent resources, officials estimated that it would take about two hundred years to process the rest.

So part of Kagame's challenge was logistical. Not only did he lack for jail cells, but the cost and economic impact of locking up so many people, especially young men, was proving disastrous.

As tough as the administrative problems were, however, Rwanda's social and psychological challenges were even more daunting. On the one hand, the nation needed justice. The guilty had to be held to account; the scale and severity of their crimes demanded it. "There [was] no way to ignore the responsibility that some people, or many people, have in what happened, in the genocide," Kagame recalled a few years later.

Yet the government was also realizing that an exclusive focus on retribution—tempting though it was—could prove perilous. The experience of countries such as South Africa and El Salvador, which were just then struggling to deal with their own mass atrocities, had begun to show that trials alone would not be enough. Rwanda needed justice, but not only justice. "If one had come out of our struggle saying, 'I'm going to impose my will and that's it, and whoever is on the other end must face the consequences,'" Kagame told me in Kigali, "that would have sowed the seeds of a cycle of chaos." To avoid such an outcome, Rwanda also needed reconciliation: a somewhat nebulous term that refers to the rebuilding of civic bonds and the restoration of some sort of trust between former enemies.

But how could that be accomplished in a place that had suffered so much? Most experts who work on transitional justice agree that you're never going to get reconciliation, however you define it, unless you first establish an authoritative account of the crimes of the past. But ordinary criminal courts, with their adversarial proceedings and strict rules of evidence, turn out to be ill-suited for that task. Not only are they slow-moving and expensive to run, but by necessity they focus on the narrow facts of a particular case, excluding broader social issues. They also offer little in the way of emotional solace, since they rarely give victims a chance to confront their tormenters or tell their side of the story. Trials are good at delivering reparations or punishment. But Rwanda needed more than that, a way to deal with its history that would still "allow space for building the future," as Kagame put it. According to Stephen Kinzer, the author of a sweeping account of the genocide and its aftermath, the government was slowly recognizing that for the country to do what Kagame hoped, it needed a way to help victims "forgive those who slaughtered their families and even live beside them in newfound brotherhood."

But that, as Kinzer put it mildly, was "not a rational thing to do."

So Kagame decided to do what seemed, at the time, like a wildly *irrational* thing: he launched a complicated, multistage process that was all but guaranteed to make almost everyone unhappy. It was an approach rife with compromises, one that would give most Rwandans at least some of what they wanted—but satisfy next to none of them completely.

Yet it just might help them to live with one another again. Or so the government hoped.

BACK IN 2000, few who knew Kagame would have thought him capable of coming up with the kind of ambitious and subtle approach Rwanda needed. Though he'd shown himself to be a brilliant military commander and was proving to be a dedicated and hardworking administrator, he had a pronounced dark side as well. Hard-edged and gaunt—at the war's end, the six-foot-two general reportedly weighed just 128 pounds—Kagame could be ruthless, impatient, and severe.

Such traits weren't unexpected in a man who'd been practically weaned on bitterness. Though he'd been born into relative luxury in 1957—his parents were Tutsi aristocrats closely related to Rwanda's then royal family—the good times had come to a crashing end just two years later. In 1959 the country's Hutu majority had overthrown the Tutsi monarchy, and, with the acquiescence of Belgium (the colonial power), launched a series of massacres that had sent Kagame's family and many other Tutsis fleeing over the border into Uganda. There the Kagames found their comfortable life replaced by the hardscrabble, hand-to-mouth existence of refugees. By the time the future president hit adolescence, privation had made him sullen and rebellious. After graduating from high school in 1975 with bad grades and no prospects, Kagame decided to join the newly formed rebel army of Yoweri Museveni, who was then mustering his forces next door in Tanzania.

In war, Kagame found his calling. The young Rwandan quickly rose through the rebels' ranks. When Museveni toppled Idi Amin, Uganda's cannibalistic dictator, in April 1979, Kagame was at his side, and when Museveni installed himself as Uganda's president a few years later, he named Kagame his chief of military intelligence. In the fall of 1990, when the newly formed RPF invaded Rwanda, Kagame was studying at the US Army Command and General Staff College at Fort Leavenworth, Kansas. But the head of the rebel Tutsi army was killed on the first day of the war, and Kagame was called home to take his place.

All these experiences had produced a fierce and cunning fighter. Somehow, however, they'd also turned Kagame into a highly rational pragmatist—a trait that would serve him well in peacetime too. That would become clear in the years after the genocide, when Kagame began to work out Rwanda's recovery plan.

The strategy ultimately involved four parts. The first of these was already well under way by 2000: the RPF would establish a monopoly of force in Rwanda and build a unified garrison state with firm control over the country, enough to ensure that an event like the genocide could never be repeated. This process would involve ruthlessly stamping out the still-simmering Hutu insurgency, and would ultimately entangle Rwanda in a series of brutal and bloody military interventions in the DRC, Rwanda's giant, chaotic neighbor.

Second, Kagame's government would invest heavily in economic reconstruction and institution building. With a good deal of financial help and advice from the World Bank and aid groups, Kagame's administration launched a long list of progressive initiatives that soon made it the darling of the development world. To boost human capital, for example, it began working to extend both education and health care to the entire population—practically for free. To promote business and woo investors, it slashed red tape and embraced technology, bringing state-of-the-art cell phone and Internet networks to Rwanda. To fight corruption, it created a national ombudsman and an auditor-general's office; passed a law requiring all public officials to disclose their net worth annually; and undertook a relentless PR campaign exhorting citizens not to give or accept bribes. Finally, to improve government accountability, it set about decentralizing administrative power and created a process known as *imihigo,* which requires all government officials to publicly set performance targets for themselves.

The third and far more controversial part of Kagame's plan involved trying to turn Rwanda into a race-blind nation. The country, Kagame reasoned, had had enough talk of Tutsi, Hutu, and Twa (a minority also known as pygmies). Such divisions had taken fluid form during the precolonial era, when a Hutu could become Tutsi through intermarriage, for example. But the Belgians had later fixed them in place for their own administrative convenience. Since the Tutsi were the most European-looking of the locals, the colonists had reckoned that they had to be the most intelligent and competent and had treated them accordingly. That history, and the resentment it produced, had finally ripped the country apart in 1994—for, as Kagame put it to me, "one thing leads to another." So the old divisions were abjured and

"We are all Rwandans now" became the new state mantra. The government banned "sectarianism" and "divisionism," effectively outlawing
all discussion of communal affiliation.* It also formally forbade ethnic
discrimination; stripped all references to Hutu, Tutsi, and Twa from
government ID cards and other official documents; erased those words
from school textbooks; and wiped all tribal or national symbols from
the country's flag and its other iconography. It even redrew Rwanda's
administrative map to intermingle regions traditionally associated with
one group or another.

FINALLY, IN 2001, Kagame settled on a radical new judicial approach
for addressing the genocide. During the previous several years, his government had held a long series of weekly "reflection meetings" at the
Hôtel Urugwiro, as well as expert conferences and public town-hall
sessions, all aimed at finding the best path toward reconciliation. After
lengthy debate, it had eventually decided that it would abandon its attempts to process most of its still-incarcerated suspects—who num-
bered in the many tens of thousands—through conventional methods.

That did not mean it would go for a South African–style truth
commission, however. Such bodies, then very much in vogue, are good
at establishing a historical record in divided societies recovering from
brutality. But they generally do so by trading away justice, offering
malefactors amnesty in exchange for their honest testimony. Rwanda's
leaders were uncomfortable with that deal, for both moral and practical reasons. Among other things, they feared that simply releasing all
those suspects back into such a tiny and overcrowded country would
result in huge numbers of revenge killings.

So they decided to forgo all the existing templates and try a completely new approach instead. Drawing on an indigenous precolonial
mechanism for dispute resolution known as *gacaca* (the Kinyarwanda
term roughly translates to "justice on the grass") that dates back to the

---

* A 2001 law prohibits "any person [from making] public any speech, writing, pic-
tures or images or any symbols over radio airwaves, television, in a meeting or public place, with the aim of discriminating [against] people or sowing sectarianism."

sixteenth century, the government came up with a plan to create some twelve thousand new village tribunals throughout the country. These *gacaca* courts would be empowered to hear all but the most serious crimes (which would still be processed through Rwanda's conventional criminal justice system) and, like regular courts, would be able to mete out prison sentences, though the death penalty would be abandoned. But, in keeping with Rwandan tribal culture, these bodies, which the government began testing in 2002 and launched nationwide in 2005, would be staffed and run by local communities. And—a big selling point—they'd hear cases quickly, with trials ranging from one hour to several days.

Although *gacaca* was fast, it aimed for something far bigger than merely accelerating the backlogged trial process. Indeed, it aimed at something bigger than Western-style justice. Traditional Rwandan *gacaca* had emphasized the reintegration of wrongdoers into their communities, and its modern manifestation was designed to attempt something similar. It would seek to promote both justice *and* reconciliation, to punish the guilty *and* reintegrate them into society—and above all, to help the country heal. As Kagame explained it to me, he and his colleagues knew that peace, justice, and truth were all indispensable parts of that process. "You can't do one at the expense of the other," he said. "Maybe you have a portion of one here and portion of the other there, but all of them have to happen."

Several innovative features of the new system would allow it to serve all those ends. First, *gacaca* would give all Rwandans a stake in the process. Though the tribunals would operate under government supervision and the aegis of law, they would be homespun affairs. Communities would elect respected locals to serve as judges. Known in Kinyarwanda as *inyangamugayo* ("those who detest dishonesty"), these officials were not required to meet any educational or professional standards, but were supposed to be selected solely on the basis of their integrity. (They would, however, get three days of training before starting work.) Court officers would also be locals. Proceedings would be held in town squares, churchyards, even forest clearings—sometimes literally on the grass. Entire communities would be required to attend, with authorities shutting down area businesses on trial days to ensure that they did. And virtually everyone would be allowed to participate; all citizens would be encouraged to come forward and describe their roles in and experiences during the conflict. Such exchanges, it was hoped, would serve both to provide evidence of particular crimes and to allow for catharsis.

By offering the accused leniency if they made full confessions and apologized for their offenses, meanwhile—many cooperative perpetrators ultimately had their sentences halved, were let off with time served, or were assigned to perform community service in lieu of jail time—*gacaca* would try to establish a full accounting of what had happened during the awful spring of 1994 and then reintegrate penitent criminals back into society.

Or so the theory went, anyway. In reality, *gacaca* represented a dangerous gamble with very high stakes. Not only did it involve staging what one legal scholar, Max Rettig, has called "one of the most ambitious transitional justice projects the world has ever seen" in a country with approximately zero resources, but it would also cede control of Rwanda's main postwar legal mechanism directly to the people—a people still reeling from a massive national trauma.

The program proved intensely controversial. "Many people disagreed with me, no doubt," recalled Kagame. Tutsi survivors denounced *gacaca*'s emphasis on rehabilitation. "Even those who agreed that we needed to exercise restraint disagreed with the extent," Kagame told me. "They would say, 'That's too much, you're forgiving too much.'" The light sentences offered to cooperative perpetrators were particularly difficult to stomach. "This is government enforced reconciliation," one former victim complained. "The government pardoned the killers, not us."

Human rights groups like Amnesty International also condemned *gacaca*, in their case for its lack of due process and procedural safeguards such as defense counsel (the courts eschewed lawyers in the name of promoting community dialogue), and for the risks inherent in giving so much power to judges with so little training. Even mental health experts weighed in, warning that a public revisiting of such terrible events would retraumatize the victims.

———

THE *GACACA* COURTS would ultimately hear close to two million cases over the course of the next decade, before formally concluding their work in June 2012. The process remained contentious until the very end. In 2011, for example, Human Rights Watch released a blistering report denouncing what it called a "wide range of fair trial violations" by the tribunals, including their misuse to settle personal scores. Other critics chided the government for excluding crimes committed by Tutsis from the tribunals' jurisdiction (though Rwanda's regular courts did ultimately hear a small number of such cases). And at least one psychological evaluation found that, as feared, *gacaca* witnesses suffered from elevated levels of mental disorders like depression and PTSD following their testimony.

While all these criticisms were legitimate, however, they also all missed a larger point: *gacaca* was never meant to be perfect. As a system designed to provide what Lars Waldorf, a law professor and former Rwanda director for Human Rights Watch, has called "mass justice for mass atrocity," it *couldn't* be perfect. "You have to remember," said Rettig, who spent some ten months observing the trials in action in 2006–7, "that you had a prison system that was massively overcrowded, overflowing. You couldn't just release all these people without some form of reckoning. But neither could you hold them indefinitely. And neither could you wait for Rwanda to set up the kind of justice system that incorporates all of the due process rights you would want to see in a Western system. Given these parameters, *gacaca* was really remarkable. It was sort of genius, at least on paper."

Not only did *gacaca* have to deal with impossible circumstances; it also had to struggle toward an impossibly contradictory set of objectives, what the program's framers called *ukuri*, *ubutabera*, and *ubwiyunge* (truth, justice, and reconciliation). It was thus inevitable that *gacaca* would involve a great many compromises, some of them extremely painful. "Whenever a country responds to horrific events, especially on the scale we're talking about in Rwanda, there's not going to be a perfect solution," Rettig told me. There can't be. "You have to make choices, and those choices are going to come with costs and benefits," he said. Flaws in execution, for example, were guaranteed given the scale of the project, as well as the fact that it was run by untrained civilians. Raw encounters between victims and their tormentors were bound to prove traumatic. And a system that split the difference between punishment and reconciliation, between retributive and restorative forms of justice, was bound to elicit howls of protest from partisans of each.

But all this controversy was, in another sense, a testament to *gacaca*'s brilliance. An absolutist approach would never have worked in a country that had been so thoroughly rent in two. To avoid perpetuating those splits, *gacaca* gave all sides something—enough (if sometimes only just) to allow them to move forward. As Peter Uvin, a development expert commissioned by the Belgian government to evaluate the program, concluded in 2000, *gacaca* was "simultaneously one of the best, most dangerous, and possibly last chances Rwanda has." (On the basis of Uvin's report, Brussels ultimately decided to help fund the courts, as did several other Western governments.)

Phil Clark, a University of London professor who has conducted extensive fieldwork in Rwanda, suggests that one reason that *gacaca*, despite the incredibly difficult context, was nevertheless criticized so stridently is that many outsiders "misinterpreted its aims and methods" and so blamed it "for failing to achieve goals for which it was never intended." Rather than analyze *gacaca* on its own terms, Clark told me, "the critics injected a very foreign framework of analysis. And that framework came from a legal and human rights perspective that expected justice to be delivered according to a set of international standards."

But *gacaca* was not designed to provide a conventional, Western-style legal accounting—or at least not only that. Instead, by forgoing the models provided by ordinary criminal trials, war crimes tribunals, and truth commissions in favor of something new, *gacaca* helped Rwanda secure goods that such proceedings couldn't have provided. By allowing—indeed, encouraging—freewheeling, often raucous public debates, for example, the *gacaca* tribunals promoted "active engagement between parties previously in conflict," which gave one-time antagonists a chance to reestablish some form of civil relationship, Clark argues. By encouraging everyone to speak and relaxing the rules of evidence, *gacaca* helped establish a clear record of what had gone wrong and where the bodies were buried. And by emphasizing community service—including the rebuilding of survivors' homes and the maintenance of communal gardens—as punishment for various crimes, *gacaca*, according to Clark, "reintegrate[d] perpetrators more rapidly into the community" than would have resulted if all the *génocidaires* and their allies had been left to rot in prison. Forbearance also made economic sense: in the words of Ignace Rukiramacumu, a former *génocidaire* who was amnestied in 2003, "reconciliation naturally promotes the sowing of every productive field."

While *gacaca* may not have been pure or satisfying, in other words, and while it definitely wasn't pretty, it worked—at least well enough, and in the particular ways Rwanda needed it to. Indeed, for all its flaws, *gacaca* performed better than just about any other conceivable approach could have under the circumstances. Philip Gourevitch, a *New Yorker* staff writer and the author of a book on the genocide, argues that the key question to ask is, "Did *gacaca*, in its own terms and in comparison to any other proposed possible solution, move things forward in a significant way? And the answer is yes. None of *gacaca*'s critics ever came up with a better idea, except that it should have been more perfectly implemented. But even with all the shortcomings, failures, and grievances, even with all the endlessly debatable complications and compromises, *gacaca* did an enormous amount to advance Rwanda's reckoning with the inheritance of genocide."

STILL, *GACACA* WAS just part of Kagame's larger recovery plan. To evaluate the success of that broader effort, you have to take a broader look at Rwanda today.

What such a view reveals is a highly imperfect but also remarkably well functioning state. The scars of the genocide have not disappeared. And modern Rwanda gets some things wrong—some of them very wrong. Yet in many other important respects, the country today is thriving, and in ways unimaginable just a few years ago.

A visitor to Rwanda today can't help but be struck by how prosperous, neat (plastic bags were banned in 2008), and orderly the place seems. Kigali, especially, is vibrant and bustling, with new construction everywhere. While the country at large remains poor and heavily dependent on aid, to a tune of about 40 percent of its annual budget, that figure is down from almost 100 percent in 1995. And that's because Rwanda's economy is booming, having grown by an average of more than 7 percent a year since 2010. Such growth has helped lift more than a million people out of poverty over the last decade and tripled per capita income. At the same time, Rwanda has also become one of the least corrupt countries in Africa (in fact, Transparency International ranks it ahead of some European states like Italy and Greece), and it came in third in the region in the World Bank's latest Ease of Doing Business Index. Meanwhile, universal health care has helped cut child mortality by 70 percent since 2005. Life expectancy has risen by ten years in that period, and deaths from HIV, TB, and malaria have all fallen by four-fifths. Rwanda has even come to excel in unexpected areas like gender parity. Women currently hold half the seats on its Supreme Court and 64 percent of the seats in its parliament: the highest level of female representation anywhere in the world.

Trying to gauge the country's progress in less material areas is somewhat harder. Reconciliation is especially tough to measure, in part because the concept remains so hazy and in part because the country's ban on the use of communal terminology can inhibit open discussion. As Cassius Niyonsaba, a survivor from a town called Nyamata, described the problem to the French journalist Jean Hatzfeld, "the harsh politics of reconciliation forbid survivors to speak in any fashion about the killings, except when invited to give evidence, during ceremonies, mourning periods, or the *gaçaça* trials. . . . Separatists are threatened with punishment."

Yet Rwandans *do* still talk about the past, and a few recent studies have tried to capitalize on that fact in order to measure how well they feel the country has overcome its history. Here too, these reports suggest, Rwanda has made enormous progress. In 2010 the National Unity and Reconciliation Commission interviewed three thousand Rwandans and found that more than 80 percent of them thought ethnic relations had improved since 1994. Because this survey was sponsored by the government, some skeptics have dismissed it, but several more recent independent studies seem to confirm its core findings. In

2012, for example, Gallup found that 93 percent of Rwandans were optimistic about the direction in which their country was headed. And research done around the same time by the academics Joanna Pozen, Richard Neugebauer, and Joseph Ntaganira found that while Rwandans had lots of specific complaints about the way in which *gacaca* had been conducted, a vast majority of them—again more than 90 percent—held positive views about the overall process and its contribution to Rwanda's rebuilding.

Even if one discounts all these findings, chalking them up to the public's internalization of government propaganda, another type of evidence is harder to dismiss: the fact that Rwanda today seems so stable and secure. Hutus and Tutsis, including former *génocidaires* and their victims' families, now live and work side by side throughout the country. According to Francine Niyitegeka, a genocide survivor, "at the market, we sell to one another without a qualm. In the *cabaret* [bar], we talk about farming, the weather, reconciliation; we share bottles and we exchange civil words of agreement." Many Hutus now serve in government and the military; the last few prime ministers have all been Hutu, and even some former armed opponents of the regime currently hold high office. (For example, General Paul Rwarakabije, who led the postwar insurgency against the RPF, is now commissioner of prisons.) Meanwhile, violence has become extremely uncommon and personal crime is strikingly low: in another Gallup poll, this one from 2011, 89 percent of Rwandan women and 94 percent of men said they felt safe walking home at night. The country seems to be at little risk of collapse or a return to large-scale violence—at least, not anytime soon.

Now, all this may still only add up to what social scientists call "thin reconciliation," meaning mere peaceful coexistence, as opposed to something more redemptive (like true forgiveness). But achieving that higher standard takes years, Clark and other experts argue. In the meantime, the peaceful coexistence Rwanda has established represents a great accomplishment for a country just two decades removed from genocide and civil war. And the fact that this tranquillity may have been imposed from above does not erase its value. As Angélique Mukamanzi, a Tutsi survivor, puts it, "the state has clamped down on our lives." But the benefit of such constraints, she said, is that "when we realize that we cannot kill one another, that we cannot squabble all the time, we choose to forget a little."

"Can enforced unity be real?" Gourevitch asked when we spoke. "I think that the history of social change everywhere indicates that yes, both for better and worse, it can."

DESPITE THESE ACHIEVEMENTS, any general discussion of Rwanda today has to grapple with a difficult problem: the very complicated nature of the man who still leads the country. Kagame has become an extremely polarizing figure in the last few years, one celebrated and pilloried in almost equal measure. The world of Rwanda studies is a small and feverish one, and it has come to be dominated by two warring camps. One views Kagame as a great savior; the other, as one of modern history's archvillains.

Kagame's fans—and he has many, including leaders such as Tony Blair, Bill Clinton, Bill Gates, Rick Warren, and Paul Farmer (the founder of Partners in Health)—tend to focus on his accomplishments in the realm of economic and human development. Over the years, Rwanda's president has grown into a wonky, almost professorial technocrat, a data-driven tinkerer with an inexhaustible appetite for policy minutiae—and Rwanda has benefited accordingly. His openness to innovation has led Farmer, for example, to say that "we get more done in Rwanda than anywhere else in the world," and such enthusiasm is widely shared. Clinton has called Kagame a "brilliant man" who "freed the heart and the mind of his people."

Kagame's many critics focus on his troublesome human rights record and marked intolerance for dissent. The charge sheet here is disturbingly long. Over the years, the RPF government has been credibly accused of killing tens of thousands of Hutu soldiers and civilians, both during the war and after—especially in the DRC. Kagame, who won his last two elections (in 2003 and 2010) by more than 90 percent, has also shown little interest in allowing Rwanda to become a real democracy, even as the threat of war—which might once have justified some restrictions on speech and political activism—has receded and the country has stabilized. Journalists, for example, complain of frequent harassment, and a few of them have been sentenced to long prison terms on charges of "divisionism" or "promoting genocide ideology." So have a number of opposition politicians, including Kagame's predecessor as president, Pasteur Bizimungu (a Hutu). Several political parties have been banned. And to the dismay of many critics, including the Obama administration, Kagame recently announced plans to run for a third term as president in 2017 (a move made possible by a recent constitutional referendum).

Finally, and perhaps most alarming, a few of his former confidants have recently broken with their boss, denounced him—and then turned up dead under murky circumstances. In January 2014, for example, Patrick Karegeya, a former chief of intelligence, was found strangled in a Johannesburg hotel. And Kayumba Nyamwasa, a former chief of staff of the Rwandan army who fled the country in 2010 after splitting with the president, has survived three assassination attempts by mysterious assailants.

Such charges are too serious to brush aside. In the years immediately following the genocide, Kagame could perhaps have been forgiven for his reluctance to tolerate fractious democracy—but the time for such caution has passed. While he has loosened some restrictions in recent years, such as the limits imposed on Rwanda's media, these liberalizing measures have not gone nearly far enough. More and more, the president's repressive tendencies seem to betray not strength but weakness. And that weakness, in turn, raises the fear that Rwanda's progress could be set back or undone if Kagame were to exit the scene. "Until there's a stable succession, how stable can one say Rwanda is? As long as what's happening there is as mortal as the man himself, it's not secure enough, not solid enough to be sure," says Gourevitch.

Still, the problems with Paul Kagame's rule don't negate all his accomplishments. The point of this story is not to paint him as a saint. The point is that some key aspects of Kagame's administration—in particular, the way he faced the very hard problem of how to recover from civil war and genocide—have been remarkably successful, and it is those aspects of his tenure that offer valuable lessons for other nations struggling with similar problems today. Rwanda's model, stripped of its excesses and shorn of its missteps—many of which were incidental, not integral, to its success—still offers vital insights that other states should study as they emerge from their own civil wars. Indeed, a number of them, such as the Central African Republic, Côte d'Ivoire, Somalia, and South Sudan, have already figured that out and have sent delegations to Rwanda for this very purpose.

As they no doubt learned, Kagame's formula can be boiled down to three key insights. First, he recognized that a crisis as obliterating as a civil war or genocide provides a unique opportunity to take a radically new approach, one more conventional circumstances would make impossible. Cataclysms like Rwanda's create space for dramatic social reengineering. And whether that space is used to eliminate racial barriers, increase the role of women in society, or make health care and education universal, such opportunities must not be wasted.

Second, local problems require local answers. As Clark argues, one "lesson from Rwanda's postgenocide recovery is that there's plenty of scope for states to innovate. In an era where states' options are narrowing because of the advent of the International Criminal Court, with its insistence on prosecutions in faraway courtrooms, and the influence of NGOs that emphasize a predetermined list of options for transitional justice, Rwanda shows that it's possible to construct mechanisms tailor-made to the specific needs of postconflict societies. There is substantial room for creativity, even in the face of immense international pressure to conform to current—especially legal—orthodoxies." Or as Gourevitch puts it, "It is misguided to think that there are universally applicable models—including the West's post–World War II and post–Cold War consensus on human rights, justice, and democracy— that can be imposed instantaneously in a place where they are not already deeply rooted." What this means is that, while *gacaca* itself would likely make no sense in a country like Sri Lanka or Syria, the strategy that underlay it—of rejecting prebaked templates in favor of an authentic, organic, and locally rooted solution to the problem of transitional justice—would. Indeed, such local approaches are more likely to be seen as legitimate by a given population—and thus more likely to succeed.

Kagame's most important insight, finally, was this: that leaders dealing with crises like Rwanda's can't be afraid to compromise, to split the difference. In fact, they should make a virtue of it. Rather than letting the great be the enemy of the good by searching for an idealized solution that would have made everyone happy—when, after all, such solutions rarely exist—Kagame essentially embraced the politics of satisficing. He recognized that when confronted with an impossible situation, wisdom often lies in forgoing the optimal for the acceptable. And when people are as bitterly divided as Rwanda's were following its war, the best approach is to give something to everyone—but not give everything to anyone. Following such a path is bound to be messy and guaranteed to make people unhappy. Sure enough, no constituency in Rwanda today feels completely content with the way the nation has accommodated its genocide.

But that is a big part of the reason why Rwanda now works as well as it does.

5

ASSUME THE WORST

How Singapore Conquers Corruption

F PROSTITUTION IS THE WORLD'S OLDEST PROFESSION, COR-
ruption must be among its most ancient vices. Ever since the first
Neanderthal figured out that he could secure a better spot in the
cave by giving his chief an extra big slab of mastodon meat, corruption
has been a constant feature of human organization. And unlike some
of the other problems discussed in this book, it probably always will
be—at least until humans evolve into a higher life-form.

In the meantime, no matter where you live, you're likely accustomed
to seeing signs of corruption all around you. The revelations never seem
to stop. In February 2014, for example, the Asian media were full of
stories about Edwin Yeo, a high-ranking official who'd been busted
for stealing some $1.4 million in public money to fund his extravagant
gambling habit. Superficially, Yeo's case looked all too familiar, but one
thing made it unusual: the country where it occurred. Yeo was from
Singapore, where he worked (ironically) for the city-state's anticorruption agency. Yeo was also the first of his colleagues to be charged with
such malfeasance in twelve years. That's not because Singapore usually
overlooks such crimes—it's because they almost never take place there.

Singapore has come closer to eradicating corruption altogether
than just about any other country. In 2014 Transparency International
ranked it the least corrupt state in all of Asia and seventh in the world.
And that's typical. Singapore has scored near the top of the rankings
every year since the watchdog first started compiling them, in 1995.

What makes Singapore's record especially striking is that it didn't
start out as a paragon of clean government—anything but. And that
makes it a particularly good model for other places trying to clean up

their acts (unlike, say, virtuous Sweden, which beats Singapore on Transparency International's league tables but which has been a constitutional democracy for more than two hundred years).

When Singapore first won home rule from Great Britain in 1959, the city was famous not for its incorruptibility but for its debaucherous embrace of vice and iniquity. Not for nothing was the place known as "Sin-galore." Chinese triads and secret societies openly operated scores of opium dens and bawdy houses, and their henchmen fought turf wars in the streets. The British Military Administration, which ran the place after World War II, had been so notoriously venal that most locals referred to it as the "Black Market Administration." And Singapore's bureaucrats, especially its police, were hopeless; a 1949 Colonial Office report referred to them as "an ill-clad, badly equipped and poorly disciplined rabble." Things were so bad the year Singapore first became self-governing that, if you were unlucky enough to get hit by a car on its chaotic streets, you'd have to pay off the ambulance crew before they'd take you to a hospital.

All that helps explain why, when a prominent young barrister known as Harry Lee decided to run for prime minister that year, he resolved to make corruption the focus—indeed, the obsession—of his campaign.

HARRY HAD BEEN born Lee Kuan Yew to a middle-class Singapore Chinese family in 1923. Obviously brilliant, he'd distinguished himself early as a star pupil, excelling at the prestigious Raffles Institution (an independent British-style high school) and dreaming of attending university in the United Kingdom. But in 1942 the Imperial Japanese Army had swept into town, dashing Harry's hopes and dealing the British one of their sharpest setbacks of the war. Like many Singaporeans, Lee survived the hard years of occupation by learning Japanese and scrounging a living on the black market (he specialized in pawned jewelry).

The Japanese were brutal overlords and the city suffered mightily under their rule. Just when it seemed like life would never improve, however, Tokyo surrendered, and on September 2, 1945, the war was over. Singapore was quickly liberated—which meant, among other things, that Lee could finally sail for England. On arrival in the imperial capital, Harry dove into student life at the London School of Economics, where he was swept up in the heady anticolonialism and Fabian socialism of the day; among his tutors was the same Harold Laski who would make such a big impression on the young Pierre Trudeau. One year later, Lee transferred to Cambridge, where his brothers were also studying, to read law.

After scoring a rare double first on his finals, Harry returned to Singapore in 1950, where he resumed his given name, entered private practice, and remarried the woman he'd secretly wed in England three years earlier. On the day of their second nuptials, the British registrar they'd hired for the ceremony made the grave error of arriving fifteen minutes late. Incensed, the groom—betraying the extreme intolerance for inefficiency that would soon make him famous—proceeded to berate the hapless civil servant.

Though Lee proved good at the practice of law, private life left him feeling restless. Bored with his commercial cases and infuriated with the island's complacent and incompetent colonial administrators, he got involved first in the labor movement and then in local politics, and in 1954 he and some friends founded the People's Action Party (PAP). Apart from pushing for independence from Great Britain, the PAP would make fighting corruption one of its top concerns when it ran in the country's first free legislative elections in 1959.

Choosing clean government as a campaign theme was a risky proposition at the time. After all, corruption wasn't just commonplace in the Singapore of that era; it was ubiquitous. As Lee himself would write some years later, "the percentage, kickback, baksheesh, slush, or whatever the local euphemism, [was] a way of life in Asia: People openly accept[ed] it as part of their culture."

Attempts to change such deeply ingrained habits usually flop. Yet Lee and his comrades were determined to try, for several reasons.

First, they recognized that graft had so thoroughly infected and enfeebled their island's institutions that it risked poisoning the fledgling state before it ever got off the ground.

Second, casting the PAP as a band of arch–corruption fighters gave the party a handy way to distinguish itself from the island's other political factions, which Lee denounced as "supine, feeble, self-serving, [and] opportunistic." During the campaign, the PAP even accused members of its main rival, the Singapore People's Alliance, of taking payoffs from foreign powers. Focusing on corruption also helped Lee outflank the island's powerful communist movement, which had made the issue its cause as well.

The strategy ended up working brilliantly. On May 30, 1959, the PAP won the election and an exultant Lee—then just thirty-five years old—suddenly found himself Singapore's first prime minister. Never one for understatement, he declared the results "a victory of right over wrong, clean over dirty, righteousness over evil."

IT WAS A triumphant moment. Yet as Lee surveyed his new domain, he quickly discovered that, politics and moralizing aside, there was another, even more pressing reason to push for sweeping reform: the city was in desperate shape.

As a colony, Singapore had been important; thanks in part to its enormous port, "the Gibraltar of the East" had been Britannia's key administrative, commercial, and military outpost in the region. But as the British Empire receded, Singapore quickly sank into poverty and obscurity, becoming what Raj Vasil, author of several books on the country, called just another "undeveloped country of the Third World." In 1965, after a brief and unhappy union with its big sibling, Malaysia, Singapore became fully independent. The new country was tiny, with just 1.58 million people crammed onto a landmass about half the size of New York City. Its population—split uneasily between ethnic Chinese, Tamils, Malays, and whoever else had washed up on the territory's shores—was diverse and divided. An island, Singapore had almost no freshwater. And unlike Malaysia, the country had no sizable markets or industry to build on and no commodities or other natural resources to exploit.

As a result, conditions at independence were grim. Per capita GDP was just $443. Unemployment was high and, with the population growing fast, rising; Albert Winsemius, Lee's chain-smoking Dutch economic adviser, warned that it could top 14 percent by 1966. Most Singaporeans were poorly educated, and half of them lived in squalid slums. The place was a malarial swamp, and everything seemed to be getting worse fast. As Winsemius warned his boss, "Singapore is walking on a razor's edge."

Rather than lament these circumstances, however, Lee realized that they offered him, and Singapore, a tremendous opportunity. His breakthrough insight, which would lay the foundation for his country's many eventual accomplishments, was that Singapore's poverty of resources could be turned into an asset—by giving its leaders the freedom to think and act radically. The one thing newly independent Singapore *could* offer, he reasoned, was good governance. Singapore needed to industrialize to survive, and that meant attracting lots of foreign investment. If Lee could enshrine the rule of law and what he called "First World standards of reliability and predictability" in a corner of the world utterly lacking in them, it might just give the city-state a comparative advantage—and a fighting chance.

Lee therefore set out to create a nation "different from our neighbors: clean, more efficient, more secure," as he put it. Spurred on by desperation—as Lee said, without rapid reform, "then verily shall we perish"—he moved fast. Just days after he was sworn in, dressed in white to symbolize his purity, he launched what the political scientist Robert Rotberg calls an "absolute jihad" against bribery and graft, constructing one of the most effective and comprehensive anticorruption systems the world has ever seen.

LEE STARTED BY building on one of the few positive legacies the departing British had bequeathed him: Singapore's Corrupt Practices Investigation Bureau (CPIB), which the colonial government—having been badly embarrassed by a particularly egregious case of police malfeasance in 1951—had been forced to create a few years earlier. (The story had involved the theft of eighteen hundred pounds of opium by a gang that included several dirty cops.) The original CPIB was tiny and relatively toothless, however, so Lee set about enhancing its powers.

The Prevention of Corruption Act (POCA), which his new government passed in June 1960, did this in several ways. First, it defined corruption very broadly: as the giving of virtually anything of value (which the law calls "gratification") in exchange for any sort of benefit from the government. Gratification could be monetary, taking the form of gifts, loans, fees, rewards, commissions, or release from a debt; or it could be something nonmonetary, such as property, a job, or "any other service, favour, or advantage of any description whatsoever." The law even criminalized bribe paying within the private sector to cover cases where no government officials were involved.

Second, the POCA created several powerful new legal presumptions. These included permitting the CPIB to treat the mere fact that an official was living beyond his or her means, or had assets that he or she couldn't properly account for, as prima facie evidence that the official was on the take. The law also put the burden of proof on any government worker who received a gift to establish that it had come with no strings attached, and that the recipient hadn't returned the favor in any way.

Third, the new legislation granted the CPIB great independence, giving it the power to investigate, search, and arrest suspects all on its own, without having to rely on the country's untrustworthy police. A few years later, Singapore's legislature also granted the CPIB the ability to force witnesses to testify. And to free the agency from meddling by politicians, the bureau was removed from the attorney general's supervision in 1969 and placed in the prime minister's office. (Since this move created the theoretical opportunity for the prime minister himself to manipulate the CPIB, the rules were amended again some years later to give Singapore's directly elected president the right to overrule the prime minister in such a case.)

To show how the bureau would actually work and to send the message that, as Lee put it, "the disinfecting has to start from the top," the new government went after some high-profile targets, including a few of the prime minister's close friends. Thus in 1966, for instance, the bureau targeted an old Lee crony named Tan Kia Gan, who was then serving as Singapore's director on the board of Malaysian Airways and whom investigators suspected of taking bribes to favor a particular aircraft supplier. (Though Tan's coconspirators refused to testify against him, making a conviction impossible, Lee fired and ostracized him anyway.) In 1975 Wee Toon Boon—a comrade of Lee's from their trade union days, then serving as minister of state for the environment—was sent to prison for accepting gifts from a property developer. And Teh Cheang Wan, another Lee ally who'd become minister for national development, was investigated in 1986 for taking bribes. Rather than face trial, Teh wrote a note announcing, "As an honourable oriental gentleman, I feel it is only right that I should pay the highest penalty for my mistake"—and took a deadly overdose of sleeping pills. Even Lee's own family would come to be investigated after he left office, though all his relatives were exonerated.

As intended, these and other prominent inquiries sent a powerful message to Singapore's public, gradually rewriting the permissive cultural values that the PAP had so deplored. As K. Shanmugam, the country's minister for law, put it to me when we met in his office on a steamy September morning not long ago, because Lee was "completely incorruptible, and chose people who were incorruptible, and when they strayed, he came down hard, that became an internalized norm." Ordinary folk, Rotberg explains, quickly came to appreciate "that the governing elite were not routinely (as elsewhere) taking advantage of their official positions to enrich themselves. . . . That robust message had its impact on lesser officials"—and on the public at large.

EVEN JIHADS CAN take time to accomplish, however, so Singapore has continued to refine its anticorruption system in the decades since independence. The CPIB has been greatly expanded: an organization that had just 8 staffers when Lee took power in 1959 now has 177, and its budget, which was barely a million Singapore dollars in 1978, has since increased by almost 5,000 percent.

The government has also developed an extremely large toolkit for detecting wrongdoing. For instance, today police officers are required to report whatever petty cash they have in their pockets at the beginning and the end of each shift; those found with more than they started out with are assumed to have taken a bribe. CPIB inspectors regularly troll racetracks looking for any official who seems to be throwing around too much money and require civil servants to declare visits to casinos. The agency has also made it extremely easy for ordinary citizens to report suspected payoffs (anonymously, if they wish) via the CPIB's website and its twenty-four-hour toll-free hotline.

To be effective, of course, deterrence requires punishment, not just detection. Singapore has thus frequently increased the penalties facing anyone still reckless enough to break the rules. Today those convicted of corruption can face lengthy prison terms and fines of up to S$100,000 (US$70,000); they're also forced to pay back the bribe. The government has even started punishing the *supervisors* of corrupt officials: after Yeo was nabbed in February 2014, for example, Prime Minister Lee Hsien Loong formally reprimanded his boss and reassigned the CPIB's director.

Political scientists distinguish between two types of corruption: the "petty" or "lubricating" sort (which involves paying a small sum to a low-level official to encourage him or her to issue a passport, say, or a vending permit), and the "administrative" or "grand" kind, which occurs at the national level and can involve the purchase of construction tenders, import permits, or a contract to supply the state with tanks or telephone lines. Singapore makes no such distinction and goes after both types with equal zeal, differentiating between them only in the sanctions it imposes. So while an official at the Singapore Land Authority got twenty-two years in 2011 for skimming some S$12.5 million (US$8.7 million) from the public purse, the next year another Singapore resident was fined S$3,000 (US$2,093) for offering a S$40 (US$27) bribe to a street cop.

Tough as it is on malefactors, the government prefers to avoid resorting to punishment and so has crafted various means of encouraging citizens not to stray in the first place. Well-funded educational and public outreach programs extend all the way down to the elementary school level, and the CPIB even runs slickly produced trailers (tagline: "Don't Stray. Corruption Never Pays.") before Hollywood movies in cinemas. The government also rewards officials who reject bribes by giving them public commendations and cash bonuses.

To reduce bureaucrats' temptation to supplement their incomes, Singapore's government has gradually increased their pay, such that it now compensates its officials more generously than virtually any other state in the world. Civil servants get a range of cushy benefits, from golf club memberships to discounted vacation packages, and their compensation is pegged to two-thirds the prevailing wage for equivalent private-sector work. New government ministers can earn about S$935,000 (US$650,000) a year—almost twice what the US president takes home. The state also regularly rotates its employees into new posts to prevent them from developing cozy relationships with the public, and it has eliminated whole classes of fees and tariffs (such as import duties) to reduce the amount of cash that passes between the public and officials. Finally, it has worked hard to take money out of politics—the source of so much corruption in so many other places, including the West—by imposing strict spending limits, keeping elections very short (they generally last only nine days), and banning political ads.

As SINGAPORE'S STRATOSPHERIC cleanliness rankings attest, this multifaceted system has paid off handsomely. Lee's "First World standards," along with a host of other good governance initiatives, have turned this once nearly destitute city into a world-beating economy. In 2015 the World Bank named Singapore the easiest place on the planet in which to do business. The country now boasts a $300 billion economy, which is slightly larger than that of the Philippines (a nation with about ninety million more citizens). In per capita purchasing-power terms, Singapore is now the world's sixth-richest country. Not bad for a state that got such a rocky start barely fifty years ago.

Still, this book is about role models, not just success stories, and so it's important to acknowledge that—despite Singapore's many accomplishments—its record comes with several asterisks.

First, some analysts, such as Simon Tay (a law professor and former MP who now chairs the Singapore Institute of International Affairs), warn that the country may have done *too* good a job fighting corruption, if such a thing is possible. Tay worries that complacency is setting in. As he told me over tea in his high-rise office above Singapore's Orchard Road, "the government feels that, having hired the right people and inculcated the right values, they no longer have to watch themselves. And I think there are a lot of signs"—such as the recent Yeo case—"that they still *do* have to watch themselves." Another former senior official (who asked for anonymity given the sensitivity of the subject) suggested that while the current administration is indeed beyond reproach when it comes to many *formal* types of corruption, it has a big blind spot when it comes to at least one *less formal* sort: nepotism. It's surely no coincidence, for example, that the current prime minister happens to be Lee Kuan Yew's oldest son.

Real as these problems are, however, they are relatively good ones for a country to have. Few people question the younger Lee's competence. And the frantic housecleaning the CPIB performed after the embarrassment of the Yeo trial suggests the government hasn't started resting on its laurels just yet. (After another CPIB scandal in 1997, the agency's then director ordered his entire staff, including himself, to take polygraph tests.)

A second, more serious question about the applicability of the Singapore model stems from the country's idiosyncrasies. It is unusually rich, and, with a tiny landmass and just 5.5 million inhabitants, unusually small. Both those attributes offer it advantages that bigger, poorer neighbors like China, India, and Indonesia—which would like to follow Singapore's lead—don't enjoy.

The issue of wealth is easy to dismiss. Though Singapore is very rich today, it wasn't when it first declared war on corruption—yet its poverty didn't prove an insurmountable impediment. And while the country does use its money to help keep clean these days—by paying government employees extremely well and generously funding anti-corruption efforts—the high salaries and big budgets are fairly recent developments, which suggests that fighting corruption needn't be an expensive undertaking. Lee actually reduced government pay during the early, lean years of his tenure, yet corruption declined anyway due to the legal strictures he put in place.

Singapore's small size represents a thornier problem. Jon S. T. Quah, a former professor at the National University of Singapore and a world-renowned corruption expert, has documented how the country's microscopic geography made communications and administration unusually straightforward, especially in the predigital age. It's also much easier to oversee a small, unitary bureaucracy than a huge federal one. Still, Quah and other experts argue that even big, administratively complex countries like India could follow Singapore's path if they started on a limited scale—launching programs on the local or state level and only expanding them outward after they'd proved successful there. When Narendra Modi, now India's prime minister, was chief minister of Gujarat from 2001 to 2014, he managed to cut corruption significantly, which shows how committed leaders can make a difference. Though it won't be easy, there's no necessary reason he or other like-minded politicians can't replicate such success on a national level.

The third problem with the Singapore model is the hardest to dismiss. Clean, honest, efficient, and successful as it is, the country is no liberal democracy. Although Lee first won office in a free election, he tolerated only token opposition during his subsequent decades in power, and used a variety of sometimes brutal means to enforce his writ and keep his enemies weak and off guard. During a valedictory 2010 interview, he admitted to having done "some nasty things" during his long reign (though he insisted they'd all been done for "honorable purposes"). And during the 1990s, he became infamous for promoting the "Asian Values" thesis—which holds that Confucian societies are culturally unsuited to the messiness of political pluralism and should be content to be led by elites—to justify his rule.

Lee resigned from Singapore's top job in 1990, gave up his last residual title (Minister Mentor) in 2011, and died in 2015. And his country has slowly edged closer toward real democracy in recent years. Yet advocacy groups continue to criticize its restrictions on opposition parties, the media, and the right to assembly; despite years of nominal reforms, Freedom House, the US-based human rights monitor, still ranks the country as only "Partly Free."

Such concerns might diminish the appeal of Singapore's corruption-fighting strategy for other, more enlightened countries. They shouldn't. Although Lee's reliance on repression is unpleasant to contemplate, it wasn't a core part of the country's cleanliness campaign. Indeed, most of the city-state's tactics in that battle could work just as well in a non-authoritarian setting.

It's true that a few of Singapore's corruption-fighting methods—like its occasional detention of suspects without speedy trial—clash with Western norms of fairness and due process. But the bulk of the system—from its reliance on high salaries and public education to the "reasonable grounds" standard the CPIB uses to search or arrest suspects without a warrant—doesn't. (American cops, for example, can also perform warrantless searches in some cases.) It's also important to stress that Singapore's corruption prosecutions have to pass through the country's well-respected courts, which follow basic British procedure, guarantee the right to counsel, and allow opportunities for appeal. Finally, while some of the CPIB's powers may look ripe for abuse, experts such as Robert Klitgaard, an American economist and corruption specialist, argue that various safeguards (especially the fact that the bureau is supervised by two oversight boards and by Singapore's directly elected president) have prevented such misuse. A 2005 survey found that ordinary Singaporeans overwhelmingly agree.

All that helps explain why, over the years, so many other countries—including a long list of democracies—have sent representatives to Singapore to study its success. Since 1992 the island has provided anti-corruption training to more than eighty thousand officials from 170 other states. Governments from Argentina to Hong Kong to Thailand have all tried to implement Singapore-style systems, and in just the last few years, high-ranking figures from Brazil, India, and Turkey have traveled to the island to scrutinize its methods.

What these officials have no doubt learned is that most of the means Singapore uses to fight corruption are eminently exportable, and some of Lee's leadership lessons are even more so. First among them is his demonstration of the fact that lofty rhetoric, good training, smart monitoring, and a whole range of carrots and sticks are important, but they're only necessary, not sufficient, conditions for achieving truly clean government. The real key is unflinching determination at the top. As K. Shanmugam, the law minister, points out, numerous countries already have anticorruption laws that are, on paper, stronger than Singapore's—yet their systems don't work. That's because, he says, "you can have the best rules, the best anticorruption agency, but if your politicians are corrupt . . . nothing is going to save the system. It's as simple as that." Rotberg argues that "leadership precedes institutional safeguards." It also creates a culture that can permeate an entire society over time—and must, if that society is to truly conquer such a virulent virus.

Singapore's history offers another, more fundamental moral as well. Lee's decision to stake his legacy on fighting corruption during one of the most inauspicious moments in the country's history underscored a powerful insight that leaders of all stripes would benefit from internalizing: the value of starting with nothing. Beginning at the bottom, as he did, can free a leader to turn absence into opportunity, and liberate him or her to try something radically new. All it takes is courage. Or if that's too much to hope for, simple fear or desperation will do.

6

DIAMONDS AREN'T FOREVER

How Botswana Defeated the
Resource Curse

IFTY YEARS AGO, BOTSWANA WAS WHAT YOU'D HAVE
generously called a backwater. If it had had much water. Which
it didn't. On the eve of independence from the United Kingdom, this parched, landlocked, France-size swath of southern Africa seemed the most luckless of nations. It had no natural resources
beyond a little copper and coal, and hardly any arable soil; most of
Bechuanaland, as it was then known, was made up of Kalahari desert.
There *were* a lot of cows—three times more of them than there were
people (the one industry was ranching). But even they were nothing to
boast about, suffering as they did from near-constant bouts of anthrax,
rinderpest, and hoof-and-mouth disease passed on by migrating wil-
debeests.

The place was so unappealing that even the insatiable European
powers had all but ignored it during their great African landgrab of
the preceding century. Only in 1885, after a few local chieftains lob-
bied London for protection (they were worried about encroachment
by Cecil Rhodes and the Boers), had the British Empire reluctantly
planted its flag there. And even then, its ambivalence remained profound: the United Kingdom's first local representative cabled home
shortly after arriving in the territory, "We have no interest in the country . . . except as a road to the interior." The empire, he argued, should
limit its role to preventing anyone else from grabbing the place, while
doing "as little in the way of administration or settlement as possible."

Over the following decades, Britain closely followed this advice. It never upgraded Bechuanaland to full colonial status (the
place remained a protectorate, a much more minimal arrangement).

It restricted its involvement there to collecting taxes, keeping order, and defending the borders. It barely sent any settlers: as of 1921 there were only 1,743 Europeans living in the vast country, and that number would just barely double over the next forty years. And it invested virtually nothing. The neglect was so profound that when Sir Robert Peter Fawcus took over as high commissioner in 1954, he angrily wrote home that London's spending—which totaled about £140,000 at that point—was "far below an acceptable level for a territory administered by Imperial Britain."

But the Colonial Office remained unmoved. And when Bechuanaland's indigenous inhabitants started pushing for self-rule in the 1960s, the empire didn't argue. Its local administrators basically just shrugged their shoulders, packed their bags, donned their pith helmets, and headed home.

Botswana declared its independence in September 1966 and promptly became one of the poorest nations on the planet—and one with no discernible prospects for improvement. It had no real civil service, just twenty-two university graduates, and only one doctor for every twenty-six thousand people. Botswana's infrastructure consisted of a single abattoir, one railway (which it didn't own), eight kilometers of paved roads, and virtually nothing else: no power grid, no phone lines, no sewage system. The black-ruled country was surrounded on all sides by hostile, white-supremacist regimes in South Africa, Namibia, and Rhodesia. It didn't even have a proper capital city: the Brits had run Bechuanaland remotely, from over the border in South Africa, and had only broken ground on Gaborone a year or two before quitting the territory. As the economists Charles Harvey and Stephen R. Lewis Jr. put it, "everything needed doing, and there was money for none of it." A cartoon published in *Punch* that year portrayed the new-born nation as a naked, emaciated child sitting forlorn in the grassland while a British officer strode away, saying, "You'll be all right—you'll be among friends"—even as lions and snakes approached on all sides.

Just when it seemed things couldn't get any worse, they did. At about the same moment that Botswana achieved self-rule, the rains failed, the maize and sorghum shriveled in the fields, and the cattle started to die off in droves.

And then—with the population teetering on the brink of starvation—something *truly* terrible happened. Prospectors rooting around under the stunted thornbush trees on the savanna stumbled on one of the richest diamond deposits the world had ever seen.

You can guess what happened next. Following the standard developing-world road map, the new nation's novice leaders proceeded to steal the jackpot as fast as they could claw it out of the ground. What they didn't pocket directly or stash in Swiss bank accounts they blew on wasteful white elephants and the establishment of a brutal security apparatus—even as they neglected the tedious work of nation building and left their impoverished constituents to fend for themselves. The economy soon cratered. And local chiefs, infuriated by the theft of their patrimony, took up arms against the capital and set the grasslands ablaze. Botswana, in short, became yet another victim of the infamous Resource Curse, the influence of which has caused one country after another to squander its geological wealth and slide into misrule and misery.

That, at least, is what should have happened, judging from the histories of most mineral-rich countries in Africa and elsewhere. But it didn't in Botswana. Instead, the country bucked history, development theory, and the law of averages—and prospered wildly.

For more than three decades now, Botswana has ranked as the world's number one diamond producer by value, mining and exporting millions of high-quality carats and earning billions of dollars in the process. In 2014 alone, its largest mine churned out some two metric tons of gemstones. Such numbers usually spell calamity, but not here; instead, Botswana has used them to turn itself into the envy of Africa. The country's leaders have built and maintained a democratic government that holds regular free and fair elections and is closely monitored by honest courts and a boisterous free press. Despite living in a very rough neighborhood, Botswana has never fought a war, foreign or civil; it didn't even have a military until 1977.

Botswana's economic accomplishments, meanwhile, have been just as astonishing. For the first thirty-five years of the country's existence, its GDP grew faster than any other nation's, often topping 14 percent a year. (Though it's slowed somewhat in the last decade, it's still increasing at a respectable pace.) Since independence, per capita income has jumped from $50 a year to over $7,000, vaulting Botswana to the top of the global middle class and putting it on roughly the same level as Bulgaria, an EU member. And unlike, say, Angola—which also has vast diamond and oil wealth and yet suffers from among the highest infant mortality rates in the world and an extreme poverty rate of close to 50 percent—most of Botswana's citizens have benefited from its boom. Although, like its neighbors, the country has been hit hard by HIV/AIDS, its people are otherwise very well off. Literacy, for example, stands at 87 percent—an impressive figure for a country that had just two full-fledged secondary schools at independence—and the Social Progress Index, which measures how well a country provides for the basic needs of its citizens, ranks Botswana second in sub-Saharan Africa. The country also boasts among the lowest corruption scores in the region. Independent Botswana has never suffered a prolonged recession, a bout of hyperinflation, or a famine, despite its harsh climate. It's hard to think of another African state that can say the same.

The trickiest thing about explaining these accomplishments is that they didn't involve any tricks. The inhabitants of Botswana are no more angelic than those of Nigeria, Equatorial Guinea, or the Democratic Republic of the Congo—all poster children for misrule and misused mineral wealth. Botswana's leaders didn't discover some talisman that wards off the Resource Curse. Instead, they protected the country by doing the painstaking work of good government: building and maintaining an open, transparent political system with limits on individual power, checks against corruption, and solid, competent institutions able to act wisely and withstand the economic shocks and seductions resource windfalls usually entail.

It may sound simple. And on a theoretical level, it was. But as Botswana's story will reveal, making it all happen was anything but.

ONE OF THE things that makes the Resource Curse so hard to deal with is that great mineral riches can damage poor countries in a lot of different ways. Sudden surges of cash drive up inflation. They screw up exchange rates. They kill off nonextractive industries, encourage waste and corruption, undermine democracy, erode the rule of law, and provoke conflict.

Botswana's not-so-magic formula for avoiding these woes involved three ingredients: luck, leadership, and shrewd political and economic policymaking. (If that doesn't sound sexy, that's part of the point.)

Of the three, the first—good fortune—might seem the most unlikely. Botswana had pitifully little going for it in its earliest days. Yet its great disadvantage—poverty—would also prove among its greatest assets. For that poverty would convince the country's territorial masters to do it one big favor and leave it alone. And that neglect allowed Botswana to develop a progressive political culture all its own, free from the noxious effects that European interference had in most other places.

To track how that came about, we need to rewind to the eighteenth century, when the eight tribes of the Tswana nation, a group of Bantu-speaking cattle herders, were chased north into present-day Botswana by the Zulus. Though capable fighters, the Tswana generally favored negotiation, accommodation, and assimilation over conflict. And they managed their internal affairs using a remarkable system known as *kgotla*.

In precolonial times, the Tswana used *kgotla* to work out personal disputes, make financial decisions, and answer other administrative questions. Whenever a *kgosi* (king or chief) needed to resolve such a matter, he'd convene his tribe in a designated enclosure surrounded by fence posts topped with rhino or cattle skulls. There the Batswana* would hash out business. And they would also use the meetings to hold their rulers to account, questioning and challenging the *kgosi*'s decisions. Such questioning was, to be sure, an unusual feature for a premodern, formally monarchical system. But according to J. Clark Leith, a Canadian economist and the author of one of the few good books on the country, it was a practice the Tswana *kgosi* were forced to accept by the fact that their people were highly mobile nomads who could (and would) simply abandon them and wander off if they didn't agree with

---

* Note on usage: the plural word used for Tswana tribesmen or the citizens of Botswana is "Batswana"; the singular is "Motswana"; the language and culture are "Setswana."

their rule. To hold the tribes together, Leith writes, the Batswana and their *kgosi* struck an implicit bargain: "The chief provided leadership, but the people required accountability."

As the pioneering anthropologist Isaac Schapera, one of the first outsiders to study the Tswana tribes, recounts, following the arrival of the British, the Batswana took advantage of London's indifference by building *kgotla* into a more expansive protodemocratic institution. In order to ensure the kind of accountability Leith describes, the tribes allowed all married men to participate in the meetings, and they encouraged free speech; as the Tswana saying held, "*Ntwa kgolo ke ya molomo*" ("The highest form of war is dialogue"). All major issues facing the tribe were debated, and while the *kgosi* technically retained the right to set policy on his own, any leader foolish enough to ignore the will of his people would soon find himself out of a job. Indeed, unlike medieval Europeans, the Batswana considered their rulers eminently fallible human beings, a sentiment summed up by the words spoken to every new monarch at his inauguration: "*Kgosi ke kogsi ka morafe*" ("The king is king by the grace of the people.") Though the selection of new chiefs was officially governed by heredity, the tribes became expert at sidelining unpromising aristocrats and replacing them with more competent commoners.

Had the British been more interested in actually ruling the place, it's unlikely they would have allowed such a fractious and unpredictable system to develop; instead, they'd have resorted to their standard strategy of suppressing the popular will and empowering whatever local leaders were willing to execute their orders—no matter how venal or repressive those satraps were. Botswana's poverty, however, allowed it to escape that fate. And that history helps explain the remarkably smooth and peaceful manner in which the country achieved independence in 1966, with none of the carnage that racked so many of its neighbors. Meanwhile, the enduring institution of *kgotla* ensured that Botswana's first generation of leaders were people who valued responsible rule, public participation in government, and limited power—all keys to the country's eventual success.

SERETSE KHAMA, WHO would become Botswana's first president and then lead the country until his death in 1980, had, in a literal sense, been born to rule. Khama, whose first name means "the clay that binds together," came into the world in 1921 as crown prince of the Bangwato, the largest of the Tswana tribes. And he formally inherited his throne at the age of four, when his father died and his uncle, Tshekedi, stepped in as regent.

Although the Khamas were noblemen, they saw leadership as a duty, not a right. From the time Seretse was little, Tshekedi carefully steeped him in the principles of *kgotla,* often bringing his charge with him to tribal councils so the youngster could watch them in action. When Seretse hit the age of ten, his uncle decided to supplement this education with a more formal Western one. To that end, he sent the young prince to a series of British-style boarding schools in South Africa. Then, in 1945, Tshekedi made the fateful decision to ship Seretse off to England, where he would study law: first at Balliol College, Oxford, and then at London's Inner Temple.

Seretse's time in the heart of the empire would have a profound impact on the future president—just as it did on Singapore's Lee, who arrived that same year, and on Canada's Pierre Trudeau, who showed up a few years later. In Lee's case, studying in England would imbue in him a new respect for the value of clean governance and the rule of law. In Trudeau's, it helped transform a somewhat parochial ethnic nationalist into a cosmopolitan and a progressive. As for Khama, Oxford and London would give him a deep respect for Anglo-Saxon constitutional democracy—one that meshed well with his own Setswana politics.

But that would come later. First Khama had to confront the realities of life in cold, impoverished postwar Britain. Nineteen forty-five was a tough year for the country, and an even tougher one if you happened to be black—royal blood notwithstanding. Ostracized by most of his fellow students (apart from a few Jewish classmates who became lifelong friends), the young Khama turned for companionship to other African expats he found in Oxford and London. This group included men like Hastings Banda (the future president of Malawi) and Jomo Kenyatta (who would become the founding father of an independent

Kenya), whose influence would help turn Khama into an ardent anti-colonialist.

The influence of a different sort of acquaintance ultimately proved even more decisive, however. In June 1947 Khama attended a missionary dance in London and met Ruth Williams, the very white daughter of a very proper British army officer. The two soon started dating and fell in love. They made a striking couple: Khama was tall, handsome, and impeccably mannered, with an easygoing charm and the muscular shoulders of a star rugby player; Ruth was pale and elegant, with strawberry blond hair and freckles. As good as they looked together, however, not everyone was taken with their union. Their 1948 wedding—which had to be held at Kensington Town Hall after the Bishop of London denied them the use of a church—sparked an enormous scandal, earning the obscure African princeling and his bride international notoriety (they were featured in *Life, Ebony,* and newspapers around the globe). Ruth's father turned his back on her. Tshekedi Khama was infuriated by his nephew's breach of custom and ordered him home. White South Africa, which had just elected its first apartheid government and was about to ban mixed marriages, was enraged. And Britain's Labour government under Clement Attlee was panicked, desperate to appease its powerful former colony lest it lose access to South Africa's gold and newly discovered uranium (vital to London's fledgling nuclear weapons program). So when the young couple tried to settle in Bechuanaland in 1950, the British government tricked them into returning to England—and then banished them from the protectorate for life.

Khama was devastated by the episode, a business so grubby that even Winston Churchill—no stranger to realpolitik—deemed it "a very disreputable transaction." Rather than succumb to bitterness, however, the young prince only redoubled his determination to fight for pluralistic rule. Yet something in him did change: this determination was now matched by a fierce hatred of racial discrimination in all its forms. When, in 1956, the British finally relented and allowed him to return home—with his wife, but without his crown, which he had to renounce—Seretse did so at once. But on arrival, he immediately entered politics as a commoner, intending, as he told the press, to "develop a democratic system, raise the standard of living, and establish a happy healthy nationhood" in his homeland.

Khama was soon joined in these efforts by the man who would become his professional partner for the rest of his life: Quett Masire. Together they would found the Botswana Democratic Party (BDP) in 1961, manage the country's transition to independence in 1966, and then steward it through its initial decades, with Masire serving as Khama's vice president and minister of finance until the latter's death in 1980, and then as president himself until 1998. In many ways, the two men were opposites. Khama was highborn, Masire wasn't; Khama was university trained and a barrister (Botswana's first), while Masire had a high school education and worked as a farmer, teacher, and journalist before entering politics. But the two were similar where it mattered most: they were deeply committed to building a nonracist, freestanding, truly democratic state. Perhaps just as important, both were men of extraordinary moral character. Although founding fathers are almost always painted in flattering colors, Khama and Masire earned their reputations. According to all evidence, the two were openminded, incorruptible, and fiercely committed to creating a nation that would serve their people's interests—not their own.

So BOTSWANA GOT lucky: it was blessed by history and by the character of its first leaders. While that good fortune may have helped the new nation, however, it wouldn't have been sufficient to get it over the huge hurdles it faced at birth. Doing so would take more than just a few happy twists of fate.*

---

* Consider that, while Botswana did enjoy good luck in several key respects, so did various other ex-colonies in Africa—and yet none of them have managed to capitalize on it anywhere close to the way Botswana has. Lesotho, for example, is culturally very similar to Botswana, right down to the tradition of consensus building through frequent public meetings (called *pitso* there). Somalia, meanwhile, enjoyed a similarly light-handed British colonial administration. And the Democratic Republic of the Congo also enjoyed vast resource wealth and elected an enlightened politician as its first leader. But none of those countries have enjoyed anything resembling Botswana's success.

The primary task facing Khama and Masire, well before the first gemstone was ever unearthed, was to get Botswana's politics right. That meant finding ways to consolidate democracy, accountability, and the rule of law—features that would help armor the new state against misrule once the diamond money started pouring in a few years later.

Their first key move in this area grew out of Khama's determination not to replicate Britain's discriminatory policies. Shortly after independence, he announced that anyone would be eligible for citizenship in the new country so long as he or she accepted its values. "Our nation is defined by its common ideals and not by narrow ethnic criteria," he declared.

This message was meant for two audiences. The president was keen to reassure whites living in the country that they needn't flee along with the departing colonial administration. He and Masire had seen what had happened next door in Zambia—which, right after independence in 1964, fired all its foreign civil servants and nearly foundered as a result—and they had no intention of falling into the same trap. So they ignored the temptation to quickly "indigenize" the bureaucracy, which at independence was just one-quarter black. And according to the Harvard political scientist James Robinson, they "called on anyone who would help," no matter where they came from or what they looked like. The new government enlisted "foreign professors, academics, and consultants. For years, they had lots of foreigners"—including scores of young advisers from the Ford Foundation and the British Overseas Development Institute—"helping them answer all the big questions," Robinson told me. Indeed, the first governor of the Bank of Botswana would be Quill Hermans, a naturalized *lekgowa* (white person), and for years the government's top macroeconomic planner was Norwegian.

Such policies allowed Botswana to avoid the unrest that the harsh treatment of whites caused elsewhere. It also helped Botswana build an extremely competent civil service in record time. But Khama's "non-racialism," as he called it, had another goal: to prevent the fledgling state from fracturing along tribal lines. To evade the fate of countries like Nigeria—which suffered a horrendously bloody civil war shortly after independence—Botswana moved quickly to reduce the salience of divisions among the Tswana and between them and minority tribes.

The government made English and Setswana its sole official languages (with an emphasis on English in all formal settings), banned the use of racial or tribal categories in census taking, and outlawed hiring discrimination of any sort. The idea, Khama told his constituents a few years later, was that "we cannot remain a stable and peaceful nation unless we are united. If we fail to think of ourselves as Batswana, and continue to categorise ourselves as Bangwato, Bakwena, Bakgatla or Bakalaka [all Tswana tribes], we will have lost the opportunity of building a viable nation in this country." Khama was right—and his policy worked. In the years since, though Botswana has often overlooked the rights of its small San Bushmen minority, it has otherwise achieved a remarkable level of ethnic harmony, avoiding the fractures that have done so much damage elsewhere in Africa.

Botswana also owes its stability to the speed with which its early government moved to centralize power and ease most prerogatives out of the hands of the chiefs. Before independence, the *kgosi* had controlled land use, education, and many other legal matters. To prevent them from interfering with the modernization of the new administration or otherwise creating trouble, Botswana's new leaders quickly stripped them of these powers. They also banned the *kgosi* from running for political office (unless, like Khama, they abandon their titles first), gave the government the sole right to hire and fire them, and relegated the headmen to a newly formed House of Chiefs—technically the upper house of Botswana's parliament, but in reality a body with very little power. Most important, in 1967 they passed the Mineral Rights in Tribal Territories Act, which transferred ownership of underground resources from local chiefs (who'd held them in the colonial system) to the national government—a move that would keep the *kgosi* from trying to grab the spoils for themselves when the diamond dollars started streaming in. The *kgosi*, of course, were not happy about any of these changes. But the fact that they were all promoted by the hereditary heir of the largest tribe—who therefore had the most to lose, especially after diamonds were found on Bangwato land—helped persuade the other chiefs to accept the reforms.

Concentrating the government's authority in these ways was necessary, but it was also dangerous; doing so could easily have led

Botswana down the authoritarian path that so many other African states were then treading. Indeed, given Khama's revered status among his countrymen, most Batswana would likely have acquiesced had he and Masire adopted the Big Man style of Zambia's Kenneth Kaunda, Tanzania's Julius Nyerere—or even of Singapore's Lee Kuan Yew, who was building his highly centralized state at just the same time. Yet Botswana's leaders rejected such temptations. Even as they worked to enhance their new government's effectiveness, they moved to restrain its power in ways rarely seen in the developing world.

From the time they first took office, both Khama and Masire ensured that *kgotla* and the values that underlay it—collaboration, transparency, and accountability—would be central features of the new state. As president, Khama avoided dictating policy; decisions were made collectively instead. According to Stephen Lewis, the economist, who lived and worked in Gaborone in the 1970s and 1980s, "everything"—at least, all major initiatives—"had to go through cabinet." First an expert or senior civil servant would prepare a memorandum outlining a new policy, he explained to me. The memo would then be circulated to all ministers and their top civil servants. It would also be discussed in Parliament's all-party caucus and at *kgotla* meetings held throughout the country. Only after consensus had been achieved would cabinet vote on a measure. And only then would the government act on it.

According to Masire, this pattern was a product of necessity. In May 2015 I flew to Gaborone—today an orderly (if somewhat drab) city of well-paved streets, shiny Chinese-built office parks, and tidy suburbs—to meet with the former president. At eighty-nine, Masire was still sharp and spry, with twinkling green eyes and an easy laugh that split his face into a thousand creases. "Remember," he told me one evening as we talked in his living room, "we were an amalgam of tribes that for many years had lived in a state of mutual suspicion, with cattle raiding and so forth. So to convince everyone to invest in the new nation, we had to make sure that everyone was consulted, everyone was a part of the decision-making process." This was undoubtedly true, but Masire was also underselling his and Khama's self-sacrifice. As Robinson points out, "Seretse Khama was the hereditary chief of the largest of the Tswana tribes. He could have done whatever he wanted. Yet he went around the country defending his policies to the people in *kgotla*. And he wasn't going around handing out patronage. He was rationally defending his policies, trying to explain what he was doing and why. What other postindependence African leader did anything like that?"

THE NEW GOVERNMENT'S emphasis on collaboration and openness would pay predictable political dividends. But it also paid economic ones: by ensuring that the new state made economic policy in a responsible, informed, and intelligent way, both before and after diamonds were discovered.

In the half-dozen or so years following independence and before minerals made it rich (the first diamond mine, at Orapa, wouldn't open until 1971), the government's top economic priority was stabilizing its finances. Though conditions were extremely tough, and Botswana's needs were enormous—it had to build everything from scratch—Khama and Masire insisted that their government live within its very limited means.

Their thrift started at the top: the two men were so frugal that when Masire would travel outside Gaborone, he would only telephone his boss at the crack of dawn, when the long-distance rates were lowest. Thanks to such parsimony and a few other deft moves, like the 1969 renegotiation of a customs union with South Africa (a vestige of the colonial era), the government soon managed to balance its books, reducing Botswana's reliance on foreign aid from 55 percent of its recurrent budget (i.e., all expenses other than infrastructure investment) in 1965 to zero in 1972.

Once the diamond money did start flowing, in the mid-1970s, Gaborone quickly shifted its emphasis to two other goals: maximizing its mineral earnings, and making sure that they were spent wisely.

Both tasks were daunting. Though Botswana's gemstones are unusually profitable—they're extremely high quality and relatively cheap to extract (sort of like Saudi oil)—the diamond industry is a notoriously tough one. And so was the company that actually ran Botswana's mines and sold its stones: the South Africa–based De Beers. Undaunted,

Botswana would, over the years, manage to progressively push the giant corporation into handing over an ever larger share of its profits. The country hired the best (and most expensive) international consultants to help it negotiate. It took advantage of De Beers's keen desire to expand its operations (following the success of Orapa, it would need Gaborone's permission to open new mines at Letlhakane in 1975 and Jwaneng in 1982). And it exploited its market dominance—by 1984 Botswana was producing more than 25 percent of the world's diamonds, a huge share of De Beers's total business. Together, these tactics enabled the government to increase its slice of the country's diamond earnings from a tenth in 1967 to around 81 percent today. And it did so without ever alienating its corporate partner. "There are times I haven't liked it," Bruce Cleaver, De Beers's executive head of strategy and corporate affairs, told me when we met at the company's ultra-high-tech and ultra-high-security Gaborone facility (picture glass airlocks with body scanners and a helipad on the roof). "But everything they have done with us has always been perfectly logical."

When it came to the government's other priority—not blowing its giant windfall—here again the example of Botswana's neighbors proved instructive. "We saw what happened in Zambia and in Ghana," Masire told me. The latter "had had a healthy economy at independence in 1957, but quickly frittered away its mineral wealth through scandalous spending—I mean, one minister's wife bought a gold-plated bed from London! So we determined that whatever they did, we wouldn't do."

Above all, that meant scrupulously avoiding wasteful spending. Government thrift is never popular, especially when times seem good. But Khama and Masire were aided in this area by another aspect of local culture. The Batswana are savers by tradition. As Keith Jefferis—a former deputy governor of the Bank of Botswana who now runs a Gaborone consulting firm—explained to me, "The culture here was forged by farming or ranching on the edge of the desert" (the term "Kalahari" means "thirst-land"). "The people were quite poor, their income was very volatile. Everyone knew that a good year could be followed by a disastrous one. So when you had a good year, you didn't throw a party. You saved your surpluses, because next year, that might be what kept you alive." Or as Masire told me, "People in other countries talk about 'putting things away for a rainy day.' Well, we learned very early on that here you have to put something aside for a *dry* day."

To ensure that it could, the government eschewed flashy prestige projects. For years after independence, it would hold conferences in local hotels so as to spare itself the expense of building large facilities, and Gaborone didn't construct a modern international airport until the 1980s—a choice that kept it from hosting Henry Kissinger, who wanted to visit in 1976. (Botswana's existing runways were too short to accommodate the US secretary of state's jet.)

The government also kept state salaries low—according to Masire, when he eventually retired as president, in 1998, his annual compensation was just $24,000. And even after it started to invest heavily in all the things the country lacked, such as infrastructure, health care, and education, it kept a careful eye on what economists call "absorptive capacity": the state's ability to effectively use the money it allocates. As Jay Salkin, an American-born adviser to the Bank of Botswana, explained to me, the government recognized that even after its financial resources started growing, its human resources remained small. "So they started factoring manpower into the budgeting process, by regularly asking themselves whether they had the human capacity to actually spend the money they were considering."

To ensure calm, stable budgeting and to avoid boom-bust cycles, meanwhile, the government decided to start plotting all state outlays on the basis of multiyear National Development Plans (NDPs). Drafted by the Ministry of Finance and Development Planning, the NDPs would only be implemented after all relevant government agencies and civic groups had a chance to weigh in and Parliament approved them. Once a plan was passed, both the government's revenue projections and its priorities were locked in—and remained locked in—for the life span of that NDP. The government was (and remains, for the system is still in operation) barred by law from making any other capital expenditures without Parliament's express approval, and any individual official who spends money outside the NDP can be billed for it.

All these safeguards would prove vitally important. Yet they would not, alone, have been enough for Botswana to avoid all the unhealthy side effects of resource earnings. That's because, beyond waste and bad governance, huge mineral income tends to create a syndrome known as "Dutch disease" (after the country where it was first observed). The phenomenon works as follows. As resource exports rise, so does the value of a country's currency. That, in turn, makes imports cheaper—a seemingly good thing. But as the exchange rate goes up, the country's *exports* become more expensive for people in other countries to buy. Locally made goods soon become uncompetitive on the global market. And so non-resource-related industries like agriculture and manufacturing start to die off, leaving the country unable to produce important goods (like food) itself and dangerously dependent on its fickle resource exports for cash.

Starting early, Botswana took several steps to break this cycle. It carefully managed its exchange rate—a process made much easier by Botswana's abandonment of the South African rand (another vestige of British rule) and the creation of its own currency, the pula, in 1976. And it worked hard to avoid inflation and diversify its economy, by creating a relatively business-friendly climate and investing heavily in human development and basic physical infrastructure. Over the years, such spending has averaged between 20 and 30 percent of GDP—a very high figure—and as of 2009 Botswana's education spending (as a percentage of GDP) ranked second in the world. Such outlays have paid off directly: between 1964 and 2012, the proportion of the population that finished primary school rose from 1.5 to 98 percent. And they've paid off indirectly: between 1965 and 1980, the country's manufacturing sector grew by 12.5 percent a year (albeit from a very low base).

BIG RESOURCE PROFITS tend to expose nations to one other virulent and highly contagious pathogen: corruption. When a lot of money starts sloshing around an underdeveloped country with a lot of poor people, both the temptation and the opportunities to steal it can be overwhelming. Recognizing this danger—and that the wisest spending strategies in the world wouldn't do it any good if didn't hold on to its diamond money in the first place—Botswana's government launched a multifaceted anticorruption campaign soon after its mineral exports started to swell.

Here again, the country's top politicians led by example. Khama—
who Lewis, the American economist and adviser, says was "cleaner
than a hound's tooth"—adopted a conspicuously modest lifestyle, eschewing motorcades and most other trappings of office, banning the
use of chauffeurs by government officials, and driving himself around
town in a secondhand Plymouth Valiant. (Contrast this to modern-day
Angola, where every member of Parliament recently got a $100,000
Lexus.) Khama also barred ministers from flying first class. This rule
often bemused foreign officials. Festus Mogae, Botswana's third president, told me a story about a trip he and Masire took during the 1970s
(when Mogae was a junior finance officer) to attend a meeting in Zaire.
On reaching Kinshasa, Mogae recalled, "the local officials were waiting for us at the first-class exit. So of course they couldn't find us, because we were in the back of the plane. And when they finally did track
us down, the president of Zaire's parliament was very angry at us. 'You
can't just think of yourselves!' he shouted. 'What am I going to say to
my own people if they find out you've been flying economy?'"

Strange as such policies might have seemed to foreigners, they made
an important point at home. Yet Khama's biggest weapon in his fight
against corruption was one I've already mentioned: his and Masire's
insistence on policymaking by consensus. The two knew that however
much integrity they might possess, if Botswana's system was to survive
them and resist the temptations that resource windfalls create, it would
require restraints that didn't depend on anyone's individual goodwill.
So they decided to create a whole system of checks on individual authority. "More important than specific legislation and investigations
was that we did not give too much power to any one person," Masire writes in his memoir. Thus, for example, "no minister could make
major decisions on his or her own but had to involve one or two or three
other departments"—a rule that made it very hard for anyone to act for
personal gain. The government also publicly punished high-level officials caught committing graft, including, on one occasion, an executive
secretary of the BDP and, on another, President Khama's cousin, who
was a senior civil servant. And decades later, in 1994, it created a powerful Singapore-style watchdog—the Directorate on Corruption and
Economic Crime—armed with independent investigative, search, and

seizure powers. These measures never managed to eliminate corruption completely; none could have. But they did turn Botswana into one of the cleanest countries in Africa, effectively blocking what Lewis calls "macro corruption": the distortion of national policymaking for private gain and the kind of wholesale looting of state coffers seen in so many other resource-rich states.

IN THE SUMMER of 1981, after years of anemic growth in the United States and Europe, the sudden shock to oil markets caused by the 1979 Iranian Revolution, as well as an attempt by the US Federal Reserve to rein in high inflation, suddenly tipped the global economy into a severe recession. Consumers stopped buying diamonds. Gem prices collapsed, and Botswana's export revenues fell by 64 percent in the second half of the year. After consulting with De Beers, Gaborone reluctantly decided to stop selling its stones entirely for six months until prices started to recover.

Arriving on the heels of almost a decade of rising prosperity and blazing economic growth, the crash came as a shock to the government of President Masire, who had inherited the office less than a year before. Despite all its precautions, his administration was thrown into a panic and had to scramble to avoid going deep into debt (Botswana was also suffering yet another of its droughts at the time—the worst on record, in fact).

Unpleasant as it was, however, the episode would have several salutary effects on how Botswana managed its economy. On a psychological level, Masire told me, the crisis showed that "no matter how hard you work, anything can come along and destabilize your progress." More specifically, according to Jefferis (the former deputy governor of the Bank of Botswana), "the government learned that it needed buffers. Lots of buffers." So, soon after Botswana's diamond exports started to recover, aided by the opening of the huge Jwaneng mine in 1982, the government started creating cushions that would minimize the pain of future downturns. These took the form of several rainy-day funds: one for recurring expenses, one for debt payments, and one, called the Pula

Fund (the word *pula* literally means "rain" in Setswana), dedicated to assisting future generations.

In the years since their creation, the government has used its steady diamond profits to build these funds into enormous savings accounts; as of mid-2015, the Pula Fund alone totaled $10 billion. And the funds amply proved their worth in 2008, when the global economic crisis hit, causing another collapse in diamond sales akin to that of 1981. This time, Botswana was able to sail through largely unscathed. Though GDP fell by almost 8 percent in 2009 and the government was forced to cut spending and run a fiscal deficit of 12 percent that year, the country avoided the kind of pain felt by most other commodity exporters, and returned to running a surplus just four years later.

The 1981 crisis did Botswana one other big favor. Not only did it remind the government that diamond prices were unreliable, it also served as a sharp warning that the mines wouldn't last forever, and that Botswana had to be ready to survive without them. This wasn't exactly a revolutionary concept at the time; Masire had long emphasized that diamonds should be thought of as limited assets and therefore only be exchanged for other assets. Spending capital from beneath the ground "to create new capital assets above the ground—educated people, productive enterprises, roads, schools" was fine. Spending it on everyday expenses was not: that would be "like eating a dairy cow that should have been saved for milking." Following the '81 crisis, however, the government decided to reinforce this principle by creating a rule known as the Sustainable Budget Index. The new precept explicitly requires that all mineral earnings be used solely for "investment expenditure": roads, schools, hospitals, water systems, and the like. Recurrent spending—things like wages and salaries—has to come out of nonmineral revenues.

NOW FOR THE inevitable caveats. Nothing written above is meant to paint a picture of a perfect state. Despite all the smart moves I've described, modern Botswana still has its shortcomings. For all its years of impressive growth, inequality, unemployment, and poverty remain high. (Both the poverty and unemployment rate stand at around 20 percent—quite good for Africa, but not great for an advanced democracy.) There are several reasons for the persistence of these problems. First, the government still relies too heavily on infrastructure development and public-sector employment to provide growth. And it's built so many roads and bridges by now that that kind of construction no longer pays big returns. In a similar vein, the state already employs close to 40 percent of the workforce and knows it shouldn't expand the number any further.

Second, despite the development of a very successful high-end tourism industry and the creation of new mining-related businesses (in 2006 the government of Botswana persuaded De Beers—in which it had acquired a 15 percent ownership stake two years earlier—to move its main sorting facility from London to Gaborone, and in 2013 the company moved its main global sales facility there as well), the country hasn't diversified as much as it should have. Though mining as a share of GDP has fallen from 51 percent in 1989 to 23 percent today, most of the nonmining growth has come in the nontradable sector of the economy—that is, in services. And that's a problem because such industries won't provide the country with a new source of export earnings when its diamonds finally start to run out. (Unlike physical goods, most services can't be sold abroad.) According to most experts, the diamonds won't disappear for several more decades; the most optimistic forecasts give Botswana's mines another forty years or so. But mining revenues have already plateaued.

Botswana thus faces a tough decision: what to do next. As Jefferis put it, "A resource economy has to deal with two things. First, it has to not mess up, and we've by and large passed that test. But then you have to manage the transition to *not* being a resource economy. And we haven't managed that yet." Gape Kaboyakgosi, a Gaborone academic, explained things this way: "We were lucky enough to have diamonds and smart enough to have managed them well. But the era of diamonds is ending. What are we going to make for ourselves in the future?" Whatever the precise answer, if it hopes to generate new growth, the government is going to have to make a long list of painful reforms. These include cutting red tape, making labor laws less rigid, and privatizing the country's many inefficient state-owned enterprises.

So far, Botswana's current leaders haven't proved up to those challenges. Indeed—and this is modern Botswana's biggest problem—the current government hasn't proved up to much. Ian Khama, the man who has led the country since 2008, is a former commander of Botswana's military. He also happens to be Ruth and Seretse's oldest son. Yet he has turned out to be as unlike his father as one could imagine. The younger Khama is an incompetent manager. He's also high-handed and thin-skinned, and he shows little appetite for the kind of broad-based consultation that made his predecessors so successful; *kgotla* sessions, for example, have become less common and more perfunctory. Numerous BDP leaders have recently left the party in disgust, journalists and opposition politicians have started complaining of harassment, and even Khama's onetime mentors have turned against him. When I asked Mogae, who made Khama his vice president in 1998, about his successor, his face turned sour. "The man is a general," he told me. "He directs, he doesn't consult. So everybody is very disgruntled right now."

Yet the system Khama's father created is stronger than any one bad president, and modern Botswana's problems, while real—and a jarring departure from its past—shouldn't be overstated. Many surveys, such as the Ibrahim Index of African Governance and the Legatum Institute's annual Prosperity Index, still rank Botswana among the best-governed countries in Africa. The Economist Intelligence Unit rates Botswana's democracy ahead of South Africa's and Italy's, and Reporters Without Borders gives the country a better press freedom score than the United States. Botswana retains a vocal opposition, independent and reliable courts, and lots of loud media critics—during my time there no one hesitated to chastise the current administration. And if anything, frustration with Khama's leadership seems only to be increasing public engagement. "For years, we didn't have a civil society to speak of—none whatsoever," Modiri Mogende, a young Batswana journalist, told me. "Now we have a very active one. Unlike many places in Africa, we have unions, public service groups, and others that are growing in power, stature, wealth, and influence by the day." Indeed, all signs suggest that the BDP will lose the country's next election, in 2019, for the first time in Botswana's history.

Despite these many positive signs, a number of development experts have recently started arguing that when poor states suddenly strike gold (or diamonds, or oil, as so many African countries recently have), they should handle those resources in a radically different way. Two Stanford scholars, Larry Diamond and Jack Mosbacher, have proposed that such countries funnel most of their resource earnings directly to their citizens as taxable income. Others have suggested that states follow the example of Chad, which in 2000 signed a deal with the World Bank creating an internationally monitored account to handle its mineral wealth (indeed, in 2011, Ghana set up a similar arrangement).

But the Chad model has turned out to be a miserable failure—the government started raiding the supposedly inviolate account within just a few years. As for the direct distribution of resource revenues, while it's attractively simple—especially since, by cutting out government, it cuts down on opportunities for corruption and waste, and as chapter 1 shows, the poor tend to spend the money well—it also represents a fatalistic compromise. The plan assumes that weak governments can't be fixed and so should simply be avoided. But that's a short-term answer at best. Resource-rich states truly interested in lasting success would be better off following Botswana's lead: building a government with guardrails, one that requires broad buy-in, limits the influence of any one individual, and punishes or sidelines officials who go astray. Viewed from afar, Botswana's success can seem implausible and unrepeatable, the story of a unique place that simply got very, very lucky. But a closer look reveals that the opposite is true. Yes, Botswana started out with a number of advantages. But for every asset, it faced several enormous obstacles, and the fact that it nevertheless managed to thrive proves that others can too. As Robinson put it to me, "There's no reason why other African societies can't build effective state institutions that promote accountability and economic development." That's exactly right. The most important lesson Botswana teaches, in Robinson's words, is "that it can be done, it can be done well, it can be done in Africa, and it can be done in resource-rich states. You can reverse the curse. Botswana shows how."

7

THIS LAND IS MY LAND

Why the Shale Revolution Could Only
Happen in the USA

THE UNITED STATES COMES IN FOR A LOT OF ABUSE IN this book. In the course of describing what various other countries have done right, I've taken a lot of swipes at the US government for all the stuff it gets wrong.

But not in this chapter. For this one's about a great American success story. It's the tale of how the United States managed to foster and create the energy revolution that is now transforming the country and the world. And not only is it an American success story; it's an *only-in-America* success story, a case in which the United States has done something no other country has, or could. Many other nations are now trying to catch up. But so far, none have come close.

Three factors, apart from its uniqueness, make America's accomplishment in this area especially impressive. There's its size. Its speed. And the fact that, not long ago, almost no one dreamed it was possible.

It may be hard to remember today, in this era of cheap and plentiful fossil fuels, but little more than a decade ago most Americans were anything but optimistic about their country's power supplies. US oil and natural gas production were both dwindling. After years of false starts and billions in investment, renewables were still going nowhere fast. Officials and pundits were worrying that the United States had grown dangerously dependent on hydrocarbon imports, which totaled 52 percent of the US energy mix in 2000 and gave states like Saudi Arabia far too much influence over US foreign policy. Doomsayers, nervously eyeing the rise of energy-hungry giants like China and India, warned that we'd soon hit a moment of "peak oil," when global production would max out and then start to collapse as underground reservoirs ran dry. Matthew Simmons, a well-respected energy analyst and investor, predicted a nightmarish future in which demand outstripped supply and "energy haves and have-nots" went to war. Colin Campbell, a petroleum geologist and an academic, foresaw "starvation, economic recession, possibly even the extinction of homo sapiens." Even the normally staid Department of Energy warned Americans to brace for "major economic upheaval."

The Cassandras turned out to be right about one thing: we've had an upheaval. But it sure wasn't the one they were predicting. Instead, since US companies figured out how to unlock shale—a dense, sedimentary, carbon-rich rock that lies under much of the continental United States—as well as other forms of unconventional oil and gas, American energy production has gushed up as furiously as one of those geysers Texas roughnecks used to dream about. In short order, the United States has gone from an energy has-been to the world's largest natural gas producer and is expected to soon become one of the biggest exporters as well. In the last half decade or so, it's also increased its oil production by some 60 percent, and in 2014 its output hit its highest level in twenty-five years—since back when *Dallas* was still on TV. And thanks to an explosion of innovation, America's supplies continue to grow, exceeding what were recently the most optimistic predictions. The International Energy Agency now forecasts that the United States will become the planet's number one oil producer by 2020, surpassing Saudi Arabia, Russia, and the world's other energy heavyweights. Some experts think it could happen sooner, especially if President Trump continues to slash regulations. Even if the experts are wrong, the United States may soon be able to stop importing crude altogether, or at least limit its purchases to friendly producers like Canada and Mexico. It even started *exporting* oil in 2016.

This enormous transformation has already sent shock waves in all directions. According to a Yale study group led by Paul MacAvoy, the energy boom has pumped an estimated $100 billion into the US economy each year since 2007. America's four big airlines saved over $11 billion in fuel in 2015 alone. Edward Morse, Citi's top global commodity analyst, estimates that by the end of this decade, the revolution will have spared US homeowners some $30 billion on electricity bills. And all the new activity has created hundreds of thousands of well-paying jobs.

Even the physical environment has improved. Green activists and many ordinary Americans still worry, with reason, about the harmful side effects of our efforts to extract oil and gas from shale—a process known as hydraulic fracturing, or fracking. Fracking has developed a toxic reputation in many parts of the country (and the world), and has even been banned in some precincts, such as New York State. The anxiety is easy to understand, for when carelessly done fracking can pollute groundwater and release methane (a dangerous greenhouse gas) into the atmosphere. It's even thought to trigger earthquakes.

But the fears about fracking's environmental costs are rapidly becoming outdated. A growing body of evidence suggests that the shale boom has already reduced emissions, as cheap natural gas quickly displaces much dirtier coal as the main fuel used to generate America's electricity. (Burning gas releases 50 percent less carbon than burning coal, and much less sulfur dioxide, mercury, and other pollutants.) As for the dangers of the fracking process itself, President Obama's energy secretary, Ernest Moniz, called them "challenging but manageable." The industry—under pressure from the public, the courts, and the government, including new federal guidelines announced by Obama in 2015—has moved rapidly to reduce fracking's risks by adopting new safeguards. Measures such as closer monitoring and enhanced testing of well components, in addition to requirements that companies disclose the chemicals they use in the fracking process, have already cut methane gas leaks significantly—even as US production has skyrocketed. And there's reason to believe that safety will keep improving, at least if Trump doesn't overturn the new rules. Fred Krupp—who, as president of the Environmental Defense Fund, is hardly a shill for the energy industry—has lauded the new protocols, writing that they should "ensure that the economic windfall benefits the environment, too." The good news, in other words, far outweighs the bad, which is why a great many other countries are now eager to emulate America's remarkable success.

But before assessing whether they can, and describing how the United States pulled it off in the first place, we should pause to confront one elephant looming over the discussion.

As everybody knows, in the summer of 2014 global oil and gas prices began to collapse. Just what triggered the slide remains somewhat hazy. America's surging production, the slow recovery of Iraq's oil industry, and weakening demand from Asia definitely had a lot to do with it; in both 2013 and 2014 Asian oil consumption grew by less than it had in the previous three years. But market manipulation by Saudi Arabia, which produces some of the cheapest oil in the world and is not eager to lose its dominance as the world's top exporter, also played a major role (though to what degree remains uncertain). What *is* clear is what happened next: over the course of a year, the benchmark price for crude oil fell from close to $110 a barrel to below $40, and the cost of gas dropped by almost as much.

These declines represented another big boon for ordinary consumers; by one estimate, the fall in prices handed American automobile drivers the equivalent of a 2 percent pay raise. But the slide caused a lot less joy among those who make their living selling all that suddenly devalued energy. Indeed, by late 2014 analysts began warning that the US shale revolution itself risked stalling out as the market was flooded with cheaper, easier-to-produce conventional oil and gas (extracted by old-fashioned, less complicated wells).

So has it?

The answer is . . . sort of. The revolution has certainly slowed. But it's far from over.

The US energy industry has suffered a serious setback, no question. According to Daniel Yergin, a Pulitzer Prize–winning author and a top energy consultant, "the world of commodities has been turned upside down." New well construction has fallen sharply, and ConocoPhillips and several other "majors" (as the mammoth international oil and gas companies are known) have been forced to cut hundreds of thousands of jobs. At the same time, many of the independent firms that had leapt into the shale revolution found themselves so deeply leveraged (to a collective tune of $260 billion) that the plunge in prices and investment pushed them perilously close to bankruptcy. A fair number went under.

Yet even if prices don't quickly rebound to their pre-2014 levels, there are several reasons to bet that America's shale producers will not just weather the storm but recapture their lucrative position before too long. First, you have to understand that those producers rely on a variety of (literally) groundbreaking technologies to do their drilling—technologies that are still being refined and improved at a blistering pace. Why does that matter? Because shale oil and gas have historically been more expensive to extract than the conventional stuff (though costs vary from well to well), and these high production costs have meant that shale producers suffered the most when prices fell. But innovation is already changing this picture and leveling the field. In 2014 rapid technological advances lowered the average break-even price for shale oil—that is, the per-barrel price producers need to earn to avoid operating at a loss—from around $70 (way too high in the current climate) to $57 (still high, but only by a little). Given current pressures, further advances are inevitable. "The gains are going to accelerate," Citi's Morse told me, "since when you're under duress, you find ways to do more with less." (Morse, for one, thinks the shale industry will get the break-even price down to $40 within just a few years.)

The second reason to keep betting on American shale is that unlike the massive deepwater or otherwise remote rigs the majors focus on these days, shale wells are cheap, quick, and easy to drill. That fact has two implications. One, it means that even while prices remain low, the smaller firms that sparked the US energy revolution should be able to afford to continue drilling—if at a moderate pace and in the easier-to-access fields. And two, it means that when prices finally *do* tick up again—as they're likely to, when production slows or the Saudis get sick of spending billions of dollars a year to artificially depress prices—the independents will be able to quickly jump back into the market, ramping their production up to precrash levels and beyond. Net result: the United States should remain the world's top source of new oil supplies for years to come, as the International Energy Agency recently predicted.

HAVING EXPLORED THE *what* of the energy revolution, let's now turn
to the *how*, and examine the various ingredients that set it off in the first
place. As a species, journalists (myself included) love to focus on solitary, larger-than-life figures. It's not that we're lazy. They just make for
tidier and more dramatic narratives. The shale boom, however, was produced by a range of different actors and forces. So this chapter, unlike
many of the others in this book, will feature a variety of protagonists.

Our story begins in the early 1970s, when US oil and gas production started to slow. Understandably anxious, the majors began scrambling for new sources, looking deep under the oceans and into remote
reaches of the globe. While they soon uncovered some promising new
prospects, these were so hard to reach that tapping them would prove
hugely expensive. To manage the costs, the majors had to join forces.
In the mid-1970s, for example, Shell and Esso launched a joint oil
drilling project in the frigid waters some one hundred miles north of
Scotland's Shetland Islands. The venture, one of the most audacious
ever attempted at that point, was expected to cost about $6 billion (a
staggering amount at the time). It was soon burning through $2.7 mil-
lion a *day*, and such numbers quickly became commonplace. Over the
next twenty-five years, the majors would spend a combined total of
about $150 billion on such ambitious projects, and the need to fund
them triggered a slew of megamergers. BP bought Amoco, Exxon de-
voured Mobil, Chevron swallowed Texaco, and so on.

Although this strategy may have worked for the giants, the industry's smaller independents lacked the resources to hunt for big game
abroad. As Robert A. Hefner III, a veteran of this period as the head
of GHK, an independent Oklahoma "deep-gas" driller, recalls, companies like his were left with a stark choice. Either they could take
advantage of what Hefner calls their "classic Yankee ingenuity" and
get creative—or they could go bust. Most, like Hefner's, chose the first
option, and started looking for new ways to get at what oil and gas
remained closer to home.

It took years of trial and error before they made much progress, but
they eventually hit the mother lode: shale.

Now, as Yergin and others have pointed out, the US oil and gas industry had long suspected that shale held enormous potential, and had even known how to unlock it—in theory. The answer involved fracking: boring holes deep into the earth and then squirting down a muddy mix of liquids that would create enough pressure to shatter the rock and release all the oil and gas trapped within it.

A crude form of this technique had first been developed in the 1940s and had worked fairly well on limestone and sandstone. But because most US shale lay very deep underground (sometimes at depths of a mile or more) and because shale is a notoriously difficult rock to deal with, most companies never bothered trying. Those that did failed. Nobody could make shale wells work.

And then George Mitchell came along.

MITCHELL WAS AN independent oilman from Galveston, Texas. The son of an illiterate Greek goatherd, he was, in many ways, the antithesis of the stereotypical oil tycoons who could be seen swaggering around Houston in ten-gallon hats and shit-kicking boots. Balding, owlish, and a father of ten, Mitchell tended to dress like a shabby used-car salesman. As an undergraduate at Texas A&M (the Harvard of the oil industry), he'd studied both geology and petroleum engineering, a rare combination in those days: geologists were viewed by the oil world as its artists, its luftmenschen, while engineers were its hard-boiled, down-to-earth technicians. Even more unusual was Mitchell's fierce dedication to philanthropy and environmentalism. Later in life, he would push for tight government regulation of his own industry, and would spend some $600 million building a planned community based on the sustainability principles of Buckminster Fuller.

For all his eccentricities, however, Mitchell did fit the Texas wildcatter mold in two key respects: he could gamble like a cowboy and he was stubborn as a mule. Convinced that the peak-energy pessimists were wrong and that falling production could be reversed, he spent the better part of two long, frustrating decades obsessively struggling to squeeze gas out of the Barnett: a five-thousand-square-mile shale formation in northeast Texas, where he'd previously found a lot of conventional oil and gas at shallower depths. For seventeen years, his firm, Mitchell Energy, got nowhere. It became pretty good at fracking rock, but it couldn't make its wells produce much gas, and the process cost way more than it earned. By the mid-1990s, almost everyone at the company, including its president, Bill Stevens, and Mitchell's own son, Todd, thought they should give up. The majors, which had long since turned their sights overseas, just scoffed.

But once again fear proved the mother of invention, for Mitchell had grown desperate. At the start of 1998, he was nearing eighty, was sick with prostate cancer, had a wife with Alzheimer's, and was barely keeping his company (in which he owned more than half the stock) afloat. Declining production and low oil prices had pushed Mitchell Energy's share price down from $35 to $10 in a few short months. The family was keen to sell but couldn't find any buyers. And creditors were baying at the door.

And then a Mitchell engineer in his early thirties named Nick Steinsberger had a strange idea. Instead of fracking with sticky, sandy, guar-based gels, as most operators did at the time—the gels were good for cracking open the rock, but were expensive and tended to gum up the resulting fissures, trapping the gas—why not try something simpler and cheaper, like water? As Steinsberger had just discovered, an engineer named Ray Walker at Union Pacific Resources (UPR) had recently figured out how to use water to frack sandstone, and Walker was happy to share his secret. (Such collaboration may seem strange in retrospect, since the independents were a fiercely competitive lot all struggling to survive. But the Texas energy world was small and tight-knit, and its inhabitants liked talking shop. And besides, UPR was working on a different rock in a different region and so didn't see a reason not to help.)

In the preceding decades, oilmen had tried using just about everything to blast open underground rock formations. They'd experimented with gunpowder, napalm, rocket fuel, and even something called a "downhole bazooka," all with limited success. In 1967, in a moment of atomic-age madness, they'd even detonated a twenty-nine-kiloton nuclear bomb under New Mexico (which worked—but also rendered the recovered gas radioactive, making it a little difficult to sell). Yet even by those crazy standards, most engineers still thought Steinsberger's idea was nuts. Dumping massive amounts of water down boreholes might have worked on other, less porous minerals. But everyone knew that so-called redneck fracking wouldn't work on Barnett shale, which was so full of clay that it was likely to just suck up the water and give nothing back.

Yet Mitchell was running out of time. Besides, Steinsberger's experiment would be cheap and, if it worked, save the boss a lot of money; swapping water for gel would cut the per-well cost by more than two-thirds. So the old man gave his engineer the go-ahead.

Not only did the water, which Steinsberger mixed with a touch of sand and polymer lubricants, shatter the shale and release huge quantities of gas—but the gas kept on flowing at a furious pace for month after month. (Typical gas wells peak early and then decline sharply, which forces conventional firms to constantly drill new ones.) Within two years, Steinsberger's experiment had increased Mitchell's daily gas production by 250 percent. Word quickly spread, and led by Aubrey McClendon, the founder of Chesapeake Energy, numerous other independents soon jumped on board, using what came to be known as "slick-water fracking" to unlock other shale gas fields in Oklahoma, Louisiana, and states along the eastern seaboard. The new technique even turned out to work for oil.

The results would change the world. Between 1999 and 2013, total known North American natural gas reserves doubled, to three quadrillion cubic feet—almost twice the size of Saudi Arabia's energy inventory. As for Mitchell, he went from teetering on the edge of ruin to enjoying fantastic wealth; in August 2001, a firm called Devon Energy snapped up his company for more than $3 billion, at a stock price 350 percent greater than its 1998 low. The unlikely oilman came to be celebrated as a visionary and the father of a new industry—especially after Devon refined his process still further by drilling its wells horizontally, which allowed it to access much more shale with a single well. (If vertical drilling is like fishing with a pole, horizontal drilling is like using a dragnet.)

MITCHELL, WHO DIED in 2013 at the age of ninety-four, certainly deserved these accolades, which he earned through decades of hard, frustrating work. The man was smart, creative, brave, and dogged, as were Steinsberger and many other Mitchell Energy employees.

Even with those qualities, however, it's possible that the company, or other industry leaders like Devon or Chesapeake, would never have made their breakthroughs without the help of another hero, this one often overlooked and maligned: the US government. Pretty much from the moment shale was identified as a promising energy source, Washington had quietly worked hand in glove with the industry to help it extract more hydrocarbons from the earth. Over the decades, this relationship proved integral to most of the key innovations that allowed Mitchell and his successors to accomplish what they did—even if the oilmen themselves rarely talked about it.

Take fracking. The technique, you'll recall, was invented in the 1940s. But because it didn't work very well at first, nobody spent much time on it over the subsequent two decades, when energy from other sources was relatively cheap and abundant. In the 1970s, however, the US government grew alarmed by the combination of falling domestic gas production and the Arab oil embargo and started pushing for the development of new American sources of fossil fuels. As research by Michael Shellenberger and Ted Nordhaus has revealed, it was a Republican president, Gerald Ford, who really threw the federal government's weight behind this effort. In 1976, following a particularly cold winter during which fuel shortages had forced schools, factories, and several federal agencies to shut down, the Ford administration decided to bankroll the study of unconventional oil and gas by creating a number of new entities, including the Gas Research Institute, the Unconventional Gas Recovery Program, and the Eastern Gas Shales Project (a joint venture among universities, private firms, and the US Bureau of Mines)—and by pumping a lot of money into their projects.

Such unabashed government intervention in the development of new technologies and resources would make today's GOP shudder—remember Solyndra, the US solar company that failed in 2011 despite major government investment, and then became a regular Republican punch line during the 2012 campaign? But Ford was a centrist, and much too worried about the country's energy problems to care about something as trivial as party orthodoxy.

Especially when his efforts started paying off, as they quickly did. Over the following years, government scientists, working alone or in concert with academics and private companies, helped produce a number of technological advances that would prove very useful to cracking the shale code. These included the creation of 3-D mapping technology that helped private firms figure out exactly where the gas lurked; the invention of ultratough diamond-studded drill bits that could bore through hard shale rock without quickly breaking down; the development of horizontal drilling; and the adaptation of microseismic imaging (originally developed to prevent coal-mine collapses) to allow frackers to monitor what they were doing underground. In 1978 the US government also set a high price for unconventional gas, and in 1980 it created a tax credit as well—two forms of financial support that helped firms like Mitchell's afford experiments that would otherwise have been prohibitive.

Despite all this largesse—the Department of Energy spent some $24 billion on fossil fuel research between 1978 and 2007, not counting the tax credits or other incentives—many industry experts and energy tycoons have been coy about admitting to the ways in which they or their colleagues benefited from Washington's help. Hefner, for example, told me that he didn't think the government did all that much to fuel the energy revolution, and said that "what really made it happen wasn't anything to do with government R&D." In a similar vein, Michael Giberson, an energy analyst and a Texas Tech professor, has argued that Washington's assistance only pushed shale gas production forward by a few years at most.

But Mitchell, who sought out and heavily relied on government advice and financing, openly acknowledged the state's role, and he and his lieutenants became vocal advocates for the value of government investment in the industry. According to Dan Steward, a former Mitchell Energy vice president, the US government "did a hell of a lot of work" to help his firm crack the Barnett. "I can't give them enough credit," he has said. Federal support helped Steward and his colleagues figure out where the gas lay, how much was down there, and how to get at it. As for financing, "you could say those pricing scenarios, and the tight gas credit, created the possibility for shale gas," he told an interviewer in 2011. "If there is one key lesson from the shale revolution," adds Shellenberger, "it is that public investments in technology innovation can bring a huge benefit"—for both the environment and the economy.

As IMPORTANT AS these two forces—private ingenuity and public support—were to the coming energy revolution, however, even they don't fully explain what ultimately transpired. Several fortuitous quirks in the US legal system, and in the structure of the American economy, also played essential roles.

First among these was the fact that US law—unlike that of most other countries—grants landowners rights not just to their turf but to everything that lies beneath it as well. This rule means that American property holders—and the prospectors who buy or lease their land or its mineral rights—enjoy full title to whatever they manage to dredge up, and the profits therefrom. And that gives them an enormous incentive to allow drilling (if individuals) or to invest in new ventures (if companies). Rex Tillerson, the head of ExxonMobil, has described this arrangement as a "marvelously elegant system that ensures that all natural resources are fully developed." Hefner, who calls this legal feature "a huge, huge deal," says it explains why the United States has so many independent energy firms in the first place—approximately six thousand—unlike the rest of the world, which has only a few.

The existence of so many firms would provide the next link in the chain reaction. The crowded nature of the US oil and gas market ensured furious competition during the race for shale. And that competition led, in turn, to the widespread and frenetic technological experimentation at which companies like Mitchell came to excel. In fact, it was precisely this high-tech free-for-all that eventually allowed the firm to solve the great shale mystery, and then spurred others, like Devon and Chesapeake, to rapidly adopt, refine, and adapt its advances.

These innovators, finally, were only able to fund their experiments (even factoring in government help) because the United States has large, varied, and fluid capital markets, which, unlike those of most other countries, are good at supporting fairly small public companies. These markets enabled the US independents to connect with investors willing to bankroll their often speculative (and expensive) early efforts; without them, they could never have kept experimenting for so long before they hit pay dirt.

All of these conditions had to be present for America's energy revolution to succeed. And—key point—most of them don't prevail in other countries.

The problem has little do with a lack of mineral wealth itself: the United States' recoverable shale resources are thought to represent just 15 percent of the worldwide total. Russia's Bazhenov Shale alone is about 170 times the size of the Barnett; Poland is thought to sit on some 148 trillion cubic feet of shale gas; and China is estimated to have more of the stuff than the United States and Canada put together.

Yet whereas the United States has drilled approximately 4 million oil and gas wells over the years, the rest of the world combined has only managed to bore about 1.5 million.

What's holding everyone else back?

The answer starts with the differences between the cast of players in the United States and those elsewhere. The American energy industry is a busy, chaotic bazaar filled both with towering giants (the majors) and lots of smaller operators scurrying between their feet. But that situation is anomalous; most other national markets are dominated by a few huge, generally state-owned, corporations. Such firms are almost always slower moving, less innovative, and more risk averse than the scrappier independents. Indeed, the latter's nimbleness explains why, in the American case, they were able to beat the majors in the shale race despite the giants' much more impressive resources. And it helps explain why foreign countries, which have few of these small, dexterous companies, haven't been able to follow America's lead.

An even bigger problem in some parts, especially Europe, is popular opposition to drilling in all forms and to fracking in particular.

According to current estimates, Europe sits on about as much shale gas as the United States does. Yet it's barely begun to exploit it. The entire region produces no commercial shale gas and has sunk a mere handful of exploratory wells. BP's chief economist, Spencer Dale, has said that he doesn't expect the picture to change much for at least twenty years. Indeed, the Continent seems to be going backward: ExxonMobil, Marathon, and Chevron all recently abandoned attempts to frack in Poland, once regarded as the region's most promising prospect.

The problem is that most European citizens simply want no part of shale. Thanks in part to Europe's much higher population density (383 people per square kilometer, versus 27 people in the United States), as well as its much stronger Green movement and the fact that its land-owners don't enjoy title to the minerals that lie underground—and thus lack a profit motive—the European public remains very wary of unconventional oil and gas extraction. Despite the mounting evidence that fracking can be done safely, France has banned all shale gas opera-tions, and Bulgaria, the Czech Republic, Germany, Luxembourg, the Netherlands, Scotland, Spain, and Switzerland have imposed partial or total moratoriums—a striking case of what Paul Stevens, senior re-search fellow for energy at Chatham House, calls "popular ignorance overrul[ing] science."

It's possible that persistent high prices—Europeans still pay more than twice as much for their gas as Americans do—could eventually soften public opposition and beat some sense into the region's leaders. So could rising pollution, since the lack of cheap gas keeps Europe hooked on dirty coal. And so could geopolitics. The crisis in Ukraine has dramatically underscored how little leverage European govern-ments will have with Russian president Vladimir Putin as long as they continue to depend on him for so much of their natural gas. (Russian imports account for about a third of Europe's total consumption, and some European officials, including NATO's former secretary-general, have accused Moscow of funding European antifracking protests in order to preserve this dependence.) More scientific studies showing both the growing safety of fracking and its environmental benefits should also help.

Even then, however, Europe will still have to reform what is an extremely cumbersome licensing and regulatory system. Continental authorities currently grant exploration permits on a much smaller scale than do American regulators. That arrangement forces energy companies to cobble together an exhausting number of individual approvals before they can get to work on a well. Meanwhile, misguided government policies have already helped ruin, or at least seriously damage, Poland's chances of exploiting its shale wealth. When the majors first moved in, Warsaw insisted that they work with local partners and levied extremely high taxes on their operations even before they'd begun making money—a senseless approach that one frustrated executive compared to hunters dividing up a bear hide before they'd managed to shoot the animal.

Despite these and other blunders, determined government leadership could still lower many of Europe's barriers. Making progress in the other great shale frontier—China, which the US Department of Energy estimates has up to 50 percent more recoverable gas than the United States—will be easier in some senses but harder in others.

Unlike many European states, China at least has the appetite for change. In 2012 Beijing—anxious to reduce the smog-choked country's reliance on coal and to address its quickly growing energy needs—came out with a five-year plan for shale that pledged that by 2020 China would produce about a third as much shale gas as the United States. This was a wildly ambitious target at the time and remains one today, considering that in all of 2014 China only managed to produce as much shale gas as the United States had every two days the year before. Indeed, so far China has only drilled a total of about four hundred shale wells—the same number that tiny North Dakota drilled every two months during the height of the boom.

China does have some big advantages going for it—advantages that other potential shale powers like Europe can't match. To start with, labor in China remains very cheap, at least by rich-world standards. And there are few regulatory obstacles; indeed, there are few regulations, period, and those that exist are rarely enforced. There's also been little public opposition to fracking so far, though that may change. Finally, China's energy industry has very deep pockets. Its oil and gas market is dominated by three state-owned firms (known in industry-speak as "national oil companies," or NOCs): China National Petroleum Corporation (CNPC), China National Offshore Oil Corporation (CNOOC), and Sinopec. All three are gargantuan; in 2015, Sinopec became the second-largest company (by revenue) in the world.

Despite these assets and Beijing's encouragement, however—it recently raised the wholesale price for natural gas, created new subsidies for shale producers, and waived import duties on drilling equipment that can't be manufactured at home—the country has so far made strikingly little progress in sparking its own energy revolution.

Most explanations you'll hear for this failure focus on the country's supposedly difficult geology and geography. Although China does sit atop vast shale formations, these tend not to be conveniently arrayed in flat layers, as are many US fields. The shale rock in the massive Sichuan Basin, for example—which stretches beneath five provinces and is thought to hold 55 percent of the country's shale gas—is folded together in ridges. Many energy experts also point to the fact that China is running short on what Nick Steinsberger identified as the key ingredient to shale drilling: H_2O. According to Stuart Elliott of Platts, an energy consulting firm, most of China's shale reserves are located in the country's arid northwest. Elliott says that that fact, coupled with the water crisis looming over the country as a whole, creates "a major sticking point" preventing progress.

But it shouldn't. In reality, neither of these explanations—a lack of water or an absence of flat shale beds—adequately explains China's struggles. Yes, fracking is a thirsty process, requiring about 2.5 million gallons of water per well. But over the last few years, companies like the Houston-based Apache Corporation have shown that brackish water can be used in place of fresh, while other American independents have figured out how to recycle their drilling liquids. As for the shape of China's shale, it's not inherently more problematic than that of the formations found in Texas, Oklahoma, or Pennsylvania; it's just different. And the fact that that difference has caused such problems for China's energy industry points to the real sources of its struggles: its risk aversion, its preference for taking shortcuts, and the lack of true free-market incentives.

Owing to these traits, China's NOCs have generally tried to copy what's worked in the United States rather than develop their own shale drilling techniques and technologies. CNPC, CNOOC, and Sinopec have all struck partnerships with international firms in the hope that the foreigners can replicate their success in China.

Now, there's nothing inherently wrong with turning to outsiders for help. Foreign veterans can bring knowledge, skills, and hard-won experience—all precious commodities—to bear on a project.

The problem is with the *sort* of joint ventures China has undertaken. First, rather than work with small, agile, and innovative Western firms, the NOCs have linked up with companies almost as stodgy as themselves: the majors. Elizabeth Muller, executive director of the think tank Berkeley Earth, explains that such moves appeal to the Chinese because they seem safe. "Nobody gets fired for partnering with Shell," she told me. The problem, however, is that such collaborators aren't very creative, and so the locals don't get much innovation from the deal. Instead, the foreigners simply apply the same techniques they've used in Texas and elsewhere. "But because the two countries' geologies are so different, it doesn't work very well," Muller says.

One of the key lessons of the US shale revolution is that companies have to be willing to fail repeatedly before they eventually succeed. As Morse puts it, "If you look at the history of someone like George Mitchell, he experimented a lot to get where he got. He tinkered." But China doesn't encourage that mind-set. "I think the barrier may be that there's not a tinkering mentality ingrained in the system," Morse told me. "Communist Party–based companies"—the heads of CNPC, CNOOC, and Sinopec are all chosen by the central government—"are very bad at encouraging tinkering and free decision making."

They also dislike the kind of frenetic competition that proved so crucial to driving Mitchell and others' breakthroughs in the United States. China does have some smaller, hungrier energy firms that are eager to start a shale boom of their own, as well as billionaire venture capitalists eager to bankroll them. But until recently, the NOCs enjoyed the rights to all of China's natural gas, and they still control all of the country's pipelines and other infrastructure, which allows them to squeeze out less established but more inventive would-be competitors.

To its credit, Beijing has recently started trying to address some of these problems. A few years ago, the Ministry of Land and Resources declared shale gas a "new mineral," removing it from the NOCs' monopoly. And the government has held a few open auctions for the right to explore new shale fields. But China's market remains very far from the kind of rambunctious scene that nurtured America's shale pioneers. Thus far, the land parcels the government has sold to smaller firms have been far less promising geologically than those already controlled by the state-run giants. China's independents are also still barred by law from forming partnerships with like-minded foreign companies, which limits their access to international expertise.

In light of all this, it's no wonder that China's efforts to unlock its shale remain underwhelming. The country has managed to create some functional—but very expensive—shale gas wells in the Fuling region. While they have proved that China can extract shale, however, they haven't shown that it can do so in a cost-effective, let alone profitable, fashion. Experts estimate that it will be at least ten years before China produces shale energy in any real quantity, and at a worthwhile price—and even longer before it hits Beijing's target, which the government quietly lowered in the summer of 2014.

All of which means the great energy revolution will remain a thoroughly American one for some time to come. "You can forget about the next five to 10 years," says Stevens, the Chatham House expert. "Fifteen to 20 is a possibility." But just a possibility, and only if China and the rest of the world can learn the right lessons from the US experience—and unleash some Yankee-style ingenuity of their own.

8

MANUFACTURE YOUR MIRACLE

HOW SOUTH KOREA KEEPS ITS ECONOMY GROWING. AND GROWING. AND GROWING.

A T VIRTUALLY THE SAME TIME THAT BOTSWANA AND Singapore were struggling to survive their difficult births, another newborn nation found itself in similar straits.

Strictly speaking, Korea wasn't new, of course; the country had existed in various forms for centuries, ever since it was first unified by King Munmu in AD 668. But the Empire of Japan had invaded in 1910 and then spent the next thirty-five years trying to grind away every trace of indigenous culture. Though liberation finally arrived with VJ Day in 1945, Korea's occupation was soon replaced by division: the peninsula was split along the 38th parallel between the Soviets, who occupied the North, and the Americans, who held the South. The two superpowers swiftly set up two new states in their respective zones of influence. And in June 1950 those two states went to war.

All civil conflicts are bitter, but Korea's was especially so. In three years, it destroyed much of what the Japanese had left behind. By the time the US-led Eighth Army retook Seoul from North Korean and Chinese troops midway through the war, South Korea's capital had been reduced to a smoking ruin. Of the city's 1.5 million prewar inhabitants, only 200,000 remained; nationwide, a tenth of the population was dead. The South's infrastructure and economy were similarly devastated. It's thought that half of all houses on the peninsula were leveled, and Gregg Brazinsky, a historian at George Washington University, estimates that nine hundred factories, more than half the country's freight trucks and locomotives, and more than $3 billion in property were demolished.

This was not fertile ground on which to build a new country.

Yet in the decades since, South Korea has managed to transcend its unhappy origins and thrive beyond anyone's expectations. Unlike Botswana, say, which is wealthy by African standards but still just middle-income, South Korea has vaulted through the economic ranks to become one of the richest countries on the planet. A state that was poorer than Bolivia, Ghana, or Iraq in 1961 is now the world's seventh-largest exporter, boasts the world's thirteenth-biggest GDP, and rivals Italy and New Zealand in per capita wealth. Visit Seoul today, and you'll find few signs of the country's grim past. Futuristic skyscrapers stand where bombed-out buildings once smoldered. Well-heeled young people stroll through ritzy neighborhoods like Gangnam (yup, that Gangnam) and ride the city's gleaming, WiFi-enabled subways, fiddling with outsize, next-generation smartphones and phablets. They even *look* different than their parents did: thanks to huge improvements in the local diet, the average South Korean male now stands 3.5 inches taller than his predecessors did a mere thirty years ago.

But even more remarkable is how South Korea accomplished all this: by expanding its economy at a healthy clip for more than five decades. Such longevity is exceedingly rare. Most countries are sprinters, not marathon runners. While plenty of them have managed to boost themselves out of abject poverty in the last half century, very few—just thirteen, in fact—have figured out how to maintain their escape velocity. The vast bulk have stalled out soon after hitting the middle-income trap; some have even subsided back into penury.

South Korea is one of the rare exceptions. Not only has it gone from poor to rich, but it's also grown faster and for longer than any other state. For the forty-five years following 1963, when its economy first took off, it expanded by an average of more than 7 percent a year and contracted only twice: in 1980 (after the second global oil shock) and in 1998 (during the Asian Financial Crisis).

All that makes South Korea an inspiration for destitute nations struggling to survive, for middle-tier ones trying to make the next leap, and for rich industrialized states hoping to keep things moving.

South Korea is an especially valuable model because its ascent hasn't always been smooth. Koreans may love to talk about the "miracle on the Han River," but there was no magic involved. Nor has South Korea avoided setbacks. Just the opposite: the country has withstood more than its share of economic crises, including major stumbles in the early 1970s, the early 1980s, in 1997–98, and again in 2008–9. And then, of course, there's the current political and economic turmoil. But the thing that makes South Korea so interesting is the way it's consistently managed to *overcome* these crises—by using them creatively to rewrite the nation's rules and to make wrenching reforms that probably would have been impossible under happier circumstances. The point is not that South Korea hasn't made mistakes; it's made plenty. The point, rather, is that on each occasion it has learned from them, corrected course—and emerged better poised for growth than ever.

THE STORY OF South Korea's climb from ruin to riches can be broken it into three distinct stages: developmental dictatorship, democratization, and liberalization.

The first phase started about eight years after the end of the Korean War, in May 1961, when a general named Park Chung-hee seized power in a military coup. Though independent and at peace, South Korea was still a miserable place at the time. Its first leader, the US-backed autocrat Syngman Rhee, had proven vicious, corrupt, and—despite degrees from Harvard and Princeton—incompetent. Under his reign, and that of the short-lived democratic government that succeeded him, South Korea's economy (such as it was) had floundered, subsisting on foreign aid and virtually nothing else.

Little in Park's background suggested he'd do a better job. Born in 1917, he'd grown up poor, like most residents of Japanese-occupied Korea; later in life, he would blame his small stature (he stood about five foot three) on the malnutrition he'd suffered as a child. In 1940, after working briefly as a schoolteacher, Park took one of the few paths for upward mobility then open to Koreans: he adopted a Japanese name, Takagi Masao, and enlisted in the Imperial Army. Then—much like Seretse Khama and Lee Kuan Yew before him—he headed to his colonists' capital to study their ways. Park spent several years at a prestigious military academy in Tokyo, where he excelled, before being dispatched as a second lieutenant to Manchukuo, the Japanese puppet-state in northern China. Only when it became clear that Japan would lose the war did the young officer swap his Imperial uniform for a Korean one. After flirting with communism—a dalliance that got him thrown into prison in 1948 by the new Korean government (though Park was soon released after ratting out his former comrades)—he joined the Southern army during the civil war, eventually rising to the rank of major general.

Park had made his bones in artillery, and in some ways he would go on to govern like a gunner: battering away at the nation, much as Rhee had. But whereas South Korea's first dictator had been able to use the civil war and the huge infusions of US and UN aid to justify and paper over his neglect, Park had no such luxuries. He came into office facing a life-or-death crisis—four of them, in fact. And these would concentrate his mind, pushing him and the country in a propitious direction.

The first of Park's predicaments was basic: Rhee had left South Korea utterly impoverished. The country had virtually no industry. Nearly three out of every five citizens were subsistence farmers. And with no raw materials or energy sources to speak of, South Korea's exports—mostly rice and fish—totaled a paltry $41 million a year.

The second big problem involved national security. Though the Korean War was over, it had ended in a draw, resolving nothing. North Korea—heavily armed, relatively prosperous, generously backed by China and the Soviet Union, and itching for a rematch—lurked just thirty-five miles from the Blue House, as the president's office is known.

Of course, Pyongyang wasn't the only one with powerful friends. South Korea had a mighty patron of its own: the United States, which had led its defense during the war and remained its largest aid donor, almost single-handedly keeping its economy afloat. This patronage came at a high price, however, as Park soon discovered. Alarmed by the general's youthful dalliance with communism and unhappy with the way he'd seized power, the newly elected Kennedy administration didn't like him. From the moment he assumed office, Washington made its displeasure clear and began badgering Park to democratize— something he had no intention of doing.

Crisis number four, finally, involved Park's fellow citizens—most of whom were almost as unenthusiastic about him as were the Americans. At the time of his coup, Park had no public constituency and no experience as a politician. He wasn't a great speaker or especially charismatic. And he'd just ousted South Korea's first-ever democratic government: not the best way to endear yourself to the masses. As Marcus Noland, a Korea expert at the Peterson Institute for International Economics, sums things up, "Park was basically illegitimate from the moment he came into office. He'd just staged Korea's first military coup in something like five hundred years. The guy didn't come from the gentry class"—Park stemmed from rural peasant stock—"so he couldn't say, 'I'm part of the traditional governing elite.'" Nor, as a former officer in the Japanese army, could he appeal to his constituents' patriotism. This left the new president with what Noland describes as "a major crisis of political legitimacy." As in, he had none.

But Park was a consummate survivor, and in this case his instinct for self-preservation would benefit his country as well. The general's great insight was to realize that all four of his problems shared a single solution—and that he could use the interlocking crises to push through the kind of radical changes required to effect it. By creating a robust new economy from whole cloth, he could simultaneously bankroll his military and stand down the North, get the Yankees off his back, and start winning over the long-suffering South Korean people.

The only question was *how* to do all this. Remember that the Republic of Korea, as it was known, had few if any apparent assets at the time. It was too small and too poor to focus on domestic consumption. That meant it would have to build an export industry. But that answer only raised more difficult questions. What, for starters, could it export? As Harvard's Dwight Perkins, a former adviser to the South Korean government, explained to me, there were no natural resources to sell abroad. Agriculture wouldn't work either, since South Korea's soil wasn't very productive and its population ate most of what it managed to grow. That left one option: manufactured goods. And here the experience of Korea's former colonial master proved instructive. According to Bruce Cumings, a leading historian of modern Korea, Park had been deeply impressed by the "military-backed forced-pace industrialization" he'd witnessed the Japanese executing in occupied China, as well as by Japan's own rapid industrialization during the Meiji era (a subject he'd study obsessively after becoming president). Recognizing that one of the few assets South Korea did possess was an over-abundance of young people willing to work for a pittance—in those days, Korean wages averaged about a tenth of those in the United States—he resolved to follow Tokyo's lead and start mass-producing cheap, simple goods like toys, shoes, and textiles for sale abroad.

Now, Park's motivation in doing so was hardly lofty. He viewed his grand economic project in crudely instrumental terms: not as an end in itself, or something that would benefit the Korean people, but as a way to strengthen his own grip on power and buttress the nation militarily. His goals were always the same: to achieve *puguk kanghyông* ("rich nation, strong army")—and the first was merely a means to the second. As Park saw things, "Confrontation between democracy and Communism is an economic competition in which supremacy in development . . . matters more than frontal collision of arms."

But whatever his motives, Park's drive and his commitment to South Korea's development were unflinching. Declaring "let's fight while we work and work while fighting," he threw himself into the task of overseeing the country's transformation. And South Korea would respond even faster than the general himself anticipated.

PARK'S FIRST MOVE was to start pumping a lot of money into the country's human and physical infrastructure—building schools, highways, ports, and the like. Next, to upgrade Rhee's incompetent administration, he began building a professional, meritocratic bureaucracy, one that combined strict Japanese-style hierarchy and discipline with the technocratic competence and the can-do spirit he'd admired in the US troops he fought alongside during the civil war. To help make exports more competitive, he devalued South Korea's currency, and to gain better control over the nation's finances, he nationalized all its commercial banks.

Then he turned to business. Park knew that to make the huge developmental leap he envisaged, he was going to need some powerful partners. That meant operators with private-sector savvy, economies of scale, and deep pockets. And that, in turn, meant the *chaebol*: Korea's powerful family-owned business conglomerates (the term *chaebol* literally means "wealth-clan").

But there was a hitch: Park despised these firms, as did many ordinary Koreans at the time. Most of the *chaebol* had formed under the Japanese occupation and had then grown rich under Rhee by snapping up abandoned Japanese industrial facilities at fire-sale prices. In Park's mind that made them parasites, corrupt war profiteers who'd gotten ahead by exploiting their connections to his avaricious predecessor. Distasteful as they were, however, only these companies—which included names like Hyundai (originally a truck-repair firm), Samsung (which started out selling fruit and dried fish), and Lucky-Goldstar (then a face-cream producer)—had the size, muscle, and know-how he needed.

Park's first attempt to enlist them was characteristically heavy-handed. Just a few weeks after taking office, he had many of the *chaebol*'s CEOs thrown in prison, and even forced a few of them to parade through the streets wearing placards reading "I am a corrupt swine" and "I ate the people." Only after the unlucky executives agreed to comply with his master plan—and make large cash contributions to his government in the forms of "fines"—did he relent and release them.

The episode certainly showed business leaders who was in charge. But Park soon realized it might not have been the best way to ensure their enthusiastic cooperation. So he moderated his approach, launching a regular series of monthly coordination meetings with *chaebol* leaders to which he'd also invite key government ministers and other bureaucrats. At these sessions, according to Cho Mu hyun (a South Korean reporter who covers the conglomerates today), Park "coaxed, wheedled, intimidated, manipulated and outright threatened" the businessmen into complying with his agenda. Those who did were richly rewarded. Park would shower them with subsidies and low-interest loans, sweep aside bureaucratic obstacles, and waive taxes and tariffs on the import of raw materials.

The incentives worked. The South Korean economy soon began to hum, though there was nothing innovative or glamorous about it in those early days. Manufacturers relied almost exclusively on imported technology. Textile firms, for example, would buy old industrial looms overseas, often getting them thirdhand from the southern United States. After shipping them home, they'd run the machines around the clock and at several times their intended speed, relying on their cheap, minimally skilled, and easily replaced workers—many as young as fourteen—to keep the gears greased or snatch out bits of thread that the overstressed looms were constantly breaking. The system was ugly, but it soon began to pay off: annual exports rose from $55 million to $1.6 billion within ten years of Park's taking office.

The country made so much progress, in fact, that by the early 1970s it began to suffer from its success. Over the previous decade, the South Korean economy had grown so fast that wages had also risen sharply, increasing manufacturers' costs. In the face of inflation and new competition from neighbors like Taiwan, South Korea found it could no longer beat the world on prices for the cheap goods it had specialized in. Sensing this shift and spooked by a sudden reduction in US economic assistance, Park assigned his best technocrats to study the problem. Their conclusion: South Korea needed to move up the value chain by refocusing its industrial energies on more technically demanding—but far more profitable—goods such as steel, ships, electronics, and automobiles. Embracing their recommendations—as a soldier, Park was especially receptive to the notion that refined iron ore could be a source and symbol of national strength—the general once again led the drive. In 1973 he unveiled the Heavy and Chemical Industrialization Plan, which specified just what kinds of new facilities should be built, where they should be located, and what size and shape they should take. Park then picked a few of the most promising *chaebol*—those with "a proven track record of risk taking, managerial capability, and high performance," according to Eun Mee Kim and Gil-sung Park (two Korean academics who study the firms)—gave them their marching orders, and set them to work.

As before, companies that complied with his diktats were lavished with guaranteed loans, tax credits, and other incentives. Cooperative CEOs were feted at the Blue House, and during South Korea's annual "Export Day" celebration, top performers were awarded the "Gold Pagoda Industrial Medal." Park also carefully protected his new corporate champions, granting them effective oligopolies in key sectors, blocking out foreign competition, and creating captive markets for their goods. In 1975, for example, when a worldwide shipping slump threatened Hyundai—which had, at Park's insistence, become a major shipbuilder—with bankruptcy, the president passed a law forcing all domestic oil refineries to import their crude using Korean-built tankers. The move single-handedly kept the company afloat.

Once more, Park's strategy worked, reinvigorating the economy and ensuring that South Korea's boom continued. And yet, for all the general's achievements in this realm, holding him up as a model reformer today is awkward. To start with, the man was a bundle of contradictions: a former fellow traveler turned archconservative, a leader who fetishized capitalism but also constantly intervened in his country's economy, and the son of a farmer who hated Korea's elites but then embraced them.

More problematic, Park was also a thoroughly nasty piece of work—more Augusto Pinochet than Alexander Hamilton. Though he flirted with democracy at several points during his long reign, he also stole elections, harassed the opposition, muzzled the press, jailed thousands of innocent people, and tortured and killed many real or suspected enemies. (In a fit of pique worthy of the Persian king Xerxes, he even banned miniskirts and rock music at one point.)

It's no surprise, then, that Park is hated by a lot of South Koreans today. What's more surprising is the number of its citizens who view him fondly. A few years ago, a poll by the newspaper *JoongAng Ilbo* found that 55 percent of respondents rated him the best president in their country's history. Park's standing is so high that it even helped get his daughter, Park Geun-hye, elected president herself in 2012.

The general's modern-day supporters tend to downplay his repression and point instead to positives like his emphasis on education: by 1970 Park had increased South Korea's literacy rate from 22 percent (in 1945) to 88 percent. They credit him with building what the Harvard economist Dani Rodrik has called a "competent, honest, and efficient bureaucracy." They argue that his reliance on the *chaebol*, which strikes many people today as excessively statist, was not that different from the way dirigiste democracies like France lovingly protect and promote their own national champions. (In 2005, they note, Paris even blocked PepsiCo from taking over Danone on the grounds that yogurt was a "strategic industry.")

Above all, Park's fans point to the sky-high growth rate—an average of more than 9 percent a year—he maintained throughout his eighteen-year tenure, which is indeed hard to dismiss. By the time Park died in October 1979—his intelligence chief shot him in the face over dinner one night during an argument over whether to crush the latest flare-up of pro-democracy demonstrations—South Korea's per capita GDP had climbed from $91 to $1,857, putting it on a level with Brazil's and Mexico's.

LIKE HIM OR not, then, there's no denying that Park's economic accomplishments were as impressive as his political and human rights records were appalling. And yet, as far as he was able to take South Korea, its development remained incomplete at the time of his death. The people were no longer starving, but they were far from rich: in 1979 the per capita income of Japan, then riding the crest of its own economic miracle, was more than four times higher, and both states lagged behind the industrialized West. South Korea had also entered that dangerous middle-income zone, the doldrums where conditions become comfortable enough that politicians often stop pushing for further change.

Which is just what happened in this case. By the time Park's successor, Chun Doo-hwan (another general), left office ten years later, per capita wealth had climbed to nearly $5,000. But the *chaebol* had transmogrified themselves from obedient engines of growth into massive, overbearing *muneo kyeongyeong* ("octopus businesses"): by 1984 the top fifty of them accounted for 94 percent of South Korea's GDP. The country was slowly discovering a reality familiar to many other middle-income countries: the tactics that get you halfway to rich stop working at that point. According to John Delury of Seoul's Yonsei University, the problem in South Korea's case was that while "military mobilization is a good way to kick-start an economy, for mature, sustained growth, a more complex system is needed—especially in a global market. And those complexities are too much for an authoritarian state to manage."

Fortunately, this was precisely the moment when, thanks to yet another crisis, South Korea ceased to be an authoritarian state. In 1987 massive numbers of students flooded the streets to protest the state's torture and murder of a young activist named Park Jong-chul. Feeling constrained by intense international scrutiny—Seoul was preparing for the 1988 Olympic Games, which the government had hoped would serve as the country's global coming-out party—Chun balked at using more force. The reins slipped, things quickly spiraled out of control, the general was overthrown, and South Korea launched the second major phase in its development: democracy. For the first time in its history, the country's population freely and directly elected a president. And the new liberties that that president, Roh Tae-woo, and his successor, Kim Young-sam, would establish—the most important of which were the freedoms of expression and association—planted the seeds for future economic growth.

But those seeds would take time to sprout. In the meantime, despite the country's political liberalization, its economic problems kept growing. Roh, a former general, was too much a product of the old system to be able to change it. And Kim, a centrist who also belonged to the ruling party, just wasn't very interested in the economy, beyond pushing through enough reforms (such as opening up capital markets) to earn South Korea membership in the Organization for Economic Cooperation and Development, a club for advanced industrial democracies.

Another reason the two leaders didn't try harder to reform the economy was that everything still seemed to be going well. South Korea's economy grew by an average of 8 percent a year between 1990 and 1996, so what was there to worry about? Plenty, it turned out; under the surface, the system was sickening fast. The *chaebol* had grown so big and powerful that they could easily intimidate any reform-minded bureaucrat. And driven in part by the rising costs of winning office in a democratic system, corruption had exploded, allowing the conglomerates to virtually capture the government's policymaking apparatus. (Roh's own avariciousness was so flagrant that it eventually got him

thrown in prison.) Freed from proper supervision, the *chaebol* were able
to maintain bad practices like shunning foreign investment, which they
saw as a threat to family control over their firms. They also took advantage of Kim's liberalizing reforms—which he'd neglected to back with
new regulations—to expand into industries, such as finance, that they
didn't understand. And according Harvard's Perkins, they covered up
their bad bets and declining profitability by "going wild" and taking on
huge new foreign loans in the blithe faith that Seoul would bail them
out if they got into trouble. The system grew steadily more unbalanced,
until something had to give.

THAT SOMETHING GAVE in May 1997, when currency speculators attacked the Thai baht, causing Thailand's overinflated economy to burst
and sending shock waves ripping through the region. As what quickly
came to be called the Asian Financial Crisis spread to Malaysia, the
Philippines, Indonesia, and Hong Kong, investors began to yank out
their money and banks began to call in their loans.

Within a few months, the gathering storm reached South Korea,
where it thundered onshore like a tidal wave. First exports collapsed.
Then the won lost half its value, as did the Korean stock exchange.
Soon the *chaebol,* unable to pay their foreign debts with their suddenly
devalued currency, turned to the government for help, as they always
had. But Seoul's usable foreign-exchange reserves quickly ran dry,
leaving it with no help to offer. In a once-unimaginable scenario, the
giant corporations began to teeter. Thousands of Korean companies
went under during the crisis months, causing unemployment to hit its
highest level since the early 1960s. GDP dropped by 33 percent, and
Seoul was forced to turn to the IMF for a humiliating $57 billion bail-
out, the largest in that institution's history.

This move—the first time an OECD member had asked the IMF
for help in two decades—had a devastating psychological impact on
the fiercely proud South Koreans. But the blow would, on balance,
prove a salutary one, just as South Korea's previous crises had. Coming
two weeks before the country went to the polls, it convinced the nor-

mally staid electorate to do something radical and elect Kim Dae-jung as president.

KDJ, as he was known, was both an insider and the ultimate outsider. He was a son of Jeolla, a long-marginalized province in Korea's southwest. Like Park, he'd grown up poor. After a brief, successful career in business, he'd entered public life in the 1950s to fight for democracy and civil liberties. And in the decades that followed, Kim had paid a huge price for such principles—"as much as any political leader in the world," according to Cumings, the historian. Park and his successors would try five times to kill the man. On one occasion, government thugs smashed a heavy truck into Kim's car, crushing his driver and leaving Kim with a lifelong limp. Two years later, Park's agents snatched Kim from a Tokyo hotel room, dragged him onto a boat and out to sea, and chained him down with weights. Only a last-minute intervention by a mysterious plane (sent by the CIA, Kim later claimed) stopped Park's hit men from tossing KDJ overboard. And even that wasn't the end of his troubles. In 1980 President Chun had him arrested and sentenced to death. It took a second American intervention to spare his life, and Kim was sent into exile in the United States.

The December 1997 election was thus an electrifying moment for South Korea: in just ten years, it had gone from rule by a strongman to choosing a onetime dissident as its president. And not just any dissident: Kim had long decried not only South Korea's authoritarian state but also the insular economic system that had empowered it. His genius was to recognize that the country's still-fragile democratic transition would never be complete until its political evolution was matched by an economic one, making one sphere as open as the other. Kim loathed what he called the "collusive intimacy between business and government" that had flourished under his predecessors and propped up both sides, and he correctly blamed that collusion for constraining Koreans' new liberties and for having caused the crash. Now, suddenly, the crisis—especially the humbling of the mighty *chaebol*—had given him a once-in-a-lifetime chance to break the back of the status quo. Kim, who liked to say that "democracy and the market economy are like two sides of the same coin," pledged in his inauguration speech to "do whatever it takes to realize politics . . . in which the people truly become the masters." And with that, he embarked on a sweeping campaign of economic liberalization—the third stage in South Korea's story.

Though Kim's rhetoric appealed to many ordinary South Koreans, it frightened business leaders and pundits in the country and abroad. Conservatives feared that the new president, who'd long cast himself as a tribune of the poor and the voice of South Korea's marginalized, would pursue irresponsible populist policies, deepening the crisis. His election so panicked investors that the won promptly lost another 11 percent of its value and the stock market fell another 5 percent.

But like Lula in Brazil, KDJ had been misunderstood. Though dedicated to social justice, he too intended to pursue it in an unconventional manner. Kim believed in profit and growth, seeing them as the best tools for improving the overall welfare. Despite his reputation as a leftist, he'd never actually favored populist economic policies, and he didn't oppose the reforms being pushed on South Korea by the IMF; on the contrary, he'd long favored precisely such changes, and the crisis had only strengthened his conviction that they were what the country needed most.

Though Kim did ultimately pass a number of important political reforms—he slashed the size and power of the intelligence services, for example—and though he did expand South Korea's fairly minimal social safety net, most of his moves came straight out of a neoliberal economics textbook. Not only did he accept virtually every condition imposed by the IMF, but he went beyond them in many cases. To weaken the power of corrupt bureaucrats, he sharply cut the size of the public sector, eliminating entire government agencies and even ministries; stripped the Ministry of Finance of many of its powers; and set up strict new independent regulatory bodies. To rekindle growth, he loosened the rules on layoffs and on the use of temporary workers, though he expanded unemployment benefits to compensate. To promote competition, he threw open the doors to foreigners, easing the rules on international mergers and acquisitions and landownership and offering tax incentives to overseas firms.

Most important, Kim kicked away many of the struts that had long propped up the bloated *chaebol*. After South Korea's courts proved unable to handle all the mounting bankruptcies, the president took over the process himself, using it to force the sprawling firms to reduce their debts, get rid of their noncore subsidiaries, and start observing exacting new accounting and transparency rules.

To the shock of many Koreans, he also allowed the least competitive of the big firms to die or be acquired. The victims would ultimately include a few giants. Kia Motors, the country's oldest auto manufacturer, was bought by Hyundai at auction in 1998. And Daewoo, South Korea's second-largest conglomerate—with interests ranging from cars to electronics to hotels to shipbuilding to financial securities—was dismantled in 1999 in the face of $80 billion in unpaid debt, and its founder fled the country to avoid prosecution.

ALL THE UPHEAVAL shook South Korea to its core; the academics Stephan Haggard and Myung-koo Kang have called the breakup of Daewoo "one of the most significant events in Korea's postwar economic history," on a parallel with the September 2008 collapse of Lehman Brothers in the United States.

Traumatic as this period was, however, Kim's response caused investors' confidence to surge. Foreign direct investment rose from less than $3 billion in 1997 to more than $15 billion in both 1999 and 2000. In the next seven years, the total amount of overseas money invested in South Korea more than tripled, from $250 billion to $825 billion, and foreigners soon acquired more than 40 percent of the shares on the stock exchange. All this activity helped kick-start the rest of the economy, which rapidly recovered. The country repaid its IMF loan in just over two years (it helped that it only used $19.5 billion out of the requested $57 billion), and by 2000 GDP was growing by close to 9 percent again.

Kim's reforms also unleashed a wave of creative destruction that permanently changed South Korea's corporate culture, setting the country up for what would become two more decades of success.

Prior to the crisis, the *chaebol* had grown synonymous with crappy consumer goods. Quality got so bad in the late 1980s that Hyundai executives started insisting that they be given US-made company cars as part of their compensation—they wouldn't risk their families in Korean clunkers. And according to Euny Hong, the author of *The Birth of Korean Cool*, local hipsters started referring to Samsung as "Samsuck," owing to appliances like an electric fan so badly designed that it broke if you tried to lift it by its neck.

But all that changed after 1998. To survive the crisis and satisfy Kim's new rules, the *chaebol* were forced to become far more efficient and innovative, transforming themselves from companies that copied others to companies others copied. The *chaebol* gave up their longtime xenophobia and started welcoming outside expertise. They also returned to their core competencies. Hyundai moved away from electronics so it could focus on making better cars. Samsung did the reverse, which helped it become a world leader in emerging technologies like plasma TVs and 3G and then 4G mobile devices. Today Samsung's microchips are so good that Apple uses them in its iPhones, despite the fact that the two firms are bitter rivals in the smartphone market. Hyundai's cars now go toe-to-toe with Toyota's. And LCD flat screens made by Lucky-Goldstar—which rebranded itself as LG in 1997 to escape its low-end reputation—rival anything produced in Japan. South Korea has even forged into some entirely new domains, such as pop culture: the country's soap operas, boy bands, and video games now dominate Asia, despite the fact that virtually no one else speaks Korean. All combined, these efforts have helped South Korea's economy grow at twice the OECD average since the Asian Financial Crisis, and to rebound from the 2008 Great Recession faster than any other rich country.

This doesn't mean South Korea has reached a state of economic nirvana, however. In the last few years, growth has slowed to the 3–4 percent range. That slowdown has produced a lot of agita in the country, although it probably shouldn't. Economists like Barry Eichengreen of UC Berkeley argue that the downshift is actually a sign of success: it just means that South Korea has firmly made it into the top wealth tier, where countries almost never grow by more than 4 percent a year. (Even at 3–4 percent, moreover, South Korea still beats just about every other advanced economy.)

A more serious problem involves the extent to which Seoul remains wedded to an economic strategy that's long since outlived its usefulness.

The second big, surprising lesson of South Korea's success in avoiding the middle-income trap turns out to be that heavy state intervention in the early stages can prove extremely helpful, at least under the right conditions. On one level, that doesn't sound at all surprising. After all, making the kind of economic adaptations South Korea has is hard. As Haggard, director of the Korea-Pacific Program at UC San Diego, explains, "Transitioning from agriculture to industry is a high-risk venture." And at the start of the process, Hong points out, "companies like Samsung couldn't manufacture so much as a paper clip" on their own. To get ahead, South Korean firms needed access to capital, new equipment, and raw materials; time to develop new technical and marketing expertise; and enough breathing room to experiment without facing immediate ruin if they fumbled.

Park provided his favored companies with all these forms of aid— which might make it seem inevitable that the economy ultimately responded the way it did. Except for one thing: according to orthodox economic theory, such individualized industrial assistance is supposed to cause far more problems than it solves. Heavy-handed government intervention is thought to promote inefficiency (by shielding firms from market forces), to encourage corruption, and so on. It's supposed to turn countries into *North* Korea. Yet South Korea somehow avoided that fate and profited extravagantly instead.

How did Seoul do it? First, Park always imposed strict conditions on his corporate handouts. As Noland, of the Peterson Institute, explained it to me, many countries in the developing world lavished funds on favored businesses during the 1960s and 1970s; South Korea was hardly unique in that regard. "What *was* unique, or at least unusual," Noland says, is that in South Korea "they would track your performance very carefully. And if you lagged behind, you'd get cut off." To avoid undue influence on decision making, Park also insisted that company bosses not seek political power themselves. And to guard against complacency, he occasionally let the most inefficient *chaebol* go under as a warning to the rest.

Second, the president was very careful to limit graft. While firms did regularly make large cash gifts to the Blue House during his tenure, most historians agree that Park himself never accepted any bribes, nor did he allow the payments to influence policy. "Once basic decisions were made," Noland says, "they were implemented in an efficient way"—no matter how many palms were greased.

Finally, the constant threat of war with North Korea—which was perceived as being richer and more powerful than the South in the 1960s and 1970s—also seems to have kept everyone focused. As Perkins puts it, "Park, Chun, and the country as a whole understood that if their economic efforts failed, there was a very real prospect that South Korea would cease to exist."

Of course, South Korea ran into trouble anyway in the late 1980s and 1990s—trouble it took Kim Dae-jung and the Asian Financial Crisis to fix. What's worrying today is the mounting evidence that the country is once again headed into similar territory. Although Seoul is no longer nearly as interventionist as it once was, it still tries to micromanage. Some of its policies are beneficial: for example, although South Korea already boasts the world's highest broadband penetration rate, the government is currently wiring every home with new Internet portals two hundred times faster than those found in the United States. The trouble is that South Korea also sometimes tries to pick winners, bestowing its favor on particular firms rather than letting the market decide which will thrive. In recent years, 25 percent of the venture capital going to South Korean start-ups has come from the government purse. That's much too high.

According to Eichengreen and other economists, South Korea's earlier history shows that this type of favoritism, if handled delicately, can work during an economy's infancy, when companies mostly copy their technologies and tactics from competitors in other countries. Under such conditions, it's easy for a government to forecast which firms are most likely to succeed: it just has to look for the best mimics. When nations reach what's known as the technological frontier, however—as South Korea now has—everything changes, and so should the government's approach. At that point, there's no one left for companies to emulate. Most new business ventures become experimental. And governments just aren't very good at predicting which of those experiments are most likely to succeed. Economic research shows that markets do a much better job at identifying likely victors. States shouldn't even try; they should just lay the groundwork and get out of the way. Yet South Korea has so far failed to embrace this wisdom, and if it keeps putting its fingers on the scales, it's likely to start making some very costly mistakes.

Modern South Korea faces one other big, related challenge: despite all the reforms undertaken by KDJ and his successors, the *chaebol* remain far too powerful. In fact, though former president Park Geun-hye declared making room for Korea's small and medium-size enterprises (SMEs) among her top priorities, the *chaebol* have grown even more dominant since the Kim era. In 2012 sales by the thirty largest among them accounted for 82 percent of the country's GDP—up from 53 percent in 2002. This dominance is, in many ways, a testament to KDJ's success: his reforms set up those *chaebol* that survived for rampant growth. But their size still represents a big problem for the country going forward. That's because, no matter how good they may be, companies that are too big to fail almost always start acting that way—a form of what economists refer to as moral hazard. Just look at what's happening at Samsung today. The *chaebol* also don't provide that many jobs, currently employing just 5 percent of South Korea's working population. Yet their wealth, prestige, and job security allow them to suck up the country's best talent and crowd out start-ups. And that's dangerous. Although Bloomberg recently ranked South Korea the most innovative country in the world (Samsung alone spent $14 billion on R&D in 2014, far more than most countries), it could easily slip if it doesn't find a way to make space for small, nimble companies and the creative minds they can attract.

Ask an average South Korean about the current state of the country and the complaints won't stop there. You'll also hear some fretting about the speed at which the population is aging and about the recent political and corruption scandals. Yet for all the complaining, South Korea has become an enormously enviable country—even if its residents don't always appreciate it. "Sure, the place is not perfect," Noland told me. "They've got all sorts of problems. But there are a hundred other countries in the world that would happily swap places with them." That might be an understatement. Not only has South Korea become one of the world's richest nations, but it is also stable, relatively equitable, and, despite some recent stumbles, among the freest and most vibrant places to live in Asia, if not the planet.

Those latter traits point to one final lesson. South Korea's history eloquently demonstrates that while a country may well be able to escape dire poverty through efficient authoritarian stewardship, it's unlikely to ever grow truly rich unless it evolves an open system that allows everyone to think, act, and compete as they wish. Closed markets deter competition and promote bloat, while political repression deters all forms of self-expression, including the economic variety. Censorship inhibits the sharing and generation of new ideas. That's why the world's most innovative countries, places like Israel or Sweden, also happen to be liberal democracies. It's no coincidence; innovation requires the ability to think and compete freely. South Korea never would have been able to build its own massive knowledge economy without the political liberties that resulted from the revolution of 1987 or the economic liberalization that followed 1997. KDJ in particular proved that real, sustained prosperity requires real freedom. And that should serve as a sharp rebuke and a warning to autocrats in China and elsewhere who insist that their state-directed economies can keep growing forever despite their closed political systems. South Korea proves that good economics requires good, open government, and vice versa. The two reinforce each other, and you're unlikely to ever truly prosper without them both—whatever the mandarins in Beijing or their admirers elsewhere like to argue.

9

GIVE TO GET

How Mexico Got Its Government Going Again

ENRIQUE PEÑA NIETO HAS HAD A ROUGH FEW YEARS. AS Mexico's president has stumbled from one crisis to the next, his country has often seemed to be caught in a perilous slide back toward its inglorious, dysfunctional past. Peña Nieto has mishandled the mass disappearance of a group of college students in the drug- and violence-plagued south, allowed Mexico's most notorious drug lord to escape from a supposedly supermax prison, and has been dogged by corruption scandals. At the same time, Mexico's economy has flatlined. The country feels suffused by gloom, and public frustration with Peña Nieto personally has driven his poll numbers down to historic lows.

Underneath the headlines, however, conditions in Mexico aren't nearly as bad as they seem—or as they often feel to people living there. Contrary to its shambolic international image, Mexico has become a real, albeit flawed, democracy and a solidly middle-class country. It has the second-largest economy in Latin America, with a $1.3 trillion GDP that puts it close to South Korea and Spain in size. Mexico is also the world's most open market, and rivals China as a manufacturing hub for US, Canadian, German, and Japanese firms. Even its recent economic woes aren't entirely its fault. They owe as much to the general global slowdown and the low price of oil as to anything else.

There is one other, more fundamental, reason that Mexico, and Mexicans, should feel hopeful. Though it often seems like Peña Nieto can't get anything right these days, the president's first two years in office—2013 and 2014—were astoundingly productive ones, during which he managed to push through a sweeping slate of fundamental economic and social reforms. These changes have set Mexico up for explosive growth in the near future—a future that could materialize as soon as oil prices recover and the government brings corruption and crime under some sort of control.

What makes these accomplishments even more impressive—and important for our purposes—is *how* Peña Nieto pulled them off: by convincing the country's three warring parties to set aside their mutual hatred and actually start governing again. This achievement was so unexpected, and the results could be so beneficial, that it offers a powerful template for other countries around the world still suffering from gridlock. For if Mexico, of all places, could break out of its trap, and in such spectacular fashion, then other nations—including the United States—should be able to as well.

As RECENTLY AS 2012, few observers in Mexico or abroad had high expectations for the country. As that year's presidential election approached, Mexico's Institutional Revolutionary Party (known by its Spanish acronym, PRI)—which had ruled the country for seventy-one years before being voted out office in 2000—looked poised for a comeback. Most observers predicted that the PRI would use its return to power to engage in all the worst practices of its past: vote rigging, corrupt cronyism, tacit cooperation with the drug cartels, and suffocating statist economic policies that had produced, on average, a lowly 2.4 percent annual growth rate for three decades.

Of course, Enrique Peña Nieto, the PRI's young candidate, denied all that. Throughout the 2012 campaign, Peña Nieto, then governor of the state of México, insisted that he represented something new. He derided his party's old guard as "dinosaurs" and declared that "in the Mexico we want, there is no room for corruption, for cover-ups, and least of all for impunity."

That all sounded good, and the forty-five-year-old candidate certainly *looked* competent and presidential, with his square jaw, immaculate pompadour, and twinkly eyes that made female voters chant "*bombón, te quiero en mi colchón*" ("sweetie, I want you in my bed") at political rallies.

Still, many analysts warned that it was all an illusion—that Peña Nieto was nothing but a "political hologram," as one put it. Though he'd grown up middle class, Peña Nieto was linked by blood to the party's elite: his godfather and one of his uncles had served as PRI governors, and his political rise had been backed by a powerful clique of party insiders known as the Atlacomulco Group.

Peña Nieto also seemed to get him himself into trouble every time he opened his mouth. His command of English was shaky, in contrast to Mexico's previous presidents (many of whom had studied in the United States). And he was no intellectual. The candidate carefully avoided specifics in his stump speeches, and didn't help his case when he proved unable to name three books that had influenced his thinking or to quote the price of tortillas. And then there was his personal life. Peña Nieto had married twice—wedding a *telenovela* star the second time around—and had fathered two children with two other women along the way. His bedroom habits were so notorious that during the campaign, Ashley Madison (the dating website for adulterers) posted a billboard in Mexico City featuring his photo next to text reading "Unfaithful to his family. Faithful and committed to his country."

But Peña Nieto was convinced that his critics had him wrong and was eager to prove it. No sooner had he won the July 2012 election— though voters were ambivalent about him, they liked his opponents even less—than the president-elect found his opportunity, pulling off an impossible-seeming coup: he secretly brought Mexico's three, long-feuding political parties together to negotiate a truce and a plan of action. On December 2, 2012, the day after his inauguration, Peña Nieto and his rivals in the right-leaning National Action Party (PAN) and the leftist Party of the Democratic Revolution (PRD) surprised the country by publicly announcing the Pacto por México: an extremely aggressive, ninety-five-item reform agenda aimed at resolving the country's worst political, social, and economic problems.

The new president then set off on a tear the likes of which few countries have ever witnessed. Over the next eighteen months, he managed to bust open Mexico's smothering monopolies and antiquated energy sector, restructure the country's education system, and modernize its tax and banking laws. It's hard to capture just how momentous these changes were. But Juan Pardinas, the head of IMCO (a Mexico City think tank), has come close, describing them as "the most ambitious process of economic reform seen in any country since the fall of the Berlin Wall."

So HOW DID this underrated *bombón* do it? The first key to his success lay in his predecessors' failures. By the time Peña Nieto was elected—announcing that "we have come not to manage but to transform"—conditions in Mexico had become so parlous that they offered him an extraordinary opportunity to try something new.

Just consider those conditions for a moment. In 2012, despite the fact that it sits on the world's fifteenth-largest oil reserves, Mexico's energy output—the key to its financial survival, since hydrocarbon sales account for a full third of the government's budget—was plummeting. Due to a legacy of underinvestment, a lack of competition under what *The Economist* called "one of the most restrictive regimes in the world," and woeful mismanagement and corruption at Pemex (the state oil monopoly), production had dropped by 25 percent in the preceding decade. And as shale extraction had exploded north of the border, Mexico, which lacked the wherewithal to tap its own huge shale reserves, had only been able to watch.

As for the rest of the Mexican economy, it was ruled by a few wealthy oligarchs who strangled all would-be competitors. Businesses controlled by Carlos Slim (whom *Forbes* ranked the world's richest man between 2010 and 2013) accounted for a third of the stock market, and his phone company, Telmex, owned 80 percent of the nation's landlines and 75 percent of its broadband hookups. Corruption was leaching away some 10 percent of gross domestic product, and polls showed that three-quarters of Mexicans thought the problem was getting worse. Less than half of the country's children were graduating from high school. Life expectancy was among the lowest in the thirty-four-member OECD. And the militarized war on drugs launched by Peña Nieto's predecessor, the PAN's Felipe Calderón, had sent violence spinning out of control, causing more than sixty thousand deaths since 2006. The Pentagon had even warned in 2008 that Mexico risked "a rapid and sudden collapse" that could leave it a failed state—a Pakistan with piñatas on America's southern frontier.

Bad as things looked, however, this relentless decline had done one powerfully good thing: it had forced Mexico's long-warring parties to accept their role in creating this mess in the first place. Although the country had, to joyful acclaim, become fully democratic fifteen years earlier, the result had been perpetual political stalemate. After losing the presidency in 2000, the PRI had spent its time in the wilderness plotting vengeance on the PAN administrations that replaced it, blocking so many bills under presidents Vicente Fox (2000–2006) and Calderón (2006–12) that Mexico's Congress had, by some measures, become among the least effective in all of Latin America.

But after a decade and a half of failure and paralysis, Mexico's more moderate leaders had finally come to accept that their infighting was destroying not only their country but also their own chances at the polls.

As Peña Nieto told me in an interview, watching his party's self-destructive tantrums during its opposition years had gradually convinced him that if the PRI was ever going to recover its dominance, it needed to "learn ... to gain the support of society" with a more positive agenda, not focus on vendettas or short-term electoral calculations. When, a year later, I met with one of his top advisers, the MIT-trained economist Luis Videgaray, who went on to serve as Mexico's finance secretary, he recalled how Peña Nieto and his young circle had developed "a common feeling that we needed to do something different, that six more years of gridlock would be costly"—for the country and for the PRI. Shannon O'Neil of the Council on Foreign Relations describes the party's thinking: "They said to themselves, 'We were in power for seventy-one years. Then, oh no, we got thrown out. How do we get back? We've got to get smart about getting elected, rather than just manipulate elections to stay in power.'"

As he'd prepared his run for president, the solution Peña Nieto had hit on was to brand himself a reformer. And the strategy worked, but just barely: though he won the 2012 election, he'd squeaked in with a mere 38 percent of the vote, and the PRI had failed to score a majority in either house of Congress. This less-than-resounding mandate convinced the president-elect that if he wanted to get anything done, he'd need to find a way to work with his enemies.

Luckily for him—and for Mexico—those enemies had just then drawn a similar conclusion. The PAN's inability to accomplish much of anything during its two terms in power (along with Calderón's pyrrhic war on drugs) had so thoroughly disgusted the public that the party was crushed in 2012; its candidate, Josefina Vázquez Mota, came in third, with an embarrassing 25 percent of the vote. That drubbing had forced at least part of the PAN's leadership to concede that they'd never turn things around unless they too took a new tack. One morning in late 2014, I met Gustavo Madero—a soft-spoken former businessman who's been chairman of the PAN since 2010—for tea at a sidewalk café in Polanco, a leafy Mexico City neighborhood. When I asked what he'd learned from his party's declining fortunes, he was blunt. "We had to wait sixty-one years"—the PAN was founded in 1939— "to win Mexico's presidency," he recounted. "And then we failed to change education, we failed to change telecommunications, we failed to change the energy sector. So we had to do something different."

For Madero, that meant forgoing the chance to get "revenge" on the PRI—by undermining its new president the same way the PRI had stymied Fox and Calderón—and to instead start acting "like a responsible party that cares more for the country than for electoral calculus." Another PAN power broker, Santiago Creel—a suave corporate lawyer who'd served as Fox's interior secretary—put it to me this way: "We had two avenues. We could act like a typical opposition party, and do what the PRI did for twelve years. Or we could take a different approach and say, 'We won less than a third of the votes in the last election, but we have a very good platform. So let's see if we can negotiate.'"

Moderates within the leftist PRD were thinking along parallel lines. After their candidate, the fiery Andrés Manuel López Obrador, lost the 2006 election by half a percentage point, he'd staged massive street protests and refused to have any contact with the new government; for years afterward, he wouldn't even shake Calderón's hand. Rather than help govern, he'd engaged in "six years of confrontation," Jesús Zambrano, a leader of the party's centrist wing, told me. But the endless attacks had deadlocked Congress, creating a dangerous power vacuum that, according to Zambrano, was then filled by "monopolist firms, drug traffickers [and] the unions." And that abdication of leadership had "cost us a lot in the eyes of society," he added. So after López Obrador's second defeat in 2012, Zambrano and another PRD moderate, Jesús Ortega—the two are such close allies that Mexicans refer to them collectively as "Los Chuchos" (a common nickname for Jesús)—decided to find a more constructive path, knowing that if they failed, they risked permanently consigning the PRD to the political sidelines.

These weren't easy decisions to make. Calderón, the outgoing president, and his powerful faction within the PAN opposed any cooperation with the enemy, and though Madero and Creel ultimately won that battle, Calderón's team denounced them as collaborators—"like the Pétain government in Nazi-occupied France," Creel recalls. The Chuchos faced similar pressures. When I met with Ortega, a former socialist who resembles a professorial version of the revolutionary hero Emiliano Zapata, in his dark, antique-filled office, he said, "We had to overcome a very old maxim in Mexican politics, which is that dialogue is a synonym for betrayal." Sure enough, when López Obrador caught wind of their intentions, he bolted from the PRD in fury, forming his own, more radical leftist movement to continue the fight.

Yet the renegades persevered, their spines stiffened by one other hard truth: that not only was Mexico in crisis, but none of them were strong enough to solve it on their own. It wasn't just that they lacked majority support. To reform the country, they'd also have to take on its bullying oligarchs, huge and belligerent unions, and all the other private interests that opposed change—and had crushed would-be reformers in the past. Aurelio Nuño, another top Peña Nieto aide, who went on to serve as the president's chief of staff and then education minister, told me that "all three parties felt that the Mexican state was not strong enough to deliver. We knew that unless we stopped confronting one another, we wouldn't have the ability" to make any headway.

PEÑA NIETO MAY not have been responsible for creating these conditions—but he was the one who figured out how to take advantage of them. Despite his reputation as a lightweight and the skepticism caused by his PRI lineage, Peña Nieto had a number of assets that would soon prove extremely valuable.

Yes, he was PRI, born and bred. But he was a new sort of PRI-*ista*. As Jorge Castañeda, a former PAN foreign minister, has pointed out, Peña Nieto was the first Mexican president to have come of age professionally under the country's new democracy. And he was the first PRI president not to have been handpicked by his predecessor, which gave him an unusual degree of independence. Though it was often overlooked, Peña Nieto had also been an unusually effective governor of México State, especially when it came to working across party lines. Domitilo Posadas of the PRD has said that as governor, Peña Nieto was "open to dialogue, tolerant and [took] on proposals that didn't come from him." Such openness helped Peña Nieto rack up an impressive record in the state, shrinking its debt by about 25 percent, posting a growth rate higher than the national average, and reducing poverty at the height of the financial crisis.

Having suddenly achieved his lifelong ambition in 2012—by the skin of his teeth—Peña Nieto hoped to replicate these collaborative tactics on the federal level. So when, shortly after the election, Zambrano told an old friend in the PRI (José Murat, the ex-governor of Oaxaca) that he might be interested in some sort of deal, Peña Nieto leapt at the opening and dispatched Videgaray to hear him out.

While the will was there, the resulting negotiations could still have come to naught—and probably would have—but for the very canny way the participants handled them.

First, they kept the talks small. The conversations started quite casually, as informal chats between Zambrano and Videgaray (who would report back to his boss each night). As they got more serious, the PRD and PRI each enlisted one more representative: Zambrano brought in Ortega, his fellow Chucho, and Videgaray tapped Miguel Osorio Chong, a former governor of Hidalgo who would later serve as Peña Nieto's interior minister. Within days, each party discovered that the other had simultaneously been talking to the PAN, so for the sake of efficiency, they invited Madero and Creel to join them at the table. And a few weeks later, when the note taking became unwieldy, the delegations all brought in one more lieutenant to help them draft the emerging agenda.

Second, to foster trust, Peña Nieto insisted that the now-daily meetings, which stretched over several months at Murat's Mexico City home, be kept secret. This veil of confidentiality gave the nine participants the freedom to debate and compromise without having to guard their flanks or worry about constituents or special interests. The fact that everyone kept things quiet—there were no leaks throughout the negotiations—also helped chip away at the intense suspicions they'd all harbored toward one another. "When Madero and I first heard what the PRI was willing to do"—the far-reaching reforms they were interested in—"we didn't believe it," Creel recalls. "It was like, you know, a letter to Santa Claus." Ortega told me that he and Zambrano were similarly incredulous; the Chuchos feared they were walking into "a trap laid to legitimize the government and help the PRI consolidate power." But the fact that everyone kept mum gradually alleviated those anxieties. According to Nuño, the intimate domestic setting for the talks, which featured lots of shared meals and rounds of tequila, also helped the negotiators start to see one another as real people, not just as political adversaries.

To facilitate horse-trading, the parties agreed to put all their priorities on the table at the start. Creel also insisted that decisions had to be unanimous and that "nothing is agreed until all is agreed." As he later told me, he'd watched with dismay during his time in Fox's government as various attempts to strike one-off bargains had foundered because they couldn't produce enough flexibility or foster a spirit of reciprocity. That experience had taught him that "if you have ten things on the table, instead of one, you can weigh them and say, 'Okay, I will go with all ten, even though I may not agree on one or two.'" Madero also felt it made much more sense to "go for the whole enchilada," as he put it.

The PRI also contributed by making it clear early on that it was willing to compromise—even though it now held the most powerful cards. For example, although Peña Nieto was convinced that Mexico desperately needed to increase its tax take (the country's collection levels were then the lowest in the OECD), he acceded to the populist PRD's insistence that the VAT not be extended to food and medicine, since that would disproportionately affect the leftists' largely poor support base. And at the PAN's urging, Peña Nieto abandoned the PRI's long-standing objections to electoral reforms. According to Pamela Starr, a professor at the University of Southern California, the PRI also began leaning on powerful interest groups, including its allies in organized labor, to keep them from trying to undermine the emerging accord. (About four months after the Pact was ultimately unveiled, the government would even arrest Elba Esther Gordillo, the formerly untouchable boss of Mexico's gigantic teachers' union, on corruption charges—conveniently taking her out of the picture.)

Peña Nieto was also very shrewd when it came to sequencing. To boost everyone's confidence, he front-loaded the reforms on which all three parties agreed, such as those in education, labor, banking, and the telecom sector. Doing so, he reasoned, would help the Pact score some easy early wins, which would build momentum for the harder parts of the agenda. Peña Nieto also made sure some of the other parties' priorities were addressed before his own. These guarantees helped, in Peña Nieto's own words, to "armor plate" the deal. Staggering the order of reforms showed all sides that nothing would get accomplished unless everyone stuck to the game plan—and reassured them that no one would get stabbed in the back.

One subsequent incident drove that message home and helped keep the parties together after the Pact was announced. During the spring of 2013, PRI officials were caught manipulating government social spending for political advantage ahead of local elections in the state of Veracruz. When Madero learned of the ploy, he threatened to boycott the Pact just one day before Peña Nieto announced its financial reforms at a banking conference. The president responded by canceling his speech, firing those responsible, and attaching a PAN-drafted addendum to the Pact that reinforced the political reforms by extending term limits; creating a new, more powerful election monitor; and imposing stricter rules on campaigns.

DESPITE THESE EFFORTS, the Pact was bitterly attacked the moment Peña Nieto publicly unveiled it on December 2, 2012. Among other things, opponents were enraged by the backroom setting in which it had been conceived. When I met with Senator Ernesto Cordero, a former PAN finance secretary and a Calderón ally, in his legislative offices, he said that the deal had "substituted unelected leaders for Congress." That approach was patently illegitimate, he said. "I mean, who even knows the name of the chairman of the Republican Party in your country?" Luis Rubio, a columnist and the head of the Center of Research for Development, echoed this charge, saying that such secret negotiations among party leaders would have been anathema in the United States, where they "would have made the founding fathers turn in their graves."

Such complaints resonated in a country long used to secret accommodations among corrupt politicians and power brokers. Yet the reforms hardly represented business as usual, as many critics claimed. And as Zambrano pointed out when I asked him about Cordero's indictment, the Pact still had to pass through Mexico's Congress multiple times before becoming law—which gave rank-and-file legislators plenty of opportunities to weigh in.

Other opponents, meanwhile, lamented some of the compromises Peña Nieto had made to keep the opposition on board. The ultimate education reform, for instance, was weaker than many advocates had wanted (it gives administrators the power to reassign underperforming teachers but not to fire them). The government also signed off on a PRD-sponsored tax package that raised rates for businesses and the wealthy, capped individual deductions, and extended the full VAT to border towns (which previous governments had kept low to encourage US cross-border shopping)—changes that incensed Mexico's wealthier citizens and its business community.

But despite these flaws—or, more likely, because of them—the Pact worked amazingly well. When Congress opened for business at the start of 2013, the truce held and Mexico's leaders abandoned warfare for legislating. Working together over the next year and a half, they managed to enact eighty-five far-reaching changes (generally with 80 percent legislative support) in all the areas mentioned above—education, taxes, banking, antitrust, and elections—as well as to the criminal code and transparency standards; they even increased tariffs on junk food to fight Mexico's fast-growing diabetes epidemic. To appreciate how profound these accomplishments were, try to imagine the US Congress doing something analogous, like passing immigration, tax, banking, and campaign-finance reform—all at the same time. And then remember that the animosity between Mexico's political parties was as bitter, if not more so, than the divisions between Republicans and Democrats in the United States.

What makes the Pact's accomplishments even more impressive is the fact that many of the changes had to be passed twice: first through constitutional amendments (which require a two-thirds vote in Congress) and then via secondary, or implementing, legislation.

The parties also had to overcome the strident opposition of many segments of Mexican society, especially when it came to the liberalization of the energy sector. The Pact did three big things in this area: it allowed private firms to start bidding against Pemex for exploration and production contracts; it permitted Pemex to begin signing joint ventures with other companies; and it authorized competition among electricity providers. (The reform also created a sovereign wealth fund to handle oil revenues and sought to improve Pemex's management structure by removing union representatives from its board.) In most countries, making changes to expose the energy sector to market forces would not have seemed radical. But Mexico is not like most countries in this regard. Government control over hydrocarbon resources has been a fierce source of pride ever since President Lázaro Cárdenas nationalized the sector in 1938, and preserving the state's monopoly had become something of a religious conviction for many Mexicans, especially in the PRD (which was founded by Cárdenas's son). That conviction had remained strong even as it became increasingly obvious in recent years that state control of the sector and the lack of competition were hurting the entire country. As a result, any loosening of the reins, even in a limited fashion—under the new regime, private firms may only compete for "licenses," not "concessions," meaning they'll get title only to the oil they extract, while everything under the surface will remain the property of the state—felt downright revolutionary.

THE GREAT THING about marriages of convenience is that they allow the newlyweds to do things together that they'd never manage on their own. The problem with such arrangements is that they tend not to last, and the Pact proved no exception. In late November 2013, when the oil reform came up for a vote, the PRD announced that it was dropping out of the agreement. (Zambrano claimed the changes went further than he'd agreed to during the 2012 negotiations.) But the PRD's walkout was actually constructive, since it let the other, more market-friendly parties pass a bill that was much more effective than anything the PRD could have stomached. And despite its disagreement on that issue, the PRD continued to cooperate with the PRI and the PAN when it came to passing legislation pertaining to other parts of the Pact.

Peña Nieto formally announced the Pact's completion on August 20, 2014, but the deal's demise was no sign of failure. Its architects had always known that it would have a limited life span; maintaining unity would become too difficult once the 2015 midterm elections approached, and they had planned accordingly. "We were very clear that the Pacto couldn't survive more than one and a half or two years, no more," Nuño told me. "So that's why we were in such a hurry to pass all the reforms so quickly."

Though the Pact may be finished, moreover, the reforms should have a profound impact on Mexico for years to come—and not just on its economy or its legal code. Creel told me that the Pact has created "a new culture, in which you're not a traitor if you sit down and talk." Nuño went even further, describing the deal as "the first step down the path to a new Mexico." As he explained, "before the Pacto, you had polarization, gridlock, something very similar to US politics today. Now relations between the parties are radically different." Videgaray agrees, arguing that thanks to all the negotiating, deal making, and legislative cooperation, trust and communication "between the government and the opposition parties is better than it's ever been." That's allowed the Pact's participants, who still meet from time to time, to continue working together. "The Pacto was a team, and in a way, it very much still is," Videgaray said.

Important as that is, a few big question marks still linger over the Pact's actual effects.

First, despite its legislative accomplishments, the Mexican government has only just started some of the trickiest work: actually enforcing the new rules. And that's where the rubber will really meet the road. As O'Neil says, "It's great to put all this stuff in the law. But can you make reality match?" Starr cautions that "Mexico is trying to do a lot of stuff they've never done before, so there will be a steep learning curve." And not only for the government: "They're writing new rules for the game for Mexican businesses, and those businesses are accustomed to working under the old ones," she told me.

Sure enough, some changes have been slow to take effect. Domestic investment dropped in 2013 as angry businesses decided to sit on their hands. And several of Mexico's poorer states, led by Oaxaca, initially refused to implement the new mandatory educational standards. Meanwhile, it will take years before many of the other reforms can materially improve the lives of ordinary Mexicans, 46 percent of whom still live at or beneath the poverty level. In fact, the economy has actually softened in the last few years, though this was largely due to low oil prices and the slowdown in China and elsewhere. Falling energy prices also ensured a lackluster response to Mexico's first open oil exploration auction in July 2015. (A second auction in December 2016 did much better, however, far exceeding expectations.)

None of this should be particularly surprising. The tough thing about structural changes is that their benefits *always* take time to materialize—which is why most politicians avoid attempting them in the first place. So, for instance, while the oil reforms are starting to attract huge amounts of investment, the real payoff—in terms of output, jobs, and lower domestic prices—won't arrive for another year or two.

That said, other signs of progress have already started to appear. The government has made good headway setting up and staffing regulatory bodies to enforce the new rules on telecommunications, economic competition, and elections. And in a break with tradition, many of the officials it has nominated to these new institutions are independent technocrats—not political cronies, as in the past. Better yet, many analysts expect the economy to recover relatively soon. A report from Franklin Templeton Investments predicts that the Pact should, in short order, "encourage innovation, give entrepreneurs access to credit, [and] increase competition in key sectors." As a consequence, the World Bank has predicted that Mexico's GDP will grow by 3.5 percent in 2017.

Credit to agriculture and to small businesses has already ticked up. Foreign investment rose dramatically in 2013, and in 2014 Mexico's government bonds earned an "A" rating from Moody's for the first time. Job creation and other important metrics are also showing signs of life. New gas pipelines from the United States are already in the works. Finally, many of Mexico's markets have been so constrained for so long—thanks to Carlos Slim's telecom monopoly, for example, Mexicans paid some of the highest long-distance fees in the world and, according to Pardinas, "had more options in their choice of president than they did in choice of telephone company"—that even minor improvements are setting off tremors. For instance, the mere appearance in late 2014 of mysterious billboards from a previously unknown cell phone provider bearing a simple but provocative slogan—"¡Adiós Carlos!"—set Mexico City buzzing.

DESPITE THE SIGNS of progress, the Pact faces one more even larger problem: the things it *didn't* do. Peña Nieto decided early on that the deal wouldn't focus on the rule of law or Mexico's ongoing security problems; after all the bloodshed of the Calderón years, the new president was keen to change the subject (and shift the world's attention) to the economy instead.

That choice has turned out to be a major miscalculation. Overall violence has remained stubbornly persistent. Although the government claimed that homicides declined by 29 percent during the first two years of Peña Nieto's term, and the police and military captured a few of the country's most notorious and elusive mafia bosses, drug-related deaths spiked in some regions, armed self-defense forces began to organize in several states, kidnappings and extortion increased across the country—and, of course, Joaquín "El Chapo" Guzmán tunneled out of Mexico's most secure prison.

And then there was the horror in Iguala. On the night of September 26, 2014, forty-three leftist students from a teacher-training institute in the impoverished and violent southern state of Guerrero headed off to a protest—and were never seen again. After days of government bumbling, a huge manhunt was organized, which turned up several unrelated and previously undiscovered mass graves—but not the protesters. A few months later, authorities announced that they'd found the students' incinerated remains on a nearby riverbank. According to the government, the young people had been kidnapped, shot, and disposed of by corrupt cops and gunmen working for the Guerreros Unidos, a local drug gang—which, it emerged, had been providing muscle to Iguala's then mayor and his wife. It seems that the couple had grown concerned that the unruly protesters might disrupt a campaign speech—and so ordered the narcos to eliminate them.

Gruesome as it was, the slaughter was hardly unprecedented in Mexico. The country has suffered all too many massacres over the years; indeed, an estimated one hundred thousand people have been killed by the cartels alone since 2007. Yet there was something so brazen about this particular case—especially the revelations that Iguala's politicians were working hand in glove with the local cartels (it was as though Vito Corleone had become mayor of New York, Pardinas told me)—and the government's response was so clumsy that this time the public exploded in anger. Massive antigovernment demonstrations rocked the country for months. And many Mexicans rejected the government's account of what had transpired.

Just when this crisis was coming to a head, the Mexican media uncovered yet more bad news for Peña Nieto: evidence that his family was living in a $7 million mansion his wife had acquired from a government contractor in a murky deal. Similar allegations were soon made against Videgaray. The back-to-back revelations inflamed Mexicans' already-raw nerves, reminding them just how much work the country still needed to do to bring violence, corruption, and government impunity under control. The public outrage continued to mount and threatened to overshadow all of the government's economic and political accomplishments.

Peña Nieto was far too slow in responding to all these revelations. He did, however, eventually take a number of substantial steps to address them. He forced Videgaray to resign and reshuffled his cabinet, moved to reform the nation's police by dissolving local forces and assimilating them into new, statewide agencies; created a nationwide emergency hotline; promised greater transparency in government contracting; and set up special economic zones in Guerrero and other impoverished states. He also introduced constitutional amendments to allow the federal government to take over municipalities infiltrated by organized crime. And in 2015 he oversaw the establishment of a new National Anticorruption System that, among other things, created an independent prosecutor dedicated to fighting corruption and that requires public officials to declare their assets and potential conflicts of interest.

Critics have derided these measures as too little and too late, and have questioned the impartiality of a government inquiry that cleared Peña Nieto and his wife of any wrongdoing in relation to their housing purchases. While such skepticism is understandable—the investigator, after all, had been appointed by Peña Nieto himself—there are three reasons to remain optimistic about Mexico's future.

The first is that neither the corruption allegations nor the Iguala massacre have undermined the Pact's main *political* achievement: shattering years of gridlock and getting Mexico's government working again.

The second is that the most fundamental source for what went so terribly wrong in Guerrero wasn't crime and wasn't drugs; it was poverty. And the Pact's economic reforms should have a huge impact on that problem once they gain traction.

Finally, despite Peña Nieto's many stumbles, he could still recover his footing before his term expires in 2018. If the president and his partners in the opposition have shown the world anything in the last few years, it's a remarkable knack for surprising and confounding even their harshest critics. "Everyone who underestimated Peña Nieto, first as a candidate and then as a leader with the capacity to reform, has been proved wrong," says Pardinas. "Now he faces the greatest challenges of his presidency. But we have good reason to think he will find a way to handle them."

AND SO FOR the inevitable question: Can other countries really replicate Mexico's cure for political paralysis?

The answer is that, while doing so won't be easy, none of the obstacles are insurmountable. Some of the factors that helped Peña Nieto make his grand deal were particular to Mexico at the moment of his election. These included the low expectations that surrounded him when he took office (which made him less threatening to rivals), his slim mandate (which forced him to compromise), and all three parties' recognition that they needed to change—that constantly saying no was killing them in national polls. Mexico's political system also affords party leaders fairly tight control over their legislators, which helped them enforce a deal struck at the top (though the Pact's electoral changes have since weakened that control).

Mexico also got lucky in one other key respect. Though political scientists tend not to emphasize the role of individuals, "people matter," Videgaray told me, "and we were extremely fortunate that we had people in charge like Jesús Ortega, Jesús Zambrano, Santiago Creel, and Gustavo Madero." These leaders shared an unusual ability to recognize reality, face it directly, and deal with it in the most responsible fashion. "Had we had other people in charge, it could easily have happened that even with the same underlying trends, we would have had a very different outcome," he told me. Creel shares this sentiment: "I'm not saying I'm special, or that anyone is special. But that group was special."

Yet Mexico's political system is far from unique in most ways. For one thing, as Nuño and others point out, the Republican-Democratic split in the United States is no more venomous than the one that divided Mexico's parties before they finally came to the table. And the same goes for the disputes in other gridlocked states like Israel, India, or Italy. Meanwhile, while Mexico was spurred to action by a sense of crisis, that too is hardly uncommon; a similar sense of impending doom has descended on Europe, the United States, and most emerging markets in recent years. All this suggests that a good many currently deadlocked nations could indeed follow Mexico's model—one that involved quiet negotiation, painful compromise, political leaders willing to take risks and keep their word, and above all a recognition that zero-sum politics accomplishes nothing.

Especially since, as Pardinas points out, Mexico's story has one other important moral. When I asked him what he thought was his nation's key lesson for other countries, he paused, then said, simply, "Hope."

"If you had asked ordinary Mexicans, or even the people who negotiated the Pact, whether, [a few] years ago, they would have thought something like this could happen here, they would have said no," he told me. "We went through fifteen years of frustration. But our lesson is that the impossible can happen. It happened. Sometimes you really can find water in the middle of the desert."

10

DIY DEFENSE

New York City and the Art of the Work-around

THE ONE OTHER LESSON MEXICO'S STORY TEACHES IS that the best way a government can deal with gridlock is simply to break it.

That shouldn't sound like a profound revelation. It's pretty obvious why the optimal way to fix a problem is to actually resolve it.

Sometimes doing so just isn't possible, however. Dealing with the United States' dysfunctional federal government is one such case. To excise all the petty partisanship and rampant self-dealing that have infected America's national policymaking apparatus, you'd have to establish new standards, set new rules, and create a new ethic of governance. And then—God help you—you'd have to find partners in both parties willing to cooperate.

Often leaders facing such problems can't wait for those kinds of conditions to materialize. They don't have time for the ideal solution; they need fixes now. What they need, in other words, is a work-around.

This was a scenario New York City confronted in traumatic fashion on September 11, 2001.

Minutes after the planes had lanced down through the clear blue sky, panicked officials began scrambling to interpret the events. Even before the fires had burned out, 9/11 had come to mean many different things to many different people. The United States was under attack. The nation was at war. The oceans would no longer protect it. US foreign policies could lead to, and had just produced, some searing unintended consequences. And the threat of Islamist terrorism was worse than most Americans had realized.

Michael Bloomberg—the billionaire media mogul and philanthropist then running for mayor (he'd be elected two months later)—understood all that. But even before winning the November election, he'd draw two other, grim conclusions.

The first was that the city he'd soon take charge of—with its world-famous monuments, its throngs of tourists, its huge and densely packed population, its thousands of fragile glass towers, and its many aging bridges and tunnels—was a uniquely tempting target for al-Qaeda. And as experts warned, the group still had the city in its sights.

Bloomberg's second conclusion was even scarier: New York City couldn't count on anyone else to protect it. The federal government wasn't working; it had failed the city once and would likely do so again. (Albany, home to New York State's perpetually corrupt legislature, was even less reliable.) The nation's new president, George W. Bush, was a Harvard MBA who'd campaigned on his supposed competence as a manager. But nine months into its term, his administration was already proving inept, especially when it came to national security (and worse was still to come). In the months prior to the attacks, for example, Bush and his top advisers had brushed off explicit warnings from outgoing Clinton staffers about the deadly storm sweeping out of the Middle East.

But Bush wasn't New York's only problem; America's legislative branch had also failed it. As the blue-ribbon 9/11 Commission would later conclude, in the years before the attacks Congress had been so distracted by its petty partisan fights that it "gave little guidance to executive branch agencies, did not reform them in any significant way, and did not systematically perform oversight" of the intelligence community.

In the absence of adult supervision, the CIA, the FBI, and their kin had fumbled badly. For example, in one of many lapses, the FBI had overlooked a frighteningly prescient July 2001 memo from its Phoenix office warning about Qaeda operatives enrolling in US flight schools.

All this was going through Bloomberg's mind as he prepared to take office, and the message he drew from these failures was stark. As New York entered a new, more violent era, it shouldn't expect Washington to "come riding to the rescue," as he later put it. Instead, it would have to work around the federal government and do something no modern American city had ever attempted: try to defend itself, by itself.

Doing so would mean completely rewriting a great many rules, including the very definition of the mayor's job. The old division of labor—in which City Hall focused on local issues like schools and garbage pickup while Washington handled the big stuff, like defense and diplomacy—was finished. New York needed a whole new paradigm of government.

It was an enormously difficult challenge, and one that should have been just as enormously intimidating. But the famously brash and cocky Bloomberg—who, before turning to politics, had built a multibillion-dollar media empire from scratch—was used to those.

Besides, he had no other choice.

As you'd expect, the new mayor's first preoccupation was how to strengthen the thin blue line that stretched around the five boroughs and their eight million inhabitants. Even before taking office on January 1, 2002, he went looking for a visionary cop who could help him keep New York safe.

It only took Bloomberg a few days to find his man. Ray Kelly was a career NYPD officer who knew both policing and New York City in his bones. The son of a milkman, Kelly had joined the department as a cadet and had quickly climbed the ranks, eventually holding every one of its command posts. He even looked the part of the quintessential cop: a Vietnam vet, Kelly stood ramrod straight and had a weight lifter's build, a silvery brush cut, and the kind of mug you'd expect to see in an old gangster film.

Kelly had first made NYPD commissioner in 1992, toward the end of the David Dinkins administration, but then had left New York to run the US Customs Service and serve as Bill Clinton's under secretary of the Treasury (where he oversaw the Secret Service and the Bureau of Alcohol, Tobacco, and Firearms). Kelly had used his years in Washington to cultivate close ties to some very powerful people there. The experience had also taught him how the nation's capital worked—and more important, how it didn't. "I'd seen the federal government up close," Kelly told me recently. "It is, by definition, lethargic; it doesn't move." That understanding would prove critical as he returned to the NYPD to take on a new role that Mitchell Moss, an urban studies professor at New York University, has described as the city's "secretary of defense, head of the CIA, and . . . chief architect all rolled into one."

Moss's language may sound hyperbolic, but if anything, it understates the complexity of the challenges Kelly and Bloomberg faced.

First, there was the question of resources. As both men saw it, New York was now walking point—"The federal government isn't at the front. It's cowering in the back corner of the room," Bloomberg would fume. Yet taking the lead in the city's defense would be dauntingly expensive, especially given that 9/11 had devastated New York not just physically and psychologically but also financially. The attacks and the subsequent panic had cost the city some 140,000 jobs as workers and businesses fled to the suburbs. In 2002 the city's comptroller would estimate New York's total economic losses at between $83 billion and $95 billion; by the next year, the city would face its biggest deficit in thirty years.

Next, for all the fear in the air, the new administration had very little sense of the precise threats it actually faced. As Kelly returned to his old desk at police headquarters, he was dismayed to discover that his department was flying virtually blind. The cops there "didn't know what was going on in our own city, let alone the rest of the world," he later recalled.

Much of the blame for this confusion fell to the US intelligence community, which was infamously stingy about sharing information *within* its own bureaucracy, let alone with local police. Soon after the 9/11 attacks, then mayor Rudolph Giuliani had sent a squad of NYPD detectives down to DC to gather whatever intelligence they could. But the FBI and CIA gave the cops such a runaround that they were soon recalled, empty-handed.

Another part of the problem was internal. New York City was no stranger to terrorism; though few today may remember it, Islamist extremists had attacked the World Trade Center once before. In February 1993, they'd set off a bomb under the North Tower, killing six people and injuring more than a thousand. The attack had led the Giuliani administration to make some improvements in how the city responded to disasters. Yet as Christopher Dickey recounts in his book *Securing the City,* the idea had long "settled in on the city's law enforcement agencies that stopping terror attacks was beyond their competence; basically a job for the 'three-letter guys'"—cop lingo for the CIA, the FBI, the NSA, and so on. "The police could joke about the Feds being 'Famous But Incompetent,'" Dickey writes, but only they "seemed to have the resources and the direction to take on foreign threats."

As a consequence of such deference, what little counterterrorism work was being done in the city back in late 2001 was handled by something called the Joint Terrorism Task Force (JTTF). Supposedly a collaboration between the FBI and the NYPD, in reality there was little joint or collaborative about it. The Feds totally dominated the handful of New York City cops assigned to the unit, relegating them to subsidiary, even menial, roles. And according to Thomas Reppetto, the former dean of John Jay College of Criminal Justice, "When the FBI obtained information on a possible threat, it was closely held, and the NYPD detectives on the task force were forbidden to disclose it to their department superiors." On the rare occasions when the bureau *did* share information, it invariably came too late. In one notorious episode, the JTTF had seized the computer of a terrorist suspect that had turned out to contain a trove of clues about Qaeda operations targeting New York. Yet the FBI hadn't shown the files to anyone in the NYPD command for six weeks—a lifetime in the counterterrorism business.

BLOOMBERG AND KELLY were determined to change all that, and as quickly as possible. But how could New York City actually do so, given the vastly greater power and deeper pockets of the federal government? After all, the national intelligence community spent about $50 billion each year, about ten times the NYPD's entire budget, and the CIA alone employed one hundred thousand personnel, more than twice as many as did New York's police.

Outmanned and outgunned, Kelly nonetheless decided to beard the lion in its den. He sent one hundred cops, led by a smart but famously abrasive bulldog of a police chief named Phil Pulaski, marching over to the JTTF. Their job, as Kelly later described it to me, was to "muscle their way" onto the task force and demand full access to whatever information the FBI had. Predictably enough, Kelly's pushiness, combined with Pulaski's manners—on arrival at JTTF headquarters, he immediately declared himself the new boss—infuriated the bureau, which sent the FBI's assistant director to Kelly's office to complain. But to almost everyone's amazement, the plan also worked, and the detectives were soon sending back reams of fresh intelligence.

While these materials proved valuable, however, they didn't solve New York's problems. Merely knowing what the FBI knew might not be enough to protect the city, given the likely gaps in the bureau's own knowledge; it had, remember, missed numerous clues in the months preceding 9/11. So Kelly and Bloomberg decided to build their own intelligence and counterterrorism apparatus.

At the time, the NYPD already had something called an Intelligence Division. Despite its name, however, the unit was a backwater that did virtually no counterterrorism work. It was, Kelly scoffed, merely an "escort service" that spent its time shepherding dignitaries and visiting VIPs around town—a job other cops derisively referred to as coat holding.

To transform the Intelligence Division into something worthy of its name, Kelly turned to a man who, like him, knew how the federal government worked, but who, *un*like him, was also intimately familiar with spycraft and counterterrorism. David Cohen may have looked unimposing, more like a bespectacled accountant than James Bond (or even M). But the explosively profane Bostonian had spent thirty-five years at the CIA, where he'd served as both its chief of analysis and its master of spies—the only person in agency history to hold both posts—before being sent to New York City as station chief, which is where he and Kelly first met.

Hired just a few days after his new boss, Cohen set to work right away. "It was like putting tires on a speeding car," he later recalled. Drawing heavily on his CIA background, the new intelligence chief created an Analytic Unit and filled it with young Ivy Leaguers, a former Supreme Court clerk, and refugees from the State Department, the UN, the World Bank, and Wall Street. Their job was to serve as a sort of in-house brain trust and help street cops comprehend the nuances of Islamic practice and the subtleties of tribal culture. He also created units dedicated to tracking suspicious financial movements, studying foreign media, and trolling through jihadist chat rooms. He dispatched agents to infiltrate suspected radical hangouts. And he set up something called Operation Nexus to monitor and advise local businesses—ranging from chemical wholesalers to salvage yards to scuba shops—that might prove useful to would-be terrorists.

Cohen's division would eventually reach a force strength of about six hundred. To supplement it, Kelly also created an entirely new Counterterrorism Bureau under the command of a slick-haired former Marine Corps general named Frank Libutti. If Cohen's Intelligence Division was to serve as the city's mini-CIA, Libutti's Counterterrorism Bureau would become its Department of Homeland Security. Working out of a futuristic headquarters—picture blinking electronic maps, flashing news tickers, and huge monitors streaming Arabic-language TV broadcasts—the Counterterrorism Bureau focused on threat assessment: finding and hardening weak spots in New York's landmarks, public and private buildings, and infrastructure. (It was security objections from this unit that forced the first redesign of the Freedom Tower.) The bureau also ran regular training programs for city, state, and federal officials. It initiated the now-familiar bag checks at subway entrances. And in order to keep would-be attackers off guard, disrupt their attempts to recon possible targets, and simply put the fear into them, it sent Hercules Teams—elite squads of officers clad in battle armor and strapped with automatic weapons—careening around town in black SUVs, to descend without warning on vulnerable locations like the Empire State Building, Times Square, or Columbus Circle.

TURNING THE NATION'S largest police department into something that was "part think tank, part detective agency, [and] part paramilitary organization," in the words of Lydia Khalil (a Cairo-born veteran of Cohen's Analytic Unit), required huge and sometimes wrenching attitude adjustments at City Hall and NYPD headquarters. After all, municipal policing had traditionally focused on investigating crimes *after* they occurred. As William Bratton, who would succeed Kelly in 2014, once put it, "for 30 years, [the police] measured . . . our success by how many arrests did we make, how many 911 calls did we answer, and how quickly did we respond to them." The NYPD and other police departments left deterrence to the courts and the prisons and the identification of foreign threats to the nation's intelligence agencies. Even terrorist attacks, such as the 1993 World Trade Center bombing, had been treated as isolated events and dealt with after the fact.

Throwing all that out the window, as Bloomberg and Kelly did, made sense for a lot of reasons. But it also involved serious risks.

The first was electoral. Because New York's resources were far from infinite, every cop the administration put on the counterterrorism beat meant one fewer officer available to deal with run-of-the-mill crime. Had this shift in manpower led to a citywide spike in muggings, violence, or other street offenses, it could have abruptly ended Bloomberg's experiment—and his tenure. (As it turned out, ordinary crime, which had hit record lows during the Giuliani administration, continued to drop.)

Bloomberg's habit of ignoring and excoriating Washington was also politically dangerous, even for someone as rich and powerful as he. As the mayor and his police chief took over one job after another traditionally performed by the federal government, they rarely asked anyone's permission. That approach (with its dangers) was demonstrated most dramatically in 2002, when the NYPD decided to start sending officers abroad—another first for a metro PD. With Bloomberg's go-ahead but without even mentioning it to the State Department or any other federal agency, Kelly would ultimately post detectives to eleven foreign cities, ranging from Abu Dhabi to Paris to Singapore to Santo Domingo. (Over the years, New York City cops also visited Afghanistan, India, Pakistan, the Philippines, Russia, and Turkey, as well as the US prison at Guantánamo Bay, Cuba.) On arrival, these officers would embed themselves in local police departments and start forging the kind of comfortable cop-to-cop relationships that would give them quick access to critical data if and when those cities were hit.

This was a hugely provocative move—among other reasons, because the FBI already had its own people based overseas. Sure enough, when bureau officials found out about the new policy, they were furious—so much so that they subsequently blocked other American cities from trying to follow New York's lead. (They never managed to stop the NYPD, however. As as one high-level police official told *The New Yorker*'s William Finnegan, "Do you think anybody in Washington has the balls to tell Ray Kelly he can't do something he decides to do?")

Yet even the Feds had a hard time arguing with Kelly's results. When terrorists set off four bombs on the Madrid rail system in 2004, New York was able to get an officer on the ground within eighteen hours, and that allowed the NYPD to tweak its own security protocols the same day. Similarly, when the London Tube was attacked the next year, a New York detective was already riding the system and was thus able to send his first report on the bombers' tactics and methods home within the hour—real-time intelligence that led to more quick changes to New York's own security precautions.

Such successes made it difficult for federal officials to do much more than grouse, and there is no evidence that the city was ever directly punished for its temerity. Yet it certainly didn't buy it much goodwill in Washington either. September 11 had thrown the US government into a frenzy. In its aftermath, Congress had held endless hearings and then reorganized the US intelligence community. Bush launched the Global War on Terror, invaded Afghanistan and Iraq, and dramatically increased US military operations abroad and intelligence collections overseas and at home. Yet for all this activity, Washington never seemed to try especially hard to help New York City directly—or at least, that's how the Bloomberg administration saw things.

Apart from the lack of intelligence sharing, New York's biggest gripe involved money. Many of the mayor's initial funding requests were rejected. And when Washington did open the spigots, the corrupt and pork-based system Congress used to dole out cash ensured that the city got less than it needed while other, more isolated locales got more than they could spend. In 2004, for example, Washington gave Wyoming seven times as much funding (in per capita terms) as it did New York. And Congress actually cut antiterror grants to New York City in 2006 by about 40 percent—while increasing disbursements to towns like Omaha, Nebraska, by the same proportion. "We're still defending the city pretty much on our own dime," a thoroughly embittered Kelly complained around that time. That wasn't strictly accurate. But it wasn't entirely off base.

Yet for all the frustration Washington caused the Bloomberg administration, going it alone, as Bloomberg and Kelly felt they had to, turned out to confer a number of powerful advantages.

Chief among them was speed. Free from the need to consult with anyone else, the Bloomberg administration made and executed decisions with little debate, creating, in Cohen's words, the smallest "air gap between information and action" he'd ever experienced in government. Michael Sheehan, a former Green Beret who replaced Libutti as head of the Counterterrorism Bureau in June 2003, has described working for New York during this period as closer in tempo to the Special Forces than it was to the federal bureaucracy. To illustrate the point, he recounts how the department first made its controversial call to send its officers abroad. Cohen initially raised the idea with Kelly at one of their daily 8:00 a.m. meetings. The commissioner said that it sounded like a good idea. And that was that for about two weeks, until the intelligence chief, wanting confirmation before taking such a big step, raised the subject again. Kelly's response was fast and impatient: "I thought we discussed this already," he snapped. "When will your detective be in London?" (The officer was there three days later.)

Another huge advantage of New York's solitary approach was the lack of red tape—an asset highlighted by the differences in city and federal government hiring policies. One of the biggest reasons the US intelligence community had missed so many warning signs prior to 9/11 was that it hadn't understood them. In the years immediately preceding the attacks, the FBI had employed so few bilingual staffers that it had failed to translate about a third of all the Arabic-language wiretaps it collected. These included a conversation recorded on September 10, 2001, in which a Qaeda operative told a colleague that "tomorrow is zero hour."

The problem wasn't that the United States lacked Arabic, Dari, or Pashto speakers (though few Americans studied those languages in college). The problem was that the federal government wouldn't hire them. It subjected all job applicants to absurdly strict background checks that made it needlessly difficult for foreign-born Americans to get security clearance. Almost all aspiring agents with dual citizenship or close family members living abroad were rejected, as were 90 percent of those hoping to work as translators.

The NYPD had very different rules. The department had long served as a key avenue of advancement for New York's wildly heterogeneous immigrant population. And in the days after 9/11, Kelly enhanced and exploited the department's already polyglot nature: by screening all new hires for their language skills and willingness to work undercover, and by placing recruiting ads in foreign-language newspapers. The result was that "we were able to get people who were from the backstreets of Karachi, who were able to speak the dialects," Kelly told me. By 2002 the force boasted sixty fluent Arabic speakers—nearly twice the number the FBI would reach three years later—and by 2009 the NYPD had 1,697 linguists on staff certified in fifty-six languages, including Bengali, Dari, Farsi, Fukienese, Hindi, Pashto, Punjabi, Russian, and Urdu. Even the Feds would come to acknowledge New York's superiority in this area: at different points in the last decade and a half, the FBI, the CIA, the Secret Service, and the Defense Intelligence Agency have all asked the NYPD for help navigating foreign languages and cultures.

Within just a few years, all these assets and innovations would allow the Bloomberg administration to create what Brian Michael Jenkins, a counterterrorism expert at the Rand Corporation, has called a "cutting-edge" security operation that "should be emulated across the country." Bloomberg and Kelly did overreach multiple times, and some of their innovations sparked intense controversy—not just from disgruntled federal agencies but also from minority and civil liberties groups, which took issue with the department's sometimes overbearing scrutiny of New York's Muslim community and its mosques. One particularly egregious program run by the Intelligence Division, which involved sending undercover cops into Muslim neighborhoods to eavesdrop at restaurants, stores, and mosques, produced so much ill will—without generating a single solid lead—that it was recently shut down.

Yet for all the controversy, Bloomberg and Kelly still proudly argue that the city foiled at least sixteen known attacks during their tenure, and possibly more that they never knew about. While critics dispute the tally, the fact is that New York never suffered a single successful follow-on attack during the mayor's three terms: something few would have thought possible in the frightening months following 9/11.

BLOOMBERG'S REINVENTION of the NYPD—with its colorful cops, soldiers, and spies, its heavy weapons, its international intrigue, and its high-tech intelligence work—is the most dramatic example of how, during his three terms in office, his administration dealt with dysfunction above it by working around the obstacle. But it is far from the only one. Stasis in Washington and Albany directly caused, or left unaddressed, a raft of other problems New York City also had to contend with under Bloomberg's watch. And simply complaining about them wasn't an option, though Bloomberg did plenty of that too. As he liked to remind the public, state and national politicians have the luxury of being able to spend their days squabbling, but "the mayors of this country still have to deal with the real world."

Of all the episodes that illustrate how he and the city managed to do so, three stand out for their ambition.

The first was climate change. Under normal circumstances—that is, when governments work the way textbooks say they should—safeguarding the environment is just the kind of job best left to the national authorities. Only they have enough reach and muscle to comprehensively address a problem of that scale. Yet in 2007 the Bloomberg administration—which, given New York's watery and low-lying location, was particularly sensitive to climate issues—got fed up with the slow pace of progress in Washington and decided to do what it could itself. Under an initiative called PlaNYC, the city launched 127 different efforts aimed at increasing New York's resilience and at slashing its greenhouse-gas emissions. To reach its target of a 30 percent reduction in carbon output by the year 2030, PlaNYC imposed strict new conservation and efficiency regulations on city buildings, taxis, and garbage trucks; proposed a congestion-pricing scheme similar to London's, which would increase tolls to cut the number of CO_2-spouting cars allowed into Manhattan; and (among many other things) made preparations for the introduction of sewage-eating mollusks into New York's polluted harbor. In the years that followed, some of the more esoteric ideas (although not the mollusks) were shot down or tripped up on logistical hurdles. Yet by 2014—just seven years into PlaNYC's twenty-three-year time frame—New York City had already made impressive strides, cutting its carbon emissions by almost 20 percent, lowering its sulfur dioxide levels by 69 percent, building more than three hundred miles of new bike paths, and planting close to a million new trees. None of that would be enough to save the world. But the city was doing its part.

Then there was infrastructure building: another traditional task for national governments. During the twentieth century, the vast majority of America's great construction projects were commissioned and funded at the federal level. In New York City, for example, it was Washington that either paid for or underwrote the construction of both airports, the FDR Drive, the Lincoln Tunnel, and the Triborough (now Robert F. Kennedy) Bridge. But in recent years, congressional infighting and a miserly and shortsighted fixation on budget cutting have all but ended this once-proud tradition. So when the Bloomberg administration decided in 2007 that it needed to extend the No. 7 subway line in order to improve access to the Hudson Yards, a planned commercial and residential district on Manhattan's West Side, it didn't even bother asking anyone else for help. Then deputy mayor Dan Doctoroff, who led the city's effort, described the administration's thinking to me: "We saw that there was no possible way we would ever get [federal] money for this, and that if we actually wanted to do something on the West Side, we were going to have to do it completely on our own." So despite the daunting $3 billion price tag, the city moved ahead with the venture. According to Moss, the NYU professor, had City Hall tried to get help from above, the rail extension would have met a "terminal death." The only option was to go do the thing by itself. (The new service opened for business in September 2015.)

An even bigger venture into traditional federal territory came in the realm of higher education. Like the United States' highways, bridges, airports, and tunnels, most of the country's big state universities (and some of its best private ones) were created and bankrolled by Washington. Even New York's so-called City University wasn't founded by the municipality. (It was chartered by Albany, which still pays most of its bills.)

In 2008, however, after New York was hit hard by the Great Recession—in fifteen months the city lost thirty-six thousand Wall Street jobs and $2 billion in taxes—the Bloomberg administration decided it needed to diversify New York's finance-heavy economy. After consulting with more than three hundred CEOs and a long list of experts, New York's Economic Development Corporation (EDC) determined that the best way for the city to reduce its reliance on bankers was to become a haven for high-tech innovation. And the best way to do that, EDC determined, was to train a whole new generation of local engineers and other techies. So in 2010, the city launched its Applied Sciences NYC initiative: a competition to build several new STEM (science, technology, engineering, and mathematics) campuses in New York. Some twenty-seven of the world's best universities—eager to tap into New York's size, wealth, and prestige—applied, and after a rigorous, multiround selection process, the Bloomberg administration picked four winners.

Within a few years, these projects stand to revolutionize the city's educational landscape. Carnegie Mellon is building a new center for digital media in the Brooklyn Navy Yard. An international consortium led by New York University (which also includes the elite Mumbai-based Indian Institute of Technology) has set up a Center for Urban Science and Progress in downtown Brooklyn. Columbia has established a new Data Science Institute uptown. And on Roosevelt Island, an underused sliver of land between Manhattan and Queens, Cornell University and Israel's Technion Institute of Technology are constructing a big new campus for applied media, health, and engineering studies.

EDC predicts that these projects will create tens of thousands of new construction jobs in the short term, and, when completed, will increase the number of engineering graduate students in New York by 120 percent. That's a huge jump, and one that could well transform the city into an entrepreneurial tech and research hub on par with power-houses like San Francisco and Boston—just as the Bloomberg administration hoped.

IT'S HARD TO imagine any of these initiatives—in policing, climate, infrastructure, or higher education—being undertaken by an ordinary city under ordinary circumstances. New York, of course, has never been ordinary, and neither were the circumstances it found itself in over the last decade and a half. Yet that doesn't explain how Bloomberg and his team were able to pull off what they did. Leaders hoping to follow his example are going to have to look at their tactics in closer detail.

The mayor's first secret, according to Doctoroff, was his intuition that it is not only generally necessary but also often preferable to avoid asking the state or federal government for help. Given how hard it is to get Albany or Congress to do anything constructive, odds are that such assistance won't be forthcoming, and requesting it will likely just delay a project indefinitely. Far better, Bloomberg figured out, to simply act, and to make a virtue of independence. Both New York's experiment in counterterrorism and its success with the No. 7 subway line extension confirm the wisdom of that approach; had the city tried to pursue either of these projects through normal channels, it would probably still be waiting for an answer.

Of course, there are good reasons why most cities still do look to their state capitals or Washington for assistance: only they seem to have the resources for really big jobs. Bloomberg discovered that that's not always true, however; the necessary means sometimes can be found elsewhere. Still, going it alone is enormously difficult, and requires a number of other tricks to pull it off.

First, you have to become extremely creative at finding new sources of money. During its long tenure, the Bloomberg administration developed a remarkable skill for striking partnerships with philanthropists and the private sector. City Hall convinced wealthy donors like Sting and David Rockefeller to bankroll the planting of the city's million new trees, for example. And it persuaded the nonprofit New York City Police Foundation to cover the living expenses of the detectives it stationed abroad. In cases where philanthropy wasn't enough, the administration was even more inventive. To pay for the rail extension, Doctoroff came up with a complicated and entirely novel area-specific bond issue that was guaranteed by future tax revenues from the rehabilitated Hudson Yards. The city showed similar savvy regarding its massive educational initiative. Seth Pinsky, former head of the EDC, told me, "Unlike most new campuses being set up these days in places like Singapore or Dubai, the vast majority of costs are being borne by the universities themselves." And of those that aren't, most still won't come out of the municipal purse. In order to persuade Columbia to spend some $80 million on its new data center, for example, the Bloomberg administration offered the school $15 million in incentives, but these took the form of cheap leases for city buildings, reduced electricity bills, and loan forgiveness—not cash. The city did have to promise the new Cornell-Technion center $100 million in infrastructure improvements. But that sum was a pittance compared with the project's overall price tag of $2 billion.

To find creative solutions, of course, you need some very creative people. Another key to Bloomberg's success is his ability to surround himself with brilliant, unconventional thinkers and doers. The mayor consistently hired the best people he could find for any given job, and he rarely worried about whether or not they possessed conventional credentials. For example, neither Cohen, Libutti, nor Sheehan had any police experience when Kelly brought them on board, yet all had other assets that served the city extremely well. Something analogous could be said of Doctoroff, an investment banker who'd never worked in city politics before Bloomberg tapped him in 2001. And there are many other examples (including a few failures like Cathie Black, the media executive whom Bloomberg named schools chancellor in 2011 and was forced to replace just a few months later).

Of course, once you've hired the right people you need to get the most out of them and keep them around. That's harder than it sounds, for as anyone who's worked in government will tell you, even the sharpest minds can be quickly ground down by bad management, excessive bureaucracy, and risk aversion (the pay scale doesn't help either). Bloomberg managed to avoid most of these problems by giving his lieutenants an uncommon amount of freedom, encouraging them to think big—and then standing by them if and when they failed big. Over the years, a significant number of his administration's most ambitious schemes would be defeated, sometimes in humiliating fashion. Congestion pricing was killed by Albany, and Bloomberg's attempt to lure the Olympics to New York, to build a new sports stadium on Manhattan's West Side, and to ban large sugary sodas also went down in flames. Yet because the mayor had embraced all these attempts and considered them well planned and well executed, he never fired anyone for these failures.

To illustrate the point, Doctoroff described to me how, during the city's fight to build a new stadium, the plan came under intense attack by Cablevision—one of the city's two big cable providers and, not coincidentally, the owner of Madison Square Garden. In 2005 the firm began running strident ads opposing the project and denouncing the mayor just when Bloomberg was running for his second term. Things got so ugly at one point that Doctoroff approached his boss and said that they should just drop the whole business, since the stadium wasn't worth the price of an election. Bloomberg, Doctoroff recalls, "looked at me with an anger I'd never seen before, and said, 'I don't ever want to hear you say that again. We got into this together and it's the right thing to do, so we're going to pursue it no matter what.' And after it went down to defeat about two months later, with Mike's popularity falling along with it, his only response was to turn to me and say, 'Okay, now what's plan B?'

"You have no idea what kind of loyalty that breeds," Doctoroff told me, "and more important, how it encourages people to take risks."

As effective a manager as he proved to be, Bloomberg's biggest asset as mayor lay still elsewhere: in his radical, buck-stops-here sense of responsibility for the city's welfare, and his almost ruthless determination to do whatever it took to advance it. A quintessential pragmatist, Bloomberg viewed political parties as encumbrances—he started his life as a Democrat, became a Republican to avoid a crowded primary in 2001, and then declared himself an independent in 2007. What he cared about were policies and ideas, not politics. "His secret was fairly simple," one former high-level adviser told me after asking that I not mention his name. "It was literally, just do the right thing and don't let shit get in the way." Or as Bill Cunningham, Bloomberg's former communications director, put it, Bloomberg "believed you get the data and [then] do what you believe is right. It was really like an experiment. Will people like someone who does what they believe in," and not what the polls tell them to do?

In Bloomberg's case, the answer was yes—at least most of the time. There's no avoiding the fact that his police initiatives angered both federal agencies and local rights groups. Critics also blame him for allowing income inequality and homelessness to grow on his watch. And Bloomberg, who developed a sort of genius for needlessly offending people over the years, could sometimes act as his own worst enemy. While many New Yorkers found his refusal to pander refreshing— unlike ordinary politicians, for example, the mayor spent most of his weekends out of town instead of pressing the flesh at sweaty street festivals—his behavior could also grate, especially toward the end of his administration. Late-model Bloomberg became infamous for his tetchy press conferences—he once singled out and humiliated a disabled reporter, for example, to the horror of everyone else in the room. And though he won a third term in office after clumsily forcing a change to the city's electoral law, Bloomberg "never seemed quite to get the outrage, even among friends, that greeted his Machiavellian move," according to Benjamin Barber, the author of *If Mayors Ruled the World*.

Still, Bloomberg has achieved an extraordinarily lofty status since leaving office. Like the city he led, much about the man—his wealth, his homes, his spending, and his policies—now seem larger than life. And that points to the biggest challenge more earthbound politicians hoping to follow his lead will face. Bloomberg may have never given "a shit about what anybody else felt," but that was because "he didn't owe anything to anybody," the former aide told me. Can other, less wealthy politicians afford such independence?

Bloomberg certainly seems to think so. In 2014 he used his own cash to set up a nonprofit consulting firm that aims to help other innovative leaders around the world follow his and New York's lead on controversial issues like climate change.

Michael Bloomberg, however, is probably not the best person to judge whether other politicians can successfully follow the Bloomberg Way. Far more meaningful, therefore, are two unexpected endorsements his preference for pragmatic work-arounds received after he left office.

In 2013 Bill de Blasio ran for New York City mayor by casting himself as the anti-Bloomberg, a more caring and progressive alternative to the plutocrat incumbent. Yet since taking office, de Blasio has effectively embraced Bloomberg's core insight that cities can and should do more themselves. In his first State of the City address, de Blasio declared that New York "cannot wait for Washington to act" and must not "let the gridlock there . . . serve as an excuse" for the failure to address problems like economic inequality and immigration reform. And his administration has since engaged both issues, by increasing the city's minimum wage, for example, and by issuing New Yorkers municipal ID cards regardless of their immigration status.

Surprising as de Blasio's tacit support was, the Bloomberg model soon found an even more powerful and unlikely adherent: President Barack Obama. Midway through Obama's second term, he got fed up with years of congressional obstruction and announced that he'd start going around the House and Senate whenever he deemed it necessary. Using his executive authority, Obama moved unilaterally to push for progress on immigration reform (by halting deportations in several types of cases); on criminal law (by releasing thousands of nonviolent drug offenders); and on gay rights (by banning federal contractors from discriminating on grounds of sexual orientation). And in August 2015, he launched his biggest solo initiative yet. Declaring that climate change is "exactly the kind of challenge that's big enough to remind us that we're all in this together," the president took action on his own, directing the Environmental Protection Agency to force American power plants—the single largest source of US carbon pollution—to cut their emissions by 32 percent by the year 2030. Not only did the president's move bear a striking resemblance to the centerpiece of Bloomberg's own climate plan, which the mayor had unveiled eight years earlier, but it also represented a profound affirmation of the mayor's fundamental credo: that the failure of others to act is no excuse for one's own inaction, and that during difficult times, leaders—if they really hope to lead—must be ready to act alone, no matter the consequences.

CONCLUSION

How to Survive and Thrive in a World in Decline

HAD THREE BASIC QUESTIONS IN MIND WHEN I FIRST STARTED thinking about this book a few years ago.

Why is it, I wondered, that in this time of turmoil—this age of ISIS, inequality, populism and political dysfunction, institutional decay, emerging-market panic, and apparent global decline—a few countries are nonetheless flourishing?

Second, can other states follow their lead? That is, are the secrets of their success exportable?

And finally, do their success stories, taken together, offer any broader lessons?

As soon as I started actually researching these questions, they began to subdivide at an alarming rate, like that enchanted broom in the "Sorcerer's Apprentice." Yet even as their numbers grew—first to the ten stories that would become my ten chapters, and then into the dozens more that each narrative raised—I tried to stay focused on the answers.

This fixation on how things work is what ultimately gave this book its shape. And it grew out of my frustration with much of the literature on international affairs. Over the course of the two decades I've now spent working in this field as a reporter, an editor, and a reader, I've increasingly been struck by how much of the writing concentrates on diagnosing *problems*.

Don't get me wrong: a lot of that analysis is superb, the handiwork of some very smart people. What they do is vital.

But so is taking the next step and asking what we should *do* about all these problems. Yet too often, it seems to me, when pundits do try to answer that question, their proposals take one of two unsatisfying forms. There are the honorable but vague exhortations ("Something must be done!"), of the sort you'd find in an unsigned newspaper editorial. And there are the recommendations delivered in such an abstract way ("Citizens must rise up and demand change!") that it's hard to know what to do with them. Both types of answers remind me of that classic cartoon showing two grizzled mathematicians standing at a blackboard on which an incredibly complex equation is scrawled. One of the professors points to a passage on the board that reads, "Then a miracle occurs," and tells his colleague: "I think you should be more explicit here in step two."

That's what I've always craved from books about the world: more explicit details on how the miracles occur. In the last ten chapters, I've tried to provide some of those details. I think I've also made some headway in answering the first two of my basic questions.

Now it's time to address the third, the one about broader lessons. Doing so is worthwhile, I think, for the following reason: because a book like this one, filled with stories about how leaders have solved particular problems, is also, inevitably, a book about leadership and problem solving per se. It would therefore be a mistake to limit its relevance to government officials struggling with challenges only and exactly the same as those I've already discussed. If you read the ten preceding chapters together, you'll find that they provide broader guidance as well. Reduced to their purest, most essential forms, the tools and methods used by the politicians in this book would work for many other sorts of problems. They'd also work for many other places; after all, the success stories we've looked at span different regions, historical eras, levels of development, even regime types. And they'd work for many other types of leaders, be they heads of banks or city boroughs, of universities or foundations, of huge corporations, small family businesses, or nonprofits. As this book shows, the answers are never easy, but they're also never impossible—not if you're willing to work hard enough and in the right ways.

And if you apply the following lessons.

I. EMBRACE EXTREMITY

In the spring of 2014, I was sitting in the headquarters of Bloomberg LP talking New York politics with Dan Doctoroff—the city's deputy mayor for most of Bloomberg's first two terms—when the conversation turned to local history.

"I have this theory about New York," Doctoroff told me. "The only time we've actually produced reform here has been when the city was in desperate shape. Look back over the last eighty years. La Guardia was elected in the teeth of the Depression. He served twelve great years, but then the city began to deteriorate again. Twenty years later, everyone had gotten so frustrated that they elected Lindsay on a reform platform. Then twenty more years went by, and everything sank again, so then Giuliani was elected. And then the only reason Bloomberg got in was because of 9/11. The only time a nontraditional candidate has ever become mayor of this city has been during a great crisis."

Strip away the particulars and Doctoroff could have been talking about any of the stories in this book, for each one featured an analogous moment. Salvation arrived at a point of great—often existential—peril. Disaster, dire necessity, proved the mother of invention and made room for the solutions that followed.

The details of the crises varied from place to place, of course. In New York, it took a massive terrorist attack to set the stage for fundamental change. In Rwanda and South Korea, it was a cataclysmic civil war. For Singapore and Botswana, it was the frightful circumstances of their births. In Indonesia, it was the eruption of terrorism and radical Islamism that followed its transition to democracy. For Mexico, it was spiraling violence, runaway economic decline, and government dysfunction. For Canada, it was a fundamental culture clash and the threat of separatism; for Brazil, it was dangerously destabilizing levels of inequality; and for the United States, it was the oil shock of the 1970s. While the specifics varied, however, in all these episodes the extremity of the moment played a similar role, pushing those in charge to set aside ordinary politics and conventional policymaking and to think big—very big.

By emphasizing circumstances, I don't mean to suggest that fate, not free will and shrewd leadership, proved decisive in any of these episodes. Circumstances played an important role: the extreme conditions cleared away the institutional and political barriers that ordinarily make radical solutions impossible to effect. But governments face serious crises all the time. What separates the best from the rest is how they deal with them.

The leaders in this book all saw that their crises gave them a once-in-a-generation chance to turn adversity into advantage and rewrite the rules—and each seized it. Bloomberg did so by redefining the role of city government and redrawing the division of duties between New York, Albany, and Washington. Trudeau reinvented Canada's identity. Park Chung-hee created a whole new economy for South Korea, and then thirty years later, Kim Dae-jung broke it apart and put it back together again. Peña Nieto rewrote Mexico's political rulebook and ended two decades of legislative civil war in the process. And so on.

To be clear: none of these leaders *created* the extreme conditions in which they found themselves. But all had the vision to recognize the rare freedom those circumstances afforded them. And all had the courage to use that freedom to its utmost, acting to ensure their fellow citizens would never again face such a terrible test.

2. THE POWER OF PROMISCUOUS THINKING

As every college student knows, Ralph Waldo Emerson once wrote that "a foolish consistency is the hobgoblin of little minds, adored by little statesmen and philosophers and divines." Almost two hundred years later, his observation may be frequently quoted, but his advice is even more frequently ignored. And that's unfortunate. Emerson's warning is the first guideline aspiring problem solvers should heed, by ridding themselves of ideological handcuffs as fast as they can.

Emerson was an American, as was Charles Sanders Peirce, the mathematician and logician who coined the term "pragmatism" more than a century ago and then became its biggest promoter. But as the narratives in this book make clear, this powerful turn of mind has long since spread far beyond these shores. Pragmatism—the dogged refusal to let party, tribe, philosophy, or custom stand in the way of the search for solutions—links all of our heroes. And it offers the best single explanation for their outsize accomplishments.

Of all the leaders we've looked at, Lula da Silva—the pro-profit progressive who could also make CEOs swoon—was, for all his faults, the most adroit (and flamboyant) practitioner of this art. By the time he became Brazil's president in 2003, Lula had earned his pragmatism the hard way: ideological purity had torpedoed his three previous attempts at high office. While painful, those losses ensured that when he *did* finally take power, Lula had become uncommonly open to appropriating the best ideas from wherever he could find them—be it the left or the right. While his apparent tolerance for political payoffs would ultimately undermine his once-stratospheric standing (and get him in legal trouble), his extreme openness of mind enabled him, as president, to cobble together one of most ambitious and successful social programs ever enacted. And Bolsa Família's unusually heterogeneous composition is what (eventually) ensured its enthusiastic reception, not just among Brazil's poorest citizens but among its richest ones too.

Lula rarely missed a chance to flaunt his insouciance toward ideological constraints. Once, during his presidency, he was heckled by an opposition politician who was angry at Lula for having stolen the idea for Bolsa Família from the opposition PSDB party. "You act like you discovered Brazil and you didn't!" the man shouted. "You're right," Lula shot back, unfazed. "But only because I wasn't alive at the time."

Brazen as he was, Lula wasn't the only leader in this book to wear his iconoclasm like a badge. Pierre Trudeau advertised his pragmatism by hanging a banner reading "Reason Over Passion" in his front hall. And when, shortly after Botswana's independence, Quett Masire was asked whether his government was socialist or capitalist, he proudly replied, "If it works, we do it, and we don't care what it's called."

None of these officials paid a high price for defying political convention; indeed, they and many of the other leaders we've looked at were rewarded for it. So was President Trump. That doesn't mean pragmatism is safe or easy, however, or that all politicians pull it off as successfully as Lula, Trudeau, and Masire managed to. Sticking your thumb in the eyes of your party, clan, or erstwhile allies can cost you support, funding, and friends. For example, when Mexico's opposition leaders found the courage to drop their grudges and sign on to Enrique Peña Nieto's grand reform agenda, they were savaged by traditionalists in their own parties who branded them traitors and tried to overthrow them (and almost succeeded). Meanwhile, Michael Bloomberg's open disdain for his (nominal) Republican Party affiliation has probably helped ruin his chances of ever being elected president.

Pragmatism, finally, should not be mistaken for a lack of backbone. Many of the most practical leaders in this book were also deeply principled people. And they remained loyal to their ideals, to their chosen causes and support bases, throughout their careers—although they sometimes expressed that loyalty in unorthodox ways.

What set them apart from more hidebound thinkers was that when the stakes were greatest, they refused to let their principles or loyalties get in the way of their search for solutions. When hard-core ideologues confront a problem, they tend to put their governing philosophies first and consider only the fixes that flow directly from them. The protagonists of this book often did things the other way around. They looked outward, familiarized themselves with the facts of the case, figured out a technocratic solution, and then manipulated the policymaking process to get it implemented. Somewhere along the way they made sure their solution meshed with their convictions—but the solutions came first. As a result, they sometimes served their supporters in unexpected ways: think of Kim Dae-jung helping South Korea's poor by embracing conservative macroeconomic reforms, or Pierre Trudeau advancing French Canadians' rights by increasing the cultural protections for *all* Canadians. While the payoffs weren't always immediately obvious, their constituencies invariably benefited in the end—and so forgave them their political eccentricities.

3. Please All the People—Some of the Time

Although crises often grant leaders unusual liberties and extraordinary powers, successful policymakers still need to be extremely careful in how they wield that power. Effective leadership demands more than boldness. It also requires restraint—often when holding back is the hardest thing to do.

When Canada was almost sundered by the threat of Quebec separatism in the late 1960s, Trudeau could have responded by giving the long-oppressed francophones everything they wanted. Nearly thirty years later, Paul Kagame could have responded to Rwanda's genocide in an analogous way, by exacting the sort of vengeance many of his fellow Tutsis craved. And when Peña Nieto recaptured Mexico's presidency for the PRI in 2012, he could have used his victory to marginalize the opposition, as it had tried to do to the PRI in the past.

Yet all three leaders explicitly rejected such maximalist approaches. Instead, they and many of the other figures in this book acted with surprising forbearance.

The mere fact that they chose to compromise is not, in and of itself, what guaranteed their subsequent successes. After all, politics always involves making deals, and making deals always involves compromising. It was *how* these leaders compromised, and what specifically they conceded, that proved decisive.

I'm referring here to two things. First, all these leaders chose to act magnanimously just when they seemed to be at their strongest. For example, in 2000 Kagame had just managed to stamp out most of the lingering embers of Rwanda's civil war, and he himself had just become president. Yet rather than use his newly acquired strength to subject Rwanda's Hutus to the same brutal treatment they'd visited on Kagame and his fellow Tutsis in earlier years, he spent his capital promoting reconciliation instead.

And note how he did so: by pushing his own people, the Tutsis, to make painful sacrifices alongside the Hutus. Trudeau acted in a similar fashion. He responded to Canada's identity crisis by embracing multiculturalism—a policy that may have denied Canada's Anglos their traditional suzerainty, but also prevented Trudeau's fellow francophones from becoming dominant themselves. Peña Nieto, finally, pursued a related course: in order to convince the opposition to sign his Pact for Mexico, he forced his own party to forsake some treasured legislative priorities.

All three leaders were guided by a shared understanding: that satisficing is key to good management, especially when trying to resolve conflict. Kagame, Trudeau, and Peña Nieto could have responded to crisis by pleasing some of their people—their core constituents—all of the time, or at least by giving them all that they wanted. But because they knew that such winner-take-all tactics would only reinforce the divisions that were wrecking their societies, they chose instead to please all of the people some of the time, or at least to give them some of what they wanted. This meant that no group got everything it demanded. And everyone ended up a bit disgruntled.

But because every group got *part* of what it needed, that unhappiness stayed within limits. The compromises were broadly accepted, the deals stuck—and the countries finally started to transcend the fractures that had caused them so much trouble in the past. We can only hope that President Trump—who, for all the talk about an electoral revolution, actually squeaked in with the narrowest of mandates, having lost the popular vote and having been embraced by just 63 million eligible voters (out of a total of more than 200 million)—now takes this lesson to heart.

4. Govern with Guardrails

One of the things that make idealists in government ineffective, if not downright dangerous, is their belief that humankind can be perfected—or at least, that humans can be trusted to do the right thing most of the time. Appealing though it is, this assumption underestimates our species' uncanny ability to do the wrong thing. Realists don't fight this truth. They accept it, and that acceptance tends to make them more effective leaders. Idealists trust; realists trust but verify.

Such realism played a particularly important role in the careers of many of the leaders in this book. It drove them to impose and embed various checks and limits on the governments they led—and in some cases, created. These statesmen sought to anticipate and control for human error, rather than blithely hope such error wouldn't occur.

The story of Seretse Khama offers the clearest example of how to put this principle into practice. When designing Botswana's government, Khama incorporated several important mechanisms that would restrain not just the power of his subordinates and successors but his own as well. And what made his decision to do so especially striking is that it was completely voluntary. Khama, after all, was the hereditary king of Botswana's largest tribe *and* the father of his country *and* a world-famous and much-loved martyr of the cruelties of colonialism. Thus few in Botswana would likely have objected had he followed the authoritarian path then favored by so many other African independence leaders. Yet Khama rejected that temptation, insisting that everyone in his new government play by the same strict rules. In order to limit individual discretion and block arbitrary decisions, he required policy to be made by broad consensus. To ensure transparency, he insisted that officials hold frequent *kgotla* meetings. And he locked his and future governments into long-term spending plans to prevent the chaotic boom-bust cycles common to most other resource-rich nations. Botswana's democracy, economy, and society all flourished as a result. But these couldn't have been easy choices for Khama to make at the time.

Lee Kuan Yew was a far more complicated exemplar of limited government, since unlike Khama, he made no efforts to constrain his own power. But Lee is nonetheless important for the way he constructed Singapore's anticorruption framework. Unlike ordinary, deterrence-based systems, Lee's did not assume that human behavior could be improved. Instead, it sought to anticipate and prepare for misdeeds in advance, by eliminating opportunities for corruption before it could ever occur. Lee knew that even the best-trained citizens will inevitably stray, and so tried to limit their chances for doing so—even while otherwise preserving Singapore's fairly open climate (at least in an economic and personal, if not political, sense).

Lula, of course, was a proud populist and a democrat, yet he too understood the importance of realism and put it to work when designing Bolsa Família. Part of what ultimately made that program work so well was its simplicity. By giving cash directly to the poor—via electronic transfers—it cut out the middlemen, the bureaucrats who had hitherto undermined the effectiveness of social spending in Brazil either by allocating it inefficiently or by stealing it outright. Bolsa Família dispensed with these intermediaries. Doing so reduced corruption (in this area of government, at least), increased the impact of the money being spent, and enhanced Brazil's democracy by undermining the power of regional bosses who had long used the distribution of government benefits to accrue almost feudalistic power for themselves.

5. MAKE REVOLUTION THROUGH EVOLUTION

At first blush, this rule may sound basic. In a sense, it resembles President Obama's much-maligned second-term mantra: don't do stupid shit.

The seeming obviousness of that slogan earned it great opprobrium when administration officials trotted it out in 2014.* Were Obama's policy truly as straightforward as its critics charge, however, governments would find it easy to follow—when in actual fact, most struggle mightily to put it into practice.

The same goes for the version of the principle we're discussing here, which means something more specific: promote change in humane ways while avoiding the mistakes of your predecessors. Sensible as it sounds, this form of the rule is also surprisingly tough to execute. It requires a leader to forgo the chance to seek revenge for past wrongs (a sacrifice encouraged by Rule #3 as well). Applying it also involves voluntarily tying your hands, and thereby making your work more difficult, in order to avoid the ugly tradeoffs that shortcuts inevitably entail.

Different governments in this book applied this rule in different ways. Under Susilo Bambang Yudhoyono, Indonesia did it by resolving to fight terrorism and radical Islam without stooping to the brutal and extrajudicial methods favored by Suharto. Indonesia's democratic leaders knew full well what this would mean: that the country's newly independent courts would sometimes exonerate terrorist suspects the government desperately wanted to lock away, and that agitators would

---

* Obama's doctrine also irritated pundits and foreign leaders who saw it as an attempt to rationalize his cautious approach to foreign policy—a cautiousness many of them found exasperating.

often remain free to preach hate on the streets because the authorities lacked the legal grounds to detain them. Yet SBY and Indonesia's other democratic leaders decided that these were prices worth paying, and they largely stuck by their commitments.

In Khama's case, applying the rule required replacing Imperial Britain's arbitrary autocracy with a much more pluralistic system. For Kagame, it meant refusing to replace the oppression of Tutsis with the oppression of Hutus. And for Peña Nieto, it meant forgoing the chance to use his presidency to continue the PRI's feud with the PAN and the PRD.

In each case, such forbearance proved politically controversial. In some instances, taking the high road was emotionally traumatic; in others, it was merely unsatisfying. And in all of them, it made policy-making more difficult: it's a lot easier to simply kill, incarcerate, or ignore your opponents than it is to deal with them in a just and open manner. But by refusing to respond to past crimes or to present problems in authoritarian or undemocratic ways, these leaders helped entrench new sets of values, thereby contributing greatly to their countries' subsequent stability and success.

THESE AREN'T THE only conclusions one can draw from the stories in this book; the individual tales all offer narrower lessons as well. But these five are the big ones, and together they answer the third basic question I set for myself at the start.

As close to the end as these conclusions get us, however, this discussion has raised one other, final puzzle that also needs an answer: if the solutions to all these problems truly are out there, why aren't more countries already applying them?

It's not as though any of the places we've looked at were so radically distinctive, so uniquely well endowed by fate, that other, less fortunate polities can't hope to follow their examples.

Nor were their leaders uniquely gifted. It's true that all of them were talented politicians and policymakers—some of them unusually so. But few were clearly marked for greatness at the start of their careers: Bloomberg was fired from his first job on Wall Street, and Lula was close to becoming the perennial also-ran of Brazilian politics before he finally became president. When they and the other leaders in this book were subsequently tested, all of them did rise to the challenge. Impressive as their eventual accomplishments were, however, none required superhuman powers to pull off. I don't buy the Great Man theory of history, and these stories argue against it. What they show is that successful leaders are made—not born that way.

And that suggests that other leaders should indeed be able to emulate them. The fact that so few of them have—and that so many countries still struggle with the terrible troubles highlighted in this book—doesn't mean that progress is impossible. It just means that the leaders in question haven't yet found the wisdom and intestinal fortitude to do what's necessary.

On one level, their lack of guts is easy to understand. None of the solutions described in the preceding pages are easy—quite the opposite. Sometimes that's because they seem so counterintuitive; sometimes it's because they violate deeply held political convictions; and sometimes the problem is that they require statesmen and stateswomen to make painful personal sacrifices and convince their constituents to do so too. All of the answers, furthermore, require that leaders open their minds to strategies imported from elsewhere—something many nationalistic politicians and ordinary citizens simply find hard to stomach.

Reasonable or not, these obstacles are real, and so overcoming them will involve taking serious political risks. Taking such risks requires bravery and strength of character.

That might sound like a lot to ask from our leaders. But remember that this is what leaders are meant to provide. It's what we hire them for.

And given the generally calamitous state of the world today, it's what we *need* them to deliver.

Indeed, they—and the rest of us—are approaching the point where we'll no longer have much choice in the matter. The fixes are out there; now our leaders must act on them. Either that or the doomsayers will win the day, and things really will keep getting worse and worse.

Notes

Introduction

2   **couldn't cover an emergency outlay of just $400**: Board of Governors of the Federal Reserve System, *Report on the Economic Well-Being of U.S. Households in 2014* (Washington, DC: May 2015), 1, http://www.federalreserve.gov/econresdata/2014-report-economic-well-being-us-households-201505.pdf.

2   **72 percent of Americans still think we are in a recession**: Robert P. Jones, Daniel Cox, Betsy Cooper, and Rachel Lienesch, *Anxiety, Nostalgia, and Mistrust: Findings from the 2015 American Values Survey*. Public Religion Research Institute, November 17, 2015, http://publicreligion.org/site/wp-content/uploads/2015/11/PRRI-AVS-2015.pdf.

2   **less than a third of US citizens think**: "Right Direction or Wrong Track," Rasmussen Reports, December 7, 2015, http://www.rasmussenreports.com/public_content/politics/mood_of_america/right_direction_or_wrong_track.

2   **not just an American phenomenon**: "Global Indicators Database: Future Economic Situation," Pew Research Center, August 2015, http://www.pewglobal.org/database/indicator/56/.

3   **the global middle class topped 1.8 billion people**: Homi Kharas and Geoffrey Gertz, "The New Global Middle Class: A Cross-Over from West to East" (paper prepared for the Wolfensohn Center for Development at the Brookings Institution, 2010), 5, http://www.brookings.edu/~/media/research/files/papers/2010/3/china%20middle%20class%20kharas/03_china_middle_class_kharas.pdf.

4   **the average emerging-market growth rate fell**: Robert J. Samuelson, "A Global Recession?," *Washington Post*, September 29, 2015.

6   **residents of unequal communities**: Margot Sanger-Katz, "Income Inequality: It's Also Bad for Your Health," *New York Times*, March 30, 2015.

7   **the global wealth gap will widen:** Henrik Braconier, Giuseppe Nicoletti, and Ben Westmore, "Policy Challenges for the Next 50 Years," *OECD*

Economic Policy Paper, July 2014, 7, http://www.oecd.org/economy/Policy -challenges-for-the-next-fifty-years.pdf.

7   **the richest 20 percent of the population:** Christopher Ingraham, "If You Thought Income Inequality Was Bad, Get a Load of Wealth Inequality," *Washington Post,* May 21, 2015.

7   **America's 25 top hedge-fund managers:** Philip Bump, "The Top 25 Hedge Fund Managers Earn More Than All Kindergarten Teachers in U.S. Combined," *Washington Post,* May 12, 2015.

7   **the number of Americans living in abject poverty:** Aimee Picchi, "The Surging Ranks of America's Ultrapoor," CBS MoneyWatch, September 1, 2015.

7   **the fabled 1 percent:** Faith Karimi, "Wealthiest 1% Will Soon Own More Than Rest of Us Combined, Oxfam Says," CNN.com, January 19, 2015.

7   **so have many salaries:** Nelson D. Schwartz, "Low-Income Workers See Biggest Drop in Paychecks," *New York Times,* September 2, 2015.

8   **the average American wage:** Drew Desilver, "For Most Workers, Real Wages Have Barely Budged for Decades," Pew Research Center Fact Tank, October 9, 2014, http://www.pewresearch.org/fact-tank/2014/10/09/for -most-workers-real-wages-have-barely-budged-for-decades/.

8   **According to the economist Robert Reich:** Robert Reich, "The Practical Choice: Not American Capitalism or 'Welfare State Socialism' but an Economy That's Working for a Few or Many," RobertReich.org, May 20, 2014.

8   **According to Alan Krueger:** Alan B. Krueger, "The Rise and Consequences of Inequality in the United States," speech, January 12, 2012, http://www.whitehouse.gov/sites/default/files/krueger_cap_speech_final_ remarks.pdf.

10   **the federal government deported:** Mike Corones, "Tracking Obama's Deportation Numbers," Reuters, February 25, 2015.

10   **more than 70 percent of them:** "Broad Public Support for Legal Status for Undocumented Immigrants," Pew Research Center, June 4, 2015, http:// www.people-press.org/2015/06/04/broad-public-support-for-legal-status -for-undocumented-immigrants/.

10   **September 2015 report:** Mary C. Waters and Marisa Gerstein Pineau, eds., *The Integration of Immigrants into American Society* (Washington, DC: National Academies Press, 2015), sum-6.

10   **Immigrants are also more likely:** "Let Them In and Let Them Earn," *The Economist,* August 29, 2015.

10   **Were the United States to merely formalize:** Raúl Hinojosa-Ojeda, "Raising the Floor for American Workers: The Economic Benefits of Comprehensive Immigration Reform," Center for American Progress and the Immigration Policy Center, January 2010, https://cdn.american progress.org/wp-content/uploads/2012/09/immigrationeconreport3.pdf.

11   **the OECD estimates:** Braconier, Nicoletti, and Westmore, "Policy Challenges for the Next 50 Years," 27.

11   **conservative members of Congress rejected a bill:** "A Chilly Welcome: Congress Protects America from Canadian Pensioners," *The Economist*, March 8, 2014.

12   **an estimated thirty thousand of them:** "Foreign Fighters: An Updated Assessment of the Flow of Foreign Fighters into Syria and Iraq," The Soufan Group, December 2015, http://soufangroup.com/wp-content/up loads/2015/12/TSG_ForeignFightersUpdate4.pdf.

12   **more foreigners than had fought with the Afghans:** Peter R. Neumann, "Foreign Fighter Total in Syria/Iraq Now Exceeds 20,000; Surpasses Afghanistan Conflict in the 1980s," International Center for the Study of Radicalization, January 26, 2015, http://icsr.info/2015/01/foreign-fighter -total-syriairaq-now-exceeds-20000-surpasses-afghanistan-conflict-1980s/.

12   **And according to Seth Jones:** Seth G. Jones, *A Persistent Threat: The Evolution of al Qa'ida and Other Salafi Jihadists* (Santa Monica, CA: Rand Corporation, 2014), x.

13   **the world suffered 39 percent more terrorist attacks:** Micah Zenko, "Terrorism Is Booming Almost Everywhere but in the United States," *Foreign Policy*, June 19, 2015.

13   **The author Steven Pinker:** Steven Pinker, *The Better Angels of Our Nature: Why Violence Has Declined* (New York: Viking, 2011), 250–51 and 302.

14   **Kristian Skrede Gleditsch has shown:** "How to Stop the Fighting, Sometimes," *The Economist*, November 9, 2013.

16   **an estimated $1 trillion in bribes each year:** "Six Questions on the Cost of Corruption with World Bank Institute Global Governance Director Daniel Kaufmann," http://web.worldbank.org/WBSITE/EXTERNAL/ NEWS/0,,contentMDK:20190295~menuPK:34457~pagePK:34370~piP K:34424~theSitePK:4607,00.html.

16   **corruption is thought to leach about 5 percent:** International Chamber of Commerce, Transparency International, the United Nations Global Compact, and the World Economic Forum Partnering Against Corruption Initiative (PACI), "The Business Case Against Corruption," http://www .weforum.org/pdf/paci/BusinessCaseAgainstCorruption.pdf.

16   **child-mortality rates in highly corrupt states:** Organization for Economic Cooperation and Development, "The Rationale for Fighting Corruption," background brief, CleanGovBiz, 2014, http://www.oecd.org/ cleangovbiz/49693613.pdf.

16   **a long list of countries stands to benefit:** Larry Diamond and Jack Mosbacher, "Petroleum to the People: Africa's Coming Resource Curse—and How to Avoid It," *Foreign Affairs*, September/October 2013.

16   **Papua New Guinea could soon:** Anthony Fensom, "Papua New Guinea:

Riding the Resource Boom," *Diplomat*, February 5, 2013, http://www
.thediplomat.com/2013/02/papua-new-guinea-riding-the-resource-boom/.

17   **Mongolia has discovered new mineral reserves:** "Mineral-Rich Mongolia Grapples with 'Resource Curse,'" Agence France-Presse, April 21, 2015.

17   **Afghanistan has found underground stores:** J. Edward Conway, "How Afghanistan Can Escape the Resource Curse," *Foreign Affairs*, October 11, 2015.

17   **The McKinsey Global Institute has calculated:** McKinsey Global Institute, *Reverse the Curse: Maximizing the Potential of Resource-Driven Economies* (McKinsey & Company, December 2013), 1, http://www.mckinsey.com/insights/energy_resources_materials/reverse_the_curse_maximizing_the_potential_of_resource_driven_economies.

17   **$3 billion in stolen oil revenues:** Ibid., 89.

18   **since Zambia and Nigeria became:** Ricardo Soares de Oliveira, "Avoiding Africa's Oil Curse: What East Africa Can Learn from Past Booms," *Foreign Affairs*, April 16, 2014.

18   **Jeffrey Sachs and Andrew Warner:** Jeffrey D. Sachs and Andrew M. Warner, "Natural Resource Abundance and Economic Growth" (NBER Working Paper No. 5398, National Bureau of Economic Research, December 1995), http://www.nber.org/papers/w5398.

18   **80 percent of resource-rich states:** McKinsey Global Institute, "Reverse the Curse," 1.

18   **according to the academic Michael Ross:** Michael L. Ross, *The Oil Curse: How Petroleum Wealth Shapes the Development of Nations* (Princeton, NJ: Princeton University Press, 2012), 1.

18   **twice as likely to suffer civil wars:** Ibid.

19   **energy consumption:** Robert Kaplan, "The Geopolitics of Energy," RealClearWorld, April 3, 2014, http://www.realclearworld.com/articles/2014/04/03/the_geopolitics_of_energy.html.

19   **the United States sits on only about 15 percent:** Edward Morse, "Welcome to the Revolution: Why Shale Is the Next Shale," *Foreign Affairs*, May/June 2014.

21   **Ruchir Sharma:** Ruchir Sharma, "The Ever-Emerging Markets," *Foreign Affairs*, January/February 2014.

21   **The actual income that an average Chinese family earned:** Edward Wong, "Survey in China Shows a Wide Gap in Income," *New York Times*, July 19, 2013.

23   **a mere 31 percent of the popular vote:** Ananya Vajpeyi, "The Might of the Pen," *Foreign Affairs*, December 17, 2015.

23   **"the White House [never] committed":** Peter Baker, "Promised Biparti-

sanship, Obama Adviser Found Disappointment," *New York Times*, November 11, 2015.

24 **"the single most important thing"**: Major Garrett, "Top GOP Priority: Make Obama a One-Term President," *National Journal*, October 23, 2010, http://www.nationaljournal.com/member/magazine/top-gop-priority -make-obama-a-one-term-president-20101023.

24 **"far from helping the economy"**: Ben S. Bernanke, *The Courage to Act: A Memoir of a Crisis and Its Aftermath* (New York: W. W. Norton, 2015), 539.

24 **"gives a misleadingly diminished"**: Jonathan Tepperman, "The Scholar as Secretary: A Conversation with Ashton Carter," *Foreign Affairs*, September/October 2015.

25 **confirmed fewer federal judges**: Burgess Everett and Seung Min Kim, "Judge Not: GOP Blocks Dozens of Obama Court Picks," *Politico*, July 6, 2015.

CHAPTER 1: PROFITS TO THE PEOPLE

27 **"It sometimes bothers my educated friends"**: Unless otherwise specified, all Lula quotes are from an author interview with Luiz Inácio Lula da Silva, December 8, 2014.

29 **even tiny, benighted Haiti was more equitable**: Wendy Hunter and Natasha Borges Sugiyama, "Assessing the Bolsa Família: Successes, Shortcomings, and Unknowns" (paper presented at Democratic Brazil Emergent, Brazilian Studies Programme, University of Oxford and the Brazil Institute, King's College London, February 21–22, 2013), 2.

29 **a third of Brazil's population**: Ibid.

30 **close to forty million Brazilians**: "Almost 40 Million Brazilians Climbed to Middle Class in the Last Eight Years," MercoPress, June 28, 2011.

30 **Average household income shot up**: Rogerio Studart, "Brazil and the Global Battle to Eliminate Extreme Poverty," *Globalist*, March 26, 2013.

31 **"the hirsute lefty union man"**: Mac Margolis, "Brazil's Lulapalooza Might Be Ending," *Bloomberg View*, September 21, 2004.

31 **"Brazil has changed"**: Mauricio A. Font, *Transforming Brazil: A Reform Era in Perspective* (Lanham, MD: Rowman & Littlefield, 2003), xiv.

31 **"pro-Castro radical"**: Kenneth Maxwell, "Brazil: Lula's Prospects," *New York Review of Books*, December 5, 2002.

31 **George Soros**: "The 685 Billion Reais Question," *The Economist*, June 13, 2002.

31 **The main stock index fell by 30 percent**: "Markets Slump on Lula Speech," BBC News, October 28, 2002.

31 **Investors started dumping their Brazilian holdings**: Tiago Pariz and

Walter Brandimarte, "Brazil Posts Biggest Dollar Outflow in over a Decade," Reuters, January 8, 2014.

32 **"CEO-whisperer, amigo to the middle class":** Margolis, "Brazil's Lulapalooza Might Be Ending."

33 **started hacking away at Brazil's bloated national budget:** Jonathan Wheatley, "Lula Meant What He Said," *Businessweek*, March 2, 2003.

33 **"from policy announcements":** Ibid.

33 **they were soon copied:** Kathy Lindert, Anja Linder, Jason Hobbs, and Bénédicte de la Brière, "The Nuts and Bolts of Brazil's Bolsa Família Program: Implementing Conditional Cash Transfers in a Decentralized Context" (World Bank Social Protection Discussion Paper, May 2007), 10, http://siteresources.worldbank.org/INTLACREGTOPLABSOCPRO/Resources/BRBolsaFamiliaDiscussionPaper.pdf.

34 **Brazil's own experience had shown:** Author interview with Lena Lavinas, December 10, 2014.

34 **Most spent it quite rationally:** Christopher Blattman and Paul Niehaus, "Show Them the Money: Why Giving Cash Helps Alleviate Poverty," *Foreign Affairs*, May/June 2014, 121.

35 **contemporaneous academic research showed:** Christopher Dunn, "Intergenerational Earnings Mobility in Brazil and Its Determinants" (unpublished paper, University of Michigan, September 2003), 21.

36 **most social assistance programs:** Ariel Fiszbein, Norbert Schady, Francisco H. G. Ferreira, Margaret Grosh, Nial Kelleher, Pedro Olinto, and Emmanuel Skoufias, *Conditional Cash Transfers: Reducing Present and Future Poverty* (Washington, DC: World Bank, 2009), 63.

36 **the first time a Brazilian president:** Hunter and Sugiyama, "Assessing the Bolsa Família," 2.

36 **"The opposition said":** Jonathan Watts, "Brazil's Bolsa Familia Scheme Marks a Decade of Pioneering Poverty Relief," *Guardian*, December 17, 2013.

37 **by creating the popular impression:** Fiszbein et al., *Conditional Cash Transfers*, 10.

37 **an investigative report:** Kathy Lindert and Vanina Vincensini, "Social Policy, Perceptions and the Press: An Analysis of the Media's Treatment of Conditional Cash Transfers in Brazil" (World Bank Social Protection Discussion Paper, December 2010), 50, http://siteresources.worldbank.org/SOCIALPROTECTION/Resources/SP-Discussion-papers/Safety-Nets-DP/1008.pdf.

38 **he staffed the new body:** Natasha Borges Sugiyama and Wendy Hunter, "Whither Clientelism? Good Governance and Brazil's Bolsa Família Program," *Comparative Politics* 46, no. 1 (October 2013): 55.

38 **the MDS cut some half a million:** Brian J. Fried, "Distributive Politics

and Conditional Cash Transfers: The Case of Brazil's Bolsa Família," *World Development* 40, no. 5 (2012): 1043.

38   **by imposing rigorous conditions:** Lindert and Vincensini, "Social Policy, Perceptions and the Press," 73.

39   **"the amount spent on Bolsa Família":** "Bolsa Familia Budget Expected to Increase by $2.1 Billion USD in 2013," International Policy Center for Inclusive Growth, March 20, 2013, http://pressroom.ipc-undp.org/federal-government-announced-an-additional-2-1-billion-usd-for-bolsa-familia-in-2013/.

39   **currently costs Brazilian taxpayers:** "How to Get Children Out of Jobs and into School," *The Economist,* July 29, 2010.

39   **the 12 percent the government spends on pensions:** "Brazil's Fall," *The Economist,* January 2, 2016.

39   **a 2011 study by the British government:** Catherine Arnold, Tim Conway, and Matthew Greenslade, "Cash Transfers Evidence Paper" (United Kingdom Department for International Development, April 2011), 76, http://webarchive.nationalarchives.gov.uk/+/http://www.dfid.gov.uk/Documents/publications1/cash-transfers-evidence-paper.pdf.

39   **"a pro-market approach to combating poverty":** Lena Lavinas, "21st Century Welfare," *New Left Review* 84, no. 6 (November/December 2013): 14.

40   **an "innovative welfare program":** Jorge G. Castañeda, "Latin America's Left Turn," *Foreign Affairs,* May/June 2006.

40   **"neither left-wing nor right-wing":** Author interview with Bernardo Sorj, December 10, 2014.

40   **A close student of Lyndon Johnson:** Author interview with Matias Spektor, December 9, 2014.

40   **"financially principled populism":** Wheatley, "Lula Meant What He Said."

41   **doubled the income of Brazil's most destitute families:** Tina Rosenberg, "To Beat Back Poverty, Pay the Poor," *New York Times,* January 3, 2011.

41   **equivalent to eradication:** Raymond Colitt, "Focus on Brazil's Poor Helps Rousseff's Reelection Chances," *Bloomberg Businessweek,* January 2, 2014.

41   **"the single largest ten-year change":** Spektor interview.

42   **recent studies credit Bolsa Família:** Claire Provost, "Social Security Is Necessary and Globally Affordable, Says UN," *Guardian,* February 21, 2011.

42   **the income of the poorest 20 percent of Brazilians:** Sam Jones, "Brazil Fights Inequality with Better Education," *Mail and Guardian,* November 28, 2014.

42   **sharp contrast to the United States:** "40 Years of Income Inequality in America, in Graphs," NPR Planet Money, October 2, 2014.

42 **Bolsa Família deserves a huge amount of credit:** "How to Get Children Out of Jobs and into School."

42 **by helping increase vaccination rates:** Tereza Campello and Marcello Côrtes Neri, eds., "Bolsa Família Program: A Decade of Social Inclusion in Brazil," Institute for Applied Economic Research, 2014, 24, http://www.ipea.gov.br/portal/images/stories/PDFs/140321_pbf_sumex_ingles.pdf.

42 **by decreasing malnutrition:** "How to Get Children Out of jobs and into School."

42 **healthy weight-to-age ratio:** "Brazil and Mexico Combat Poverty and Inequality," *Global Sherpa*, May 15, 2012.

42 **one of the sharpest reductions ever seen:** Alec Liu, "How Giving Cash Directly to the Poor Paid Off in Brazil," *Motherboard*, December 31, 2013.

42 **the number of children forced to work:** Hunter and Sugiyama, "Assessing the Bolsa Família," 10.

42 **graduation rate:** Liu, "How Giving Cash Directly to the Poor Paid Off in Brazil."

42 **improving school attendance:** Alan de Brauw, Daniel O. Gilligan, John Hoddinott, and Shalini Roy, "The Impact of Bolsa Família on Schooling" (International Food Policy Research Institute Discussion Paper, January 2014), 14, http://papers.ssrn.com/sol3/papers.cfm?abstract_id=2405714&download=yes.

42 **the national literacy rate has already risen:** "Pennies from Heaven," *The Economist*, October 26, 2013.

42 **Bolsa Família has empowered Brazilian women:** Hunter and Sugiyama, "Assessing the Bolsa Família," 14–15.

43 **exclusive authority over contraception:** Ibid., 14.

43 **"lead more autonomous and dignified lives":** Wendy Hunter and Natasha Borges Sugiyama, "Transforming Subjects into Citizens: Insights from Brazil's Bolsa Família," *Perspectives on Politics* 12, no. 4 (December 2014): 7.

43 **increased faith in their country's democracy:** Hunter and Sugiyama, "Assessing the Bolsa Família," 15.

44 **Bolsa Família has increased Brazil's GDP growth:** "Bolsa Família Turns Ten," *The Economist*, October 22, 2013.

45 **an election analysis:** Wendy Hunter and Timothy J. Power, "Rewarding Lula: Executive Power, Social Policy, and the Brazilian Elections of 2006," *Latin American Politics and Society* 49, no. 1 (Spring 2007): 4.

46 **"political suicide":** Stephen Kurczy, "Social Workers Channel Indiana Jones to Deliver Welfare Checks to Brazil's Amazon," *Christian Science Monitor*, August 27, 2014.

46 **"by making transfers conditional":** Maxine Molyneux, "Mothers at the

Service of the New Poverty Agenda: Progresa/Oportunidades, Mexico's Conditional Transfer Programme," *Social Policy and Administration* 40, no. 4 (August 2006): 438.

46 **75 percent of adult Bolsa Família recipients**: Stephanie Nolen, "What Would Robin Hood Do: How Cash Handouts Are Remaking Lives in Brazil," *Globe and Mail,* December 28, 2013.

46 **"no one in their right mind"**: Author interview with Wendy Hunter, December 3, 2014.

47 **"as close as you can come"**: Celia W. Dugger, "To Help Poor Be Pupils, Not Wage Earners, Brazil Pays Parents," *New York Times,* January 3, 2004.

47 **"likely the most important"**: Tina Rosenberg, "To Beat Back Poverty, Pay the Poor," *New York Times,* January 3, 2011.

47 **"a stunning success"**: "How to Get Children Out of Jobs and into School."

47 **more than sixty-three countries**: Liu, "How Giving Cash Directly to the Poor Paid Off in Brazil."

47 **at least forty other countries**: Rosenberg, "To Beat Back Poverty, Pay the Poor."

47 **the program did significant good:** James Riccio, Nadine Dechausay, Cynthia Miller, Stephen Nuñez, Nandita Verma, and Edith Yang, "Conditional Cash Transfers in New York City: The Continuing Story of the Opportunity NYC–Family Rewards Demonstration," MDRC, September 2013, http://files.eric.ed.gov/fulltext/ED545453.pdf.

CHAPTER 2: LET THE RIGHT ONES IN

48 **"general agreement"**: Triadafilos Triadafilopoulos, "Dismantling White Canada: Race, Rights, and the Origins of the Points System," in *Wanted and Welcome?: Policies for Highly Skilled Immigrants in Comparative Perspective,* ed. Triadafilos Triadafilopoulos (Toronto: Springer Science and Business Media, 2013), 15.

49 **"You're safe at home now"**: Ian Austen, "Syrian Refugees Greeted by Justin Trudeau in Canada," *New York Times,* December 11, 2015.

49 **about 250,000 newcomers a year:** Jeffrey G. Reitz, "Pro-immigration Canada: Social and Economic Roots of Popular Views" (Institute for Research on Public Policy Study, paper no. 20, October 2011), 3, http://oppenheimer.mcgill.ca/IMG/pdf/IRPP_Study_no20.pdf.

49 **the proportion is expected to rise:** Gordon Nixon, "Canada Must See Immigration as a Competitive Edge," *Globe and Mail,* May 12, 2014.

49 **the top three countries of origin:** Government of Canada data; see http://www.cic.gc.ca/english/resources/statistics/facts2011/permanent/10.asp.

49 **immigration is one of Canada's key positive features:** Irene Bloemraad, "Understanding 'Canadian Exceptionalism' in Immigration and Plural-

ism Policy" (Migration Policy Institute paper, July 2012), 1, http://www
.migrationpolicy.org/research/TCM-canadian-exceptionalism.

49   **public support for immigration in Canada:** "Immigration support by Ca-
      nadians at all-time high," CBC News, October 20, 2011.

49   **only 20 percent of the Canadian public wants to reduce:** Bloemraad,
      "Understanding 'Canadian Exceptionalism,'" 2.

49   **even the country's immigration *critics* favor higher levels:** Reitz, "Pro-
      immigration Canada," 4–5.

50   **Canada hasn't had a single anti-immigrant riot:** Bloemraad, "Under-
      standing 'Canadian Exceptionalism,'" 6.

51   **"feared the peaceful invasion of immigrants":** John English, *Citizen of
      the World: The Life of Pierre Elliott Trudeau*, vol. 1, *1919–1968* (Toronto:
      Alfred A. Knopf Canada, 2006).

52   **"Reason Over Passion":** Jeffrey Simpson, John Gray, and Donn Downey,
      "Pierre Trudeau, 1919–2000: An Unconventional Man, a Conventional
      PM," *Globe and Mail*, September 29, 2000.

52   **close to a million French Canadians fled:** Damien-Claude Bélanger,
      "French Canadian Emigration to the United States, 1840–1930" (West-
      mount, Quebec: Marianopolis College, August 23, 2000), http://faculty
      .marianopolis.edu/c.belanger/quebechistory/readings/leaving.htm.

52   **French speakers remained underrepresented:** Jack Jedwab, "An Anglo
      Elite in Quebec? Not Anymore," *Globe and Mail*, October 15, 2013.

53   ***"Vive le Québec libre!"*:** Thomas S. Axworthy, "De Gaulle and 'Vive
      le Québec Libre,'" Historica Canada, July 23, 2013, http://www.the
      canadianencyclopedia.ca/en/article/de-gaulle-and-vive-le-quebec-libre
      -feature/.

53   **more than two hundred bombings:** Marc Laurendeau, "Front de libéra-
      tion du Québec," Historica Canada, August 11, 2013, http://www.the
      canadianencyclopedia.ca/en/article/front-de-liberation-du-quebec/.

53   **"the greatest crisis in [Canada's] history":** Richard J. F. Day, *Multicultur-
      alism and the History of Canadian Diversity* (Toronto: University of Toronto
      Press, 2000), 180.

54   **The bill formally gave French equal status:** Ibid., 182.

54   **the "Third Force":** Evelyn Kallen, "Multiculturalism: Ideology, Policy and
      Reality," in *Multiculturalism and Immigration in Canada: An Introductory
      Reader*, ed. Elspeth Cameron (Toronto: Canadian Scholars' Press, 2004),
      78–85.

54   **They represented about 26 percent:** Elspeth Cameron, "Introduction," in
      Cameron, *Multiculturalism and Immigration in Canada*, xviii.

54   **"cultural pluralism is the very essence":** "Pierre Elliott Trudeau, Federal
      Multicultural Policy," in Cameron, *Multiculturalism and Immigration in
      Canada*, 401–2.

55   **the first of its kind anywhere in the world:** English, *Citizen of the World*, 142.

55   **Trudeau steadily increased support:** "The Truth About Pierre Trudeau and Immigration," *Maclean's*, June 5, 2013.

55   **an initial funding of $3 million a year:** Bohdan Bociurkiw, "The Federal Policy of Multiculturalism," in *Ukrainian Canadians, Multiculturalism, and Separatism: An Assessment*, ed. Manoly R. Lupul (Edmonton: University of Alberta Press, 1978), 112.

55   **"If Canada is to survive":** Richard Gwyn, *The Northern Magus* (Toronto: McClelland and Stewart, 1980), 243.

55   **funding for "folk dances":** "The Truth About Pierre Trudeau and Immigration."

55   **"French culture was being downgraded":** Author interview with Jeffrey Reitz, July 28, 2014.

56   **an unconnected "chain of ethnic enclaves":** John English, *Just Watch Me: The Life of Pierre Elliott Trudeau: 1968–2000* (Toronto: Alfred A. Knopf Canada, 2009), 146.

56   **"a desire and effort":** "Pierre Elliott Trudeau, Federal Multicultural Policy," 402.

56   **one of Trudeau's main priorities:** "Forging Our Legacy: Canadian Citizenship and Immigration, 1900–1977," http://www.cic.gc.ca/English/resources/publications/legacy/chap-6.asp.

57   **"an underpopulated country":** Day, *Multiculturalism and the History of Canadian Diversity*, 185.

57   **"Canada must populate or perish":** Valerie Knowles, *Strangers at Our Gates: Canadian Immigration and Immigration Policy, 1540–2006* (Toronto: Dundurn Press, 2007), 180.

57   **Canada lost more than forty thousand professionals:** Peter S. Li, *Destination Canada: Immigration Debates and Issues* (Don Mills, ON: Oxford University Press, 2003), 25.

58   **three types of foreigners:** Triadafilopoulos, "Dismantling White Canada," 15.

58   **Asian immigrants were particularly feared:** Ibid.

58   **"Canada's northern environment":** Cameron, "Introduction," xvi.

58   **"to prohibit or limit the admission of persons":** Knowles, *Strangers at Our Gates*, 170.

58   **"an established (and most would say sensible) feature":** English, *Just Watch Me*, 110.

59   **"to prevent aggravation":** Triadafilopoulos, "Dismantling White Canada," 20.

59   **Canada formally abandoned ethnicity:** Knowles, *Strangers at Our Gates*, 187.

59 **any suitably qualified person:** Day, *Multiculturalism and the History of Canadian Diversity*, 185.

59 **Fairclough "was simply not telling the whole truth":** Ibid., 186.

59 **Ottawa would "still give preference":** Triadafilopoulos, "Dismantling White Canada," 24.

60 **Between 1946 and 1953:** Statistics from the Government of Canada, "Cultural Diversity in Canada: The Social Construction of Racial Difference," http://www.justice.gc.ca/eng/rp-pr/csj-sjc/jsp-sjp/rp02_8-dr02_8/p3.html.

60 **Asians, Caribbeans, Latin Americans, and Africans:** Triadafilopoulos, "Dismantling White Canada," 16.

60 **the idea of race-blind immigration:** English, *Just Watch Me*, 143.

60 **the public opposed *any* increase in immigration:** Mildred A. Schwartz, *Public Opinion and Canadian Identity* (Scarborough, ON: Fitzhenry and Whiteside, 1967), 86–87.

60 **more than half of Canadians surveyed:** Gallup Canada poll, October 1966, http://odesi2.scholarsportal.info/webview/index.jsp?object=http://142 .150.190.128:80%2Fobj%2FfStudy%2Fcipo-321-E-1966-10&mode= documentation&v=2&top=yes.

62 **more than $1 billion a year:** Bloemraad, "Understanding 'Canadian Exceptionalism,'" 12.

62 **Canadians' support for the country's generous immigration policies:** Jeffrey G. Reitz, "Economic Opportunity, Multiculturalism, and the Roots of Popular Support for High Immigration in Canada," in *Anti-immigrant Sentiments, Actions and Policies in the North American Region and the European Union*, ed. Mónica Verea (Mexico City: Center for Research on North America, Universidad Nacional Autónoma de México, 2012), 291–94.

62 **65 percent of newcomers to Canada:** Joe Friesen, "Canada to Open the Door Wider to 'Higher Calibre' Immigrants," *Globe and Mail*, October 31, 2014.

62 **Canada's foreign-born citizenry is more educated:** Bloemraad, "Understanding 'Canadian Exceptionalism,'" 4

62 **economic-class migrants consume less in welfare spending:** Brian Lilley, "Immigrants Use of Welfare a Mixed Bag, Documents Show," *Toronto Sun*, January 11, 2011.

63 **employment rate is among the highest in the OECD:** Clément Gignac, "For Canada, Immigration Is a Key to Prosperity," *Globe and Mail*, October 7, 2013.

63 **a large majority of Canada's unemployed feel the same way:** Bloemraad, "Understanding 'Canadian Exceptionalism,'" 3.

63 **what made them proudest of their country:** Jeffrey G. Reitz, "Pro-Immigration Canada," 7–8.

63 **it had climbed into second place:** Ibid., 7.

63   **85 percent of Canadians now see multiculturalism:** Reitz, "Economic Opportunity, Multiculturalism," 302.

63   **the most patriotic among them:** Bloemraad, "Understanding 'Canadian Exceptionalism,'" 7.

63   **"a more open or tolerant":** Reitz, "Economic Opportunity, Multiculturalism," 308.

64   **Canada has the highest naturalization rate:** "Canada Welcomes Record Number of New Canadians," *Canadian Immigration News,* April 17, 2014, https://www.migrationexpert.ca/visa/canadian_immigration _news /2014/Apr/1061/1061/canada_welcomes_record_number_of_new_ canadians.

64   **"laps gently onto Canadian shores":** Bloemraad, "Understanding 'Canadian Exceptionalism,'" 5.

66   **"designed to radically or suddenly alter":** Ibid., 13.

66   **surprisingly progressive steps on immigration:** Alex Castonguay, "The Inside Story of Jason Kenney's Campaign to Win Over Ethnic Votes: The Secret to the Success of Canada's Immigration Minister," *Maclean's,* February 2, 2013.

66   **their party needed to boost its popularity:** Ibid.

67   **the Conservatives had outpolled Trudeau's old party:** Edward Alden, "What Canada Can Teach GOP on Immigration," CNN.com, May 8, 2013.

Chapter 3: Kill Them with Kindness

68   **"facing one of the most dangerous years":** Seth Mydans, "Indonesians at a Crossroads: Democracy or Chaos?," *New York Times,* December 26, 1998.

68   **the nation would burn:** Terry McCarthy, "Indonesia Burning," *Time,* May 25, 1998.

69   **"Indonesian people have been in chains":** Mydans, "Indonesians at a Crossroads."

69   **Islamic parties scored an alarming 36 percent of the vote:** Robert W. Hefner, "Shari'a Politics and Indonesian Democracy," *Review of Faith and International Affairs* 10, no. 4 (Winter 2012): 64.

69   **some 135 million ballots were peacefully cast:** "Jokowi's Day," *The Economist,* July 24, 2014.

69   **doling out most political power to its regions:** Elizabeth Pisani, "Indonesia in Pieces: The Downside of Decentralization," *Foreign Affairs,* July/August 2014.

70   **Today fewer Indonesian Muslims:** "Sharia Do Like It," *The Economist,* April 30, 2013.

70   **Since hitting a high point:** Norimitsu Onishi, "Indonesia's Voters Retreat from Radical Islam," *New York Times,* April 24, 2009.

70   **though their tally improved slightly in 2014:** Ben Otto and Sara Schonhardt, "Islamic Political Parties Make a Comeback in Indonesian Election," *Wall Street Journal,* April 10, 2014.

70   **"If you want to know whether Islam":** Mark Landler, "Clinton Praises Indonesian Democracy," *New York Times,* February 18, 2009.

71   **Islam had traditionally looked different there:** Jeff Lee, "The Failure of Political Islam in Indonesia: A Historical Narrative," *Stanford Journal of East Asian Affairs* 4, no. 1 (Winter 2004): 88.

71   **This blending of faiths, which academics call "syncretism":** Ibid.

71   **the Muslim sultan of Yogyakarta:** Jon Emont, "Watch the Throne: The Battle over Indonesia's First Female Sultan," *Foreign Affairs,* June 9, 2015.

71   **visit the tombs of holy saints:** Avantika Chilkoti, "Indonesia: A Challenge to Tradition," *Financial Times,* August 26, 2015.

71   **Java's famous indigenous form of theater:** Pankaj Mishra, "The Places in Between: The Struggle to Define Indonesia," *The New Yorker,* August 4, 2014.

71   **a reliably incompetent one:** Joe Cochrane, "In a Nation of Muslims, Political Islam Is Struggling to Win Votes," *New York Times,* April 7, 2014.

71   **Luthfi Hasan Ishaaq:** "Indonesian Islamic Parties Head for Poll Drubbing," Agence France-Presse, March 30, 2014.

71   **captured on camera watching porn:** Endy Bayuni, "Can Indonesia's Main Islamist Party Recover from Scandal?," *Foreign Policy,* February 1, 2013.

71   **its blended approach to Islam:** Author interview with Robert Hefner, professor of anthropology and director of the Institute on Culture, Religion, and World Affairs at Boston University, August 28, 2014. All following Hefner quotations are from this interview unless otherwise specified.

72   **growing steadily more religiously conservative:** "Muslims in Indonesia May Be Becoming More Pious, but Not Necessarily More Extreme," *The Economist,* September 10, 2009. See also "Chapter 1: Beliefs About Sharia," Pew Research Center, April 30, 2013, http://www.pewforum.org/2013/04/30/the-worlds-muslims-religion-politics-society-beliefs-about-sharia/.

72   **some 70 percent of Indonesian Muslims:** "Sharia Do Like It."

72   **most of them shudder at the harsh way it's enforced:** Saiful Mujani and R. William Liddle, "Muslim Indonesia's Secular Democracy," *Asian Survey* 49, no. 4 (July/August 2009): 588.

73   **He seemed like a tired old man:** Bob S. Hadiwinata, *Politics of NGOs*

in Indonesia: Developing Democracy and Managing a Movement (London: RoutledgeCurzon, 2003), 81.

73 **he used his office to challenge:** Seth Mydans, "Abdurrahman Wahid, 69, Is Dead; Led Indonesia for 2 Years of Tumult," *New York Times,* December 30, 2009.

74 **she "makes George Bush seem like an intellectual":** "President or Princess?" *The Economist,* April 26, 2001.

74 **Megawati never showed much interest:** Author interview with Joshua Kurlantzick, senior fellow for Southeast Asia, Council on Foreign Relations, August 22, 2014.

74 **Megawati offered them a deal:** Hefner interview.

75 **even serving in East Timor:** Paul Dillon, "Profile: Susilo Bambang Yudhoyono," Al Jazeera, July 4, 2004.

75 **was never credibly accused of human rights abuses:** Ishaan Tharoor, "Susilo Bambang Yudhoyono: The Man Behind Indonesia's Rise," *Time,* July 10, 2009.

75 **his "second country":** Stanley Weiss, "Despite the Bombing: Indonesia's Progress Will Continue," *International Herald Tribune,* August 8, 2003.

75 **was immediately sacked for his defiance:** Richard C. Paddock, "Beleaguered Wahid Sacks 4 Members of His Cabinet," *Los Angeles Times,* June 2, 2001.

76 **"charismatic, hero styles of leadership":** Jane Perlez, "A Cautious Reformer as Indonesia's Next President," *New York Times,* September 22, 2004.

76 **he blasted the notion of a sharia-based constitution:** "Dispense with the Pieties," *The Economist,* May 20, 2010.

76 **The president told Charlie Rose in 2011:** "The President of Indonesia Is Interviewed About His Role as the Leader of the World's Third Largest Democracy," *Charlie Rose Show,* April 26, 2011.

76 **"always protect our minorities":** The text of Yudhoyono's speech is at http://www.appealofconscience.org/d-557/awards/H.E.%20Susilo%20 Bambang%20Yudhoyono%20%20President%20Of%20The%20Republic %20Of%20Indonesia.

77 **analysts often compare to Egypt's Muslim Brotherhood:** Endy Bayuni, "The Political Failure of Indonesian Islamists," *Foreign Policy,* October 25, 2012.

77 *peduli* **(caring) and** *bersih* **(clean):** Mujani and Liddle, "Muslim Indonesia's Secular Democracy," 582.

77 **Suharto and his family had embezzled:** Marilyn Berger, "Suharto Dies at 86; Indonesian Dictator Brought Order and Bloodshed," *New York Times,* January 28, 2008.

77   **he declared that the country would be "destroyed":** "'I Have to Face Many Fundamental Issues': An Exclusive Interview with Indonesia's New President," *Time*, October 25, 2004.

77   **convict and jail some 160 senior officials:** "Interview with Foreign Editor Greg Sheridan," *The Australian*, February 23, 2012.

77   **the father-in-law of Yudhoyono's son:** Gregory B. Poling and Blake Day, "Corruption in Indonesia and the 2014 Elections," Center for Strategic and International Studies, November 7, 2013, http://csis.org/publication/ corruption-indonesia-and-2014-elections.

77   **the KPK even nailed the head of the constitutional court:** "Indonesia President Susilo Bambang Yudhoyono Under Pressure as Corruption Investigators Arrest Top Judge," *Independent*, October 3, 2013.

78   **helped turn Indonesia's moribund market:** Pisani, "Indonesia in Pieces."

78   **the country more than doubled its exports:** Karen Brooks, "Indonesia and the Philippines: A Tale of Two Archipelagoes," *Foreign Affairs*, January/February 2014.

78   **SBY was also accused of turning a blind eye:** Author interview with R. William Liddle, professor emeritus of political science, Ohio State University, August 27, 2014.

78   **when he issued a "religious harmony" decree:** Adreas Harsono, "No Model for Muslim Democracy," *New York Times*, May 21, 2012.

79   **SBY's Democratic Party backed a loosely worded antipornography law:** Cochrane, "Political Islam Is Struggling to Win Votes."

79   **the greatest stain on his record:** Liddle interview.

80   **bringing Indonesia's Islamic parties into the political mainstream:** Jay Solomon, "In Indonesia, a Model for Egypt's Transition," *Wall Street Journal*, February 12, 2011.

80   **fighting in just one province—Maluku:** "Troops Sent After Deadly Clashes in Indonesia's Ambon," BBC News, September 12, 2011.

80   **extremists successfully staged more than one hundred attacks:** See the University of Maryland Global Terrorism Database page for Indonesia, http://www.start.umd.edu/gtd/search/Results.aspx?chart=country& casualties_type=&casualties_max=&country=93.

80   **October 12, 2002:** Brian A. Jackson, John C. Baker, Kim Cragin, John Parachini, Horacio R. Trujillo, and Peter Chalk, *Aptitude for Destruction*, vol. 2, *Case Studies of Organizational Learning in Five Terrorist Groups* (Washington, DC: Rand Corporation, 2005), 70.

80   **202 people were dead:** Sara Schonhardt, "Bali Bombings: 10 Years Later, Progress and Some Bumps Ahead," *Christian Science Monitor*, October 12, 2012.

80   **insisting that JI did in fact not exist:** "Dispense with the Pieties."

81   **a broad new antiterrorism law:** Sidney Jones, "Indonesian Government

Approaches to Radical Islam Since 1998," in *Democracy and Islam in Indonesia*, ed. Mirjam Künkler and Alfred C. Stepan (New York: Columbia University Press, 2013), 117.

81 **Densus 88 (Detachment 88):** Author interview with Sidney Jones, director of the Institute for Policy Analysis of Conflict, Jakarta, September 5, 2014. All following Jones quotations are from this interview unless otherwise specified.

81 **Indonesia's allies also flew Detachment 88 members:** Leonard C. Sebastian, *Realpolitik Ideology: Indonesia's Use of Military Force* (Singapore: Institute of Southeast Asian Studies, 2006), 176n172.

81 **Western states also provided:** Jones, "Indonesian Government Approaches to Radical Islam," 115.

81 **"one of the world's most determined campaigns":** Hannah Beech, "What Indonesia Can Teach the World About Counterterrorism," *Time*, June 7, 2010.

82 **the group has officially renounced violence in Indonesia:** Jones interview.

82 **officers apprehended a number of senior leaders:** International Crisis Group, "How Indonesia Extremists Regroup" (Asia Report, July 16, 2012), i, http://www.crisisgroup.org/~/media/Files/asia/south-east-asia/indonesia/228-how-indonesian-extremists-regroup.pdf.

82 **jailed a total of about nine hundred terrorists:** Author interview with Solahudin, Institute for Policy Analysis of Conflict, September 7, 2014.

82 **only detained terrorism suspects:** Ibid.

82 **numerous suspects widely thought guilty:** Ibid.

83 **Jakarta's use of public hearings:** Ibid.

83 **often share meals:** Hamish McDonald, "Fighting Terrorism with Smart Weaponry," *Sydney Morning Herald*, May 31, 2008.

83 **join them in prayer:** Beech, "What Indonesia Can Teach the World About Counterterrorism."

83 **the campaign has involved setting up moderate *pesantrens*:** Jones, "Indonesian Government Approaches to Radical Islam," 120.

83 **getting prominent local and Middle Eastern imams:** Solahudin interview.

83 **trotting former terrorists out on TV:** Joshua Kurlantzick, "A Muslim Model: What Indonesia Can Teach the World," *Boston Globe*, September 13, 2009.

83 **enlisting everyone from comic-book artists to pop stars:** Magnus Ranstorp, "Preventing Violent Radicalization and Terrorism: The Case of Indonesia" (Center for Asymmetric Threat Studies, Swedish National Defence College, 2009), 6–13, https://www.fhs.se/Documents/Externwebben/forskning/centrumbildningar/CATS/publikationer/Preventing%20

Violent%20Radicalization%20and%20Terrorism%20-%20The%20
Case%20of%20Indonesia.pdf.

84   **one of the most systematic and successful antiextremism initiatives:**
      Ibid., 23.

84   **one of the world's "fragile five" economies:** "Tales from the Emerging
      World: Elections 2014: How Fragile Are the 'Fragile Five'?" Morgan Stanley,
      December 3, 2013, https://www.morganstanley.com/public/Tales_from_
      the_Emerging_World_Fragile_Five.pdf.

84   **43 percent of the population:** Michael Bristow, "Can Indonesia's Jokowi
      Meet Expectations?" BBC News, August 22, 2014.

84   **the chairman and the treasurer of Yudhoyono's Democratic Party:** "The
      Great Unravelling," *The Economist*, February 25, 2012.

85   **no longer count on public or bureaucratic backing:** Kanupriya Kapoor
      and Randy Fabi, "Special Report: Indonesia's Graftbusters Battle the Es-
      tablishment," Reuters, November 18, 2013.

85   **Allegations of torture, unlawful detention, and "encounter killings":**
      Jim Della-Giacoma, "Indonesia's Police: The Problem of Deadly Force,"
      Interpreter, June 18, 2013. See also Tom Allard, "Indonesia's New Danger
      from Within," *Sydney Morning Herald*, September 13, 2010.

85   **experts put the figure at several hundred:** Chilkoti, "Indonesia: A Chal-
      lenge to Tradition."

85   **the son of a carpenter:** Mishra, "The Places in Between,"

86   **as mayor he declined to draw a salary:** Bristow, "Can Indonesia's Jokowi
      Meet Expectations?"

86   **Jokowi made merit, not religion, the core principle:** Jonah Blank, "Good
      Guy Gamble: What to Expect from Indonesia's Jokowi," *Foreign Affairs*,
      July 16, 2014.

86   **"pork-eating infidel":** Tobias Basuki, "First Ethnic Chinese Governor of
      Jakarta Takes Indonesia Forward," *Jakarta Globe*, August 22, 2014.

CHAPTER 4: LEARN TO LIVE WITH IT

87   **the Interahamwe:** Human Rights Watch, "Rwanda: Justice After
      Genocide—20 Years On," March 28, 2014, 2, https://www.hrw.org/
      news/2014/03/28/rwanda-justice-after-genocide-20-years.

87   **trained and amply equipped by its great-power patron, France:** Stephen
      Kinzer, "A Devastating Report on France's Role," *New York Times*, August
      15, 2008.

87   **the word means "the Invincibles":** Jean Hatzfeld, *The Antelope's Strategy:
      Living in Rwanda After the Genocide* (New York: Picador, 2010), 11.

87   **a nation that the World Bank had deemed "nonviable":** Philip Goure-
      vitch, "The Life After," *The New Yorker*, May 4, 2009.

87   **More than 40 percent of Rwanda's total population:** John Norris, "In the Wake of Mass Murder," *Foreign Policy,* April 7, 1994.

88   **Conditions among the general population:** Swanee Hunt, "The Rise of Rwanda's Women: Rebuilding and Reuniting a Nation," *Foreign Affairs,* May/June 2014.

88   **Malaria, HIV, tuberculosis, and other infectious diseases:** Neal Emery, "Rwanda's Historic Health Recovery: What the U.S. Might Learn," *Atlantic,* February 20, 2013.

88   **Four-fifths of them had lost at least one relative:** L. Gupta, "1998 Rwanda: Follow-up Survey of Rwandan Children's Reactions to War Related Violence from the 1994 Genocide" (UNICEF, 1998), http://www.unicef.org/evaldatabase/index_14242.html.

88   **Close to one hundred thousand minors had been orphaned:** "Ten Years After Genocide, Rwandan Children Suffer Lasting Impact," UNICEF press release, April 6, 2004, http://www.unicef.org/media/media_20325.html.

89   **some form of post-traumatic stress disorder:** Stephen Kinzer, *A Thousand Hills: Rwanda's Rebirth and the Man Who Dreamed It* (New York: John Wiley & Sons, 2009), 254.

89   **a land of "confusion, death, and despair":** "Rebooting Rwanda," *Foreign Affairs,* May/June 2014. All following Kagame quotations are from this interview unless otherwise specified.

89   **the number of suspected *génocidaires* was enormous:** Phil Clark, "The Rules (and Politics) of Engagement: The *Gacaca* Courts and Post-Genocide Justice, Healing and Reconciliation in Rwanda," in *After Genocide: Transitional Justice, Post-Conflict Reconstruction and Reconciliation in Rwanda and Beyond,* ed. Phil Clark and Zachary D. Kaufman (New York: Columbia University Press, 2009), 226.

89   **numerous ICTR administrators were accused of sexual harassment:** Barbara Crossette, "On Eve of U.N. Rwanda Trials, Reports of Misconduct," *New York Times,* January 9, 1997.

90   **RPF troops had killed tens of thousands:** Alison Des Forges, *Leave None to Tell the Story: Genocide in Rwanda* (New York: Human Rights Watch, 1999), 1052.

90   **by 2000 the number would exceed 130,000:** Human Rights Watch, "Rwanda: Justice After Genocide," 4.

90   **detainees were "underfed, drinking dirty water":** Clark, "The Rules (and Politics) of Engagement," 297.

90   **it would take about two hundred years to process the rest:** "Rwanda to Use Traditional Justice in '94 Killings," *New York Times,* October 7, 2001.

90   **the cost and economic impact of locking up so many people:** Clark, "The Rules (and Politics) of Engagement," 297.

90 **"There [was] no way to ignore the responsibility"**: Kinzer, *Thousand Hills,* 256.

91 **reconciliation: a somewhat nebulous term**: Geneviève Parent, "Reconciliation and Justice After Genocide: A Theoretical Exploration," *Genocide Studies and Prevention: An International Journal* 5, no. 3 (2010): 278.

91 **"not a rational thing to do"**: Kinzer, *Thousand Hills,* 254.

92 **the six-foot-two general**: Raymond Bonner, "How Minority Tutsi Won the War," *New York Times,* September 6, 1994.

92 **Though he'd been born into relative luxury**: Kinzer, *Thousand Hills,* 13–39.

92 **he named Kagame his chief of military intelligence**: Aimable Twagilimana, *Historical Dictionary of Rwanda* (New York: Rowman & Littlefield, 1997), 94.

93 **it began working to extend both education and health care**: Tina Rosenberg, "In Rwanda, Health Care Coverage That Eludes the U.S.," *New York Times,* July 3, 2012.

93 **it slashed red tape and embraced technology**: Nicholas Kulish, "Rwanda Reaches for New Economic Model," *New York Times,* March 23, 2014.

93 **it created a national ombudsman and an auditor-general's office**: World Bank, *World Development Report 2011: Conflict, Security, and Development* (Washington, DC: World Bank, 2011), 158.

93 **passed a law requiring all public officials to disclose their net worth annually**: Robert I. Rotberg, "Leadership Alters Corrupt Behavior," in *Corruption, Global Security, and World Order,* ed. Robert I. Rotberg (Washington, DC: Brookings Institution Press, 2009), 355.

93 **created a process known as *imihigo***: Daniel Scher and Christine MacAulay, "The Promise of Imihigo: Decentralized Service Delivery in Rwanda, 2006–2010" (Innovations for Successful Societies, Princeton University, 2010), http://successfulsocieties.princeton.edu/sites/successful societies/files/Policy_Note_ID133.pdf.

93 **Such divisions had taken fluid form**: Kinzer, *Thousand Hills,* 22.

93 **Since the Tutsi were the most European-looking of the locals**: Des Forges, *Leave None to Tell the Story,* 36.

94 **formally forbade ethnic discrimination**: Freedom House, *Countries at the Crossroads 2011: An Analysis of Democratic Governance* (New York: Rowman & Littlefield, 2012), 11:567.

94 **stripped all references to Hutu, Tutsi, and Twa**: Marc Lacey, "A Decade After Massacres, Rwanda Outlaws Ethnicity," *New York Times,* April 9, 2004.

94 **"reflection meetings"**: Hatzfeld, *Antelope's Strategy,* 125.

94 **it would abandon its attempts to process**: Phil Clark, *The* Gacaca *Courts,*

Post-Genocide Justice and Reconciliation in Rwanda: Justice Without Lawyers (Cambridge: Cambridge University Press, 2010), 57.

94   **huge numbers of revenge killings:** Author interview with Phil Clark, April 14, 2015. All following Clark quotations are from this interview unless otherwise specified.

94   *gacaca***:** Max Rettig, "*Gacaca*: Truth, Justice, and Reconciliation in Post-conflict Rwanda?," *African Studies Review* 51, no. 3 (December 2008): 25–50.

95   **Entire communities would be required to attend:** Kinzer, *Thousand Hills*, 258.

96   **"one of the most ambitious transitional justice projects":** Rettig, "*Gacaca*," 25.

96   **"This is government enforced reconciliation":** Human Rights Watch, *Justice Compromised: The Legacy of Rwanda's Community-Based* Gacaca *Courts* (New York: Human Rights Watch, 2011), 120.

96   **Human rights groups like Amnesty International also condemned *gacaca*:** Amnesty International, "*Gacaca:* A Question of Justice," December 17, 2002, https://www.amnesty.org/en/documents/afr47/007/2002/en/.

97   **close to two million cases:** Human Rights Watch, "Rwanda: Justice After Genocide," 5.

97   **"wide range of fair trial violations":** Human Rights Watch, "Rwanda: Mixed Legacy for Community-Based Genocide Courts: Serious Miscarriages of Justice Need National Court Review" (May 31, 2011), https://www.hrw.org/news/2011/05/31/rwanda-mixed-legacy-community-based-genocide-courts.

97   **elevated levels of mental disorders:** Karen Brounéus, "The Trauma of Truth Telling: Effects of Witnessing in the Rwandan *Gacaca* Courts on Psychological Health," *Journal of Conflict Resolution* 54, no. 3 (June 2010): 408–37.

97   **"You have to remember":** Author interview with Max Rettig, March 29, 2015. All following Rettig quotations are from this interview unless otherwise specified.

97   *ukuri, ubutabera,* **and** *ubwiyunge***:** Rettig, "*Gacaca*," 30.

98   **"simultaneously one of the best":** Peter Uvin, "The Introduction of a Modernized *Gacaca* for Judging Suspects of Participation in the Genocide and the Massacres of 1994 in Rwanda" (discussion paper, Belgian Secretary of State of Development Cooperation, 2000), 14, https://www.researchgate.net/publication/260399376_The_Introduction_of_a_Modernized_Gacaca_for_Judging_Suspects_of_Participation_in_the_Genocide_and_the_Massacres_of_1994_in_Rwanda_A_Discussion_Paper.

98   **"active engagement between parties":** Clark, "The Rules (and Politics) of Engagement," 315.

99 **"reconciliation naturally promotes":** Hatzfeld, *Antelope's Strategy*, 129.

99 **"Did *gacaca*, in its own terms":** Author interview with Philip Gourevitch, April 1, 2015. All following Gourevitch quotations are from this interview unless otherwise specified.

100 **Life expectancy has risen by ten years:** Swanee Hunt, "Rebuilding Rwanda: Reflections on a Nation Two Decades After Genocide," *Global Post*, December 23, 2013.

100 **deaths from HIV, TB, and malaria have all fallen:** Emery, "Rwanda's Historic Health Recovery."

100 **the highest level of female representation:** Roopa Gogineni, "Rwandan Parliament's Female Majority Focuses on Equality," Voice of America, September 26, 2013.

100 **"the harsh politics of reconciliation":** Hatzfeld, *Antelope's Strategy*, 83.

101 **held positive views about the overall process:** Joanna Pozen, Richard Neugebauer, and Joseph Ntaganira, "Assessing the Rwanda Experiment: Popular Perceptions of *Gacaca* in Its Final Phase," *International Journal of Transitional Justice* 8, no. 1 (2014): 11.

101 **"at the market, we sell to one another without a qualm":** Hatzfeld *Antelope's Strategy*, 83.

102 **"when we realize that we cannot kill one another":** Ibid., 208.

102 **"we get more done in Rwanda than anywhere else in the world":** Hunt, "Rebuilding Rwanda."

102 **"freed the heart and the mind of his people":** Kevin Sack and Sheri Fink, "Rwanda Aid Shows Reach and Limits of Clinton Foundation," *New York Times*, October 18, 2015.

103 **Patrick Karegeya:** "Rwanda's President Paul Kagame Warns Traitors," BBC News, January 13, 2014.

103 **Kayumba Nyamwasa:** Daniel Donovan, "Kagame's Iron Fist Stokes Fires in Rwanda," *U.S. News & World Report*, January 10, 2014.

Chapter 5: Assume the Worst

106 **Edwin Yeo:** Chun Han Wong, "Singapore Jails Anticorruption Official for Misappropriation of Public Funds," *Wall Street Journal*, February 21, 2014.

106 **they almost never take place there:** Alfred Oehlers, "Corruption: The Peculiarities of Singapore," in *Corruption and Good Governance in Asia*, ed. Nicholas Tarling (London: Routledge, 2005), 149.

107 **its debaucherous embrace of vice and iniquity:** Robert I. Rotberg, "Leadership Alters Corrupt Behavior," in *Corruption, Global Security, and World Order*, ed. Robert I. Rotberg (Washington, DC: Brookings Institution Press, 2009), 346.

107   **fought turf wars in the streets:** C. M. Turnbull, *A History of Singapore,
      1819–1988.* (Oxford: Oxford University Press, 1989), 138.

107   **you'd have to pay off the ambulance crew:** Lee Kuan Yew, *From Third
      World to First: The Singapore Story, 1965–2000* (New York: HarperCollins,
      2000), 158.

107   **Lee survived the hard years of occupation:** Lee Kuan Yew, *The Singapore
      Story: Memoirs of Lee Kuan Yew* (Singapore: Times Editions, 1998), 66.

108   **among his tutors was the same Harold Laski:** Ibid., 104.

108   **proceeded to berate the hapless civil servant:** Ibid., 135.

108   **infuriated with the island's complacent and incompetent colonial ad-
      ministrators:** Ibid., 137.

108   **"the percentage, kickback, baksheesh, slush":** Lee, *From Third World to
      First,* 163.

109   **"supine, feeble, self-serving, [and] opportunistic":** Lee, *Singapore
      Story,* 160.

109   **the PAP even accused members of its main rival:** Irene Ng, *The Singa-
      pore Lion: A Biography of S. Rajaratnam* (Singapore: Institute of South East
      Asia Studies, 2010), 279.

109   **"a victory of right over wrong":** Jon S. T. Quah, "Curbing Corruption in a
      One-Party Dominant System: Learning from Singapore's Experience," in
      Preventing Corruption in Asia: Institutional Design and Policy Capacity, ed.
      Ting Gong and Stephen K. Ma (London: Routledge, 2009), 134.

109   **another "undeveloped country of the Third World":** Raj Vasil, *Governing
      Singapore: A History of National Development and Democracy* (St. Leonards,
      NSW, Australia: Allen & Unwin, 2000), 45.

109   **The new country was tiny:** Quah, "Curbing Corruption in a One-Party
      Dominant System," 131.

109   **diverse and divided:** Rotberg, "Leadership Alters Corrupt Behavior," 347.

110   **"Singapore is walking on a razor's edge":** Lee, *From Third World to
      First,* 49.

110   **"First World standards of reliability and predictability":** Lee Kuan Yew,
      "Why Singapore Is What It Is" (speech to the International Bar Associa-
      tion, October 14, 2007).

110   **"different from our neighbors":** Ibid.

110   **without rapid reform, "then verily shall we perish":** Lee Kuan Yew, *The
      Wit and Wisdom of Lee Kuan Yew* (Singapore: Editions Didier Millet,
      2013), 61.

110   **an "absolute jihad" against bribery and graft:** Rotberg, "Leadership Al-
      ters Corrupt Behavior," 346.

110   **the theft of eighteen hundred pounds of opium:** Jon S. T. Quah, *Combat-
      ing Corruption Singapore-Style,* Maryland Series in Contemporary Asian

Studies, no. 2 (Baltimore: University of Maryland Franics King Carey School of Law, 2007), 15–16.

111   **"any other service, favour, or advantage":** Quah, "Curbing Corruption in a One-Party Dominant System," 136.

111   **The law even criminalized bribe paying:** Author interview with K. Shanmugam, September 9, 2014.

111   **POCA created several powerful new legal presumptions:** Ibid.

111   **the new legislation granted the CPIB great independence:** Quah, "Curbing Corruption in a One-Party Dominant System," 136.

111   **Singapore's legislature also granted:** Quah, *Combating Corruption Singapore-Style*, 20.

111   **the bureau was removed from the attorney general's supervision:** Ibid., 23.

111   **the right to overrule the prime minister:** Constitution of Singapore, part 5, chapter 1, article 22g.

111   **"the disinfecting has to start from the top":** Lee, *Wit and Wisdom*, 62.

112   **Lee fired and ostracized him anyway:** Lee, *From Third World to First*, 160.

112   **"As an honourable oriental gentleman":** Lee, *From Third World to First*, 162–63.

112   **"completely incorruptible":** Author interview with K. Shanmugam, September 9, 2014. All following Shanmugam quotations are from this interview unless otherwise specified.

112   **"that the governing elite":** Rotberg, "Leadership Alters Corrupt Behavior," 348.

112   **police officers are required to report:** Robert E. Klitgaard, *Controlling Corruption* (Berkeley: University of California Press, 1988), 129.

112   **CPIB inspectors regularly troll:** "Effective Rules, Procedures Prop Up Singapore's Anti-corruption System," Xinhua News Agency, September 8, 2014.

113   **Prime Minister Lee Hsien Loong formally reprimanded his boss:** Chun Han Wong, "Singapore Jails Anticorruption Official for Misappropriation of Public Funds," *Wall Street Journal*, February 21, 2014.

113   **Political scientists distinguish between two types of corruption:** Robert I. Rotberg, "How Corruption Compromises World Peace and Stability," in Rotberg, *Corruption, Global Security, and World Order*, 4.

113   **an official at the Singapore Land Authority:** Ann Koh and Andrea Tan, "Koh Seah Wee Sentenced to 22 Years for Singapore's Public Sector Fraud," Bloomberg.com, November 4, 2011.

113   **another Singapore resident:** Elena Chong, "Man Fined $3,000 for Offering a Bribe of $40 to a Cop," *Strait Times*, September 26, 2013.

113   **The government also rewards officials who reject bribes:** Klitgaard, *Controlling Corruption*, 128.

114   **it now compensates its officials more generously:** Quah, "Different Paths to Curbing Corruption," 245.

114   **The state also regularly rotates its employees:** Jakob Svensson, "Eight Questions About Corruption," *Journal of Economic Perspectives* 19, no. 3 (Summer 2005): 35.

114   **"the government feels":** Author interview with Simon Tay, September 10, 2014.

115   **the agency's then director ordered his entire staff:** Quah, *Combating Corruption Singapore-Style,* 42.

115   **Lee actually reduced government pay:** Quah, "Curbing Corruption in a One-Party Dominant System," 135.

115   **the country's microscopic geography:** Quah, *Combating Corruption Singapore-Style,* 5.

116   **he admitted to having done "some nasty things":** Seth Mydans, "Days of Reflection for Man Who Defined Singapore," *New York Times,* September 10, 2010.

117   **various safeguards:** Klitgaard, *Controlling Corruption,* 133.

117   **Governments from Argentina to Hong Kong:** Patrick Meagher, "Anti-corruption Agencies: A Review of Experience" (paper prepared for the World Bank, IRIS Center, University of Maryland, August 2002), 14–33, http://www1.worldbank.org/publicsector/anticorrupt/feb06course/summaryWBPaperACagencies.pdf.

118   **"leadership precedes institutional safeguards":** Rotberg, "Leadership Alters Corrupt Behavior," 343.

Chapter 6: Diamonds Aren't Forever

119   **no natural resources:** Keith Jefferis, "Macroeconomic Management in a Mineral-Rich Economy" (International Growth Center Policy Note 14/0105, March 2014), 4, http://www.thcigc.org/wp-content/uploads/2014/09/Jefferis-2013-Policy-Brief.pdf.

119   **There *were* a lot of cows:** Ibid.

119   **"We have no interest in the country":** Daron Acemoglu and James A. Robinson, *Why Nations Fail: The Origins of Power, Prosperity, and Poverty* (New York: Crown Business, 2013), 405.

120   **as of 1921 there were only 1,743 Europeans living in the vast country:** "South Africa Seeks to Annex Two States," *New York Times,* December 13, 1924.

120   **that number would just barely double:** Zdenek Červenka, *Republic of Botswana: A Brief Outline of Its Geographical Setting, History, Economy and Policies* (Uppsala, Sweden: Scandinavian Institute of African Studies, 1970), 25.

120   **"far below an acceptable level":** J. Clark Leith, *Why Botswana Prospered* (Montreal: McGill-Queens University Press, 2005), 24–25.

120   **just twenty-two university graduates:** Daron Acemoglu, Simon Johnson, and James A. Robinson, "An African Success Story: Botswana" (Massachusetts Institute of Technology Working Paper, July 2001), 1, http://economics.mit.edu/files/284.

120   **only one doctor for every twenty-six thousand people:** Charles Harvey and Stephen R. Lewis Jr., *Policy Choice and Development Performance in Botswana* (New York: St. Martin's Press, 1990), 22.

120   **eight kilometers of paved roads:** Quett Ketumile Joni Masire, *Very Brave or Very Foolish? Memoirs of an African Democrat* (Gaborone: Macmillan Botswana, 2006), ix.

120   **the Brits had run Bechuanaland remotely:** Leith, *Why Botswana Prospered,* 24.

120   **"everything needed doing, and there was money for none of it":** Harvey and Lewis, *Policy Choice and Development Performance in Botswana,* 50.

121   **some two metric tons of gemstones:** Author interview with Debswana executives, Jwaneng mine, Botswana, May 13, 2015.

121   **its GDP grew faster than any other nation's:** Leith, *Why Botswana Prospered,* 3.

122   **just two full-fledged secondary schools at independence:** Acemoglu, Johnson, and Robinson, "An African Success Story," 17.

122   **bout of hyperinflation:** Leith, *Why Botswana Prospered,* 103.

122   **famine:** John D. Holm, "Botswana: A Paternalistic Democracy," *World Affairs* 150, no. 1 (Summer 1987): 25.

124   **"The chief provided leadership":** Leith, *Why Botswana Prospered,* 20.

124   **the Batswana took advantage of London's indifference:** Isaac Schapera, "The Political Organization of the Ngwato of Bechuanaland Protectorate," in *African Political Systems,* ed. E. E. Evans-Pritchard and Meyer Fortes (Oxford: Oxford University Press, 1940), 72.

124   **"Ntwa kgolo ke ya molomo":** James Raymond Denbow and Phenyo C. Thebe, *Culture and Customs of Botswana* (Westport, CT: Greenwood Press, 2006), 22–23.

124   **any leader foolish enough to ignore the will of his people:** John L. Comaroff and Simon Roberts, *Rules and Processes: The Cultural Logic of Dispute in an African Context* (Chicago: University of Chicago Press, 1981), 26.

124   **"Kgosi ke kogsi ka morafe":** Leith, *Why Botswana Prospered,* 21.

124   **the tribes became expert at sidelining unpromising aristocrats:** Acemoglu and Robinson, *Why Nations Fail,* 407.

125   **born to rule:** Thomas Tlou, Neil Parsons, and Willie Henderson, *Seretse Khama, 1921–1980* (Braamfontein: Macmillan South Africa, 1995), 30–58.

126 **Their 1948 wedding:** Ibid., ix–84.

126 **"a very disreputable transaction":** Robert I. Rotberg, *Transformative Political Leadership: Making a Difference in the Developing World* (Chicago: University of Chicago Press, 2012), 72–73.

127 **"develop a democratic system":** Ibid., 75.

127 **none of them have managed to capitalize on it:** Acemoglu, Johnson, and Robinson, "An African Success Story," 27–29.

128 **"Our nation is defined by its common ideals":** Tlou, Parsons, and Henderson, *Seretse Khama*, 280.

128 **which at independence was just one-quarter black:** Acemoglu, Johnson, and Robinson, "An African Success Story," 17.

128 **they "called on anyone who would help":** Author interview with James A. Robinson, April 27, 2015. All following Robinson quotations are from this interview unless otherwise specified.

129 **The government made English and Setswana its sole official languages:** Lydia Nyati-Ramahobo, "The Language Situation in Botswana," in *Language Planning and Policy in Africa*, vol. 1, *Botswana, Malawi, Mozambique, and South Africa*, ed. Richard B. Baldauf and Robert B. Kaplan (Clivedon: Multilingual Matters, 2004), 44.

129 **banned the use of racial or tribal categories in census taking:** Acemoglu and Robinson, *Why Nations Fail*, 412–13.

129 **outlawed hiring discrimination of any sort:** Lawrence E. Harrison, *The Central Liberal Truth: How Politics Can Change a Culture and Save It from Itself* (Oxford: Oxford University Press, 2008), 181.

129 **"we cannot remain a stable and peaceful nation":** Sandy Grant, *Botswana: An Historical Anthology* (Cambridgeshire, UK: Melrose Books, 2012), 69.

129 **They also banned the *kgosi* from running for political office:** Holm, "Botswana: A Paternalistic Democracy," 23.

129 **gave the government the sole right to hire and fire them:** Ato Kwamena Onoma, *The Politics of Property Rights Institutions in Africa* (Cambridge: Cambridge University Press, 2010), 94.

129 **the Mineral Rights in Tribal Territories Act:** Harvey and Lewis, *Policy Choice and Development Performance in Botswana*, 114.

130 **"everything . . . had to go through cabinet":** Author interview with Stephen R. Lewis, May 4, 2015. All following Lewis quotations are from this interview unless otherwise specified.

130 **"we were an amalgam of tribes":** Author interview with Quett Masire, May 12, 2015. All following Masire quotations are from this interview unless otherwise specified.

131 **he would only telephone his boss:** Tlou, Parsons, and Henderson, *Seretse Khama*, 274.

131 **the government soon managed to balance its books:** Jerker Carlsson,

Gloria Somolekae, and Nicolas Van de Walle, *Foreign Aid in Africa: Learning from Country Experiences* (Uppsala, Sweden: Nordic Africa Institute, 1997), 18–19.

132 **by 1984 Botswana was producing:** Harvey and Lewis, *Policy Choice and Development Performance in Botswana*, 120.

132 **"There are times I haven't liked it":** Author interview with Bruce Cleaver, May 11, 2015.

132 **"The culture here was forged by farming or ranching":** Author interview with Keith Jefferis, May 12, 2015.

133 **it would hold conferences in local hotels:** Harvey and Lewis, *Policy Choice and Development Performance in Botswana*, 63.

133 **a choice that kept it from hosting Henry Kissinger:** Tlou, Parsons, and Henderson, *Seretse Khama*, 327.

133 **his annual compensation was just $24,000:** Masire interview.

133 **"So they started factoring manpower into the budgeting process":** Author interview with Jay Salkin, May 14, 2015.

133 **multiyear National Development Plans:** Keith Jefferis, "Macroeconomic Management," 6.

133 **any individual official who spends money outside the NDP:** Salkin interview.

134 **investing heavily in human development and basic physical infrastructure:** Keith Jefferis, "Botswana and Diamond-Dependent Development," in *Botswana: Politics and Society*, ed. W. A. Edge and M. H. Lekorwe (Pretoria: J. L. van Schaik, 1998), 305.

134 **such spending has averaged between 20 and 30 percent of GDP:** Acemoglu, Johnson, and Robinson, "An African Success Story," 19.

134 **the country's manufacturing sector grew by 12.5 percent a year:** Harvey and Lewis, *Policy Choice and Development Performance in Botswana*, 159.

135 **eschewing motorcades:** Robert I. Rotberg, "Leadership Alters Corrupt Behavior," in *Corruption, Global Security, and World Order*, ed. Robert I. Rotberg (Washington, DC: Brookings Institution Press, 2009), 352.

135 **a secondhand Plymouth Valiant:** Robyn Scott, *Twenty Chickens for a Saddle: The Story of an African Childhood* (New York: Penguin Press, 2008), 252.

135 **every member of Parliament recently got a $100,000 Lexus:** Michael Specter, "Extreme City: The Severe Inequality of the Angolan Oil Boom," *The New Yorker*, June 1, 2015.

135 **Khama also barred ministers from flying first class:** Rotberg, *Transformative Political Leadership*, 87.

135 **"the president of Zaire's parliament was very angry at us":** Author interview with Festus Mogae, May 11, 2015. All following Mogae quotations are from this interview unless otherwise specified.

135 **"More important than specific legislation":** Masire, *Very Brave or Very Foolish?*, 240.

136 export revenues fell by 64 percent: Charles Harvey, "Banking Policy in Botswana: Orthodox but Untypical" (Institute of Development Studies Working Paper, January 1996), 9, http://www.ids.ac.uk/publication/banking-policy-in-botswana-orthodox-but-untypical.

136 **Gaborone reluctantly decided to stop selling its stones:** Marvin Zonis, Dan Lefkovitz, and Sam Wilkin, *The Kimchi Matters: Global Business and Local Politics in a Crisis-Driven World* (Chicago: Agate Publishing, 2003), 258.

137 **"like eating a dairy cow that should have been saved for milking":** Masire, *Very Brave or Very Foolish?*, 205.

137 **all mineral earnings be used solely for "investment expenditure":** Atushi Iimi, "Did Botswana Escape from the Resource Curse?" (International Monetary Fund Working Paper, African Department, June 2006), 10, https://www.imf.org/external/pubs/ft/wp/2006/wp06138.pdf.

138 **the state already employs close to 40 percent of the workforce:** Jefferis interview.

138 **mining as a share of GDP has fallen:** Keith Jefferis, "The Botswana Development Model Since 1966: Evaluation of Diversification Efforts. What Worked? What Didn't?" (paper presented to BIDPA-UB-FES Conference, "Are Diamonds There Forever?," August 28, 2014), 5, available at http://www.fes-botswana.org/pages/conference-papers/sustainable_development.php. Current figure supplied by author.

138 **"We were lucky enough to have diamonds":** Author interview with Gape Kaboyakgosi, May 12, 2015.

140 **funnel most of their resource earnings directly to their citizens:** Larry Diamond and Jack Mosbacher, "Petroleum to the People," *Foreign Affairs*, September/October 2013.

Chapter 7: This Land Is My Land

141 **US oil and natural gas production were both dwindling:** Edward L. Morse, "Welcome to the Revolution: Why Shale Is the Next Shale," *Foreign Affairs*, May/June 2014.

141 **the United States had grown dangerously dependent:** Martin Feldstein, "Oil Dependence and National Security: A Market-Based System for Reducing U.S. Vulnerability" (paper, National Bureau of Economic Research, October 2001), http://www.nber.org/feldstein/oil.html.

142 **"energy haves and have-nots":** Matthew R. Simmons, "The Peak Oil Debate" (presentation for the EIA 2008 Energy Conference, April 7, 2008), https://www.eia.gov/conference/2008/conf_pdfs/Monday/Simmons.pdf.

142   **"starvation, economic recession":** Michael C. Ruppert, "Colin Campbell on Oil," *From the Wilderness*, October 23, 2002.

142   **"major economic upheaval":** Robert L. Hirsch, Roger Bezdek, and Robert Wendling, "Peaking of World Oil Production: Impacts, Mitigation, and Risk Management" (paper sponsored by the National Energy Technology Laboratory, February 2005), 66, http://www.netl.doe.gov/energy-analyses/pubs/Oil_Peaking_NETL.pdf.

142   **in 2014 its output hit its highest level:** Eduardo Porter, "Behind the Drop in Oil Prices, Washington's Hand," *New York Times*, January 20, 2015.

142   **stop importing crude altogether:** Gregory Zuckerman, *The Frackers: The Outrageous Inside Story of the New Billionaire Wildcatters* (New York: Portfolio, 2013), 3.

142   **According to a Yale study group:** Robert Ames, Anthony Corridore, Joel N. Ephross, Edward A. Hirs III, Paul W. MacAvoy, and Richard Tavelli, "The Arithmetic of Shale Gas" (Yale Graduates in Energy Study Group Report, June 15, 2012), http://marcelluscoalition.org/wp-content/uploads/2012/07/The-Arithmetic-of-Shale-Gas.pdf.

142   **America's four big airlines:** James Surowiecki, "Tanking," *New Yorker*, February 8 and 15, 2016.

143   **spared US homeowners some $30 billion:** Morse, "Welcome to the Revolution."

143   **the shale boom has already reduced emissions:** Mark Drajem, "Fracking Boom Has U.S. Cutting Climate Warming Emissions," Bloomberg-Business, March 27, 2012.

143   **"challenging but manageable":** Roberta Rampton and Jeff Mason, "Obama Considering MIT Physicist Moniz for Energy Secretary—Sources," Reuters, February 6, 2013.

143   **have already cut methane gas leaks significantly:** Kevin Begos, "EPA Methane Report Further Divides Fracking Camps," Associated Press, April 28, 2013.

143   **Fred Krupp:** Fred Krupp, "Drill, Baby, Drill—but Carefully," *Foreign Affairs*, May/June 2004.

144   **Asian oil consumption grew by less:** Michael Levi, "Go East, Young Oilman: How Asia Is Shaping the Future of Global Energy," *Foreign Affairs*, July/August 2015.

144   **the equivalent of a 2 percent pay raise:** "Sheiks vs. Shale," *The Economist*, December 6, 2014.

144   **"the world of commodities":** Clifford Krauss and Ian Austen, "If It Owns a Well or a Mine, It's Probably in Trouble," *New York Times*, December 8, 2008.

144   **hundreds of thousands of jobs:** Ibid.

144   **to a collective tune of $260 billion:** "Shale Oil: In a Bind," *The Economist,* December 6, 2014.

145   **"The gains are going to accelerate":** Author interview with Edward Morse, February 13, 2015. All following Morse quotations are from this interview unless otherwise specified.

145   **the United States should remain:** Alex Lawler, "U.S. Oil Output 'Party' to Last to 2020: IEA," Reuters, February 10, 2015.

146   **was expected to cost about $6 billion:** "Exxon British Unit, Shell Plan $6 Billion North Sea Program," *Wall Street Journal,* May 7, 1976.

146   **It was soon burning through $2.7 million a day:** Walter Sullivan, "North Sea Getting Its Test as Oil Drilling Site," *New York Times,* May 31, 1976.

146   **a combined total of about $150 billion:** Zuckerman, *Frackers,* 69.

146   **"classic Yankee ingenuity":** Robert A. Hefner III, "The United States of Gas," *Foreign Affairs,* May/June 2014.

146   **the US oil and gas industry had long suspected:** Daniel Yergin, *The Quest: Energy, Security, and the Remaking of the Modern World* (New York: Penguin Press, 2011), 328.

147   **A crude form of this technique:** Russell Gold, *The Boom: How Fracking Ignited the American Energy Revolution and Changed the World* (New York: Simon & Schuster, 2014), 76.

147   **son of an illiterate Greek goatherd:** Daniel Yergin, "Your Dot" blog post as quoted in Andrew C. Revkin, "Daniel Yergin on George Mitchell's Shale Energy Innovations and Concerns," *New York Times,* July 23, 2013, http://dotearth.blogs.nytimes.com/2013/07/29/daniel-yergin-on-george -mitchells-shale-energy-innovations-and-concerns/.

148   **Mitchell Energy:** Zuckerman, *Frackers,* 19–26.

148   **"downhole bazooka":** Loren King, Ted Nordhaus, and Michael Shellenberger, "Shale Gas and Innovation Policy: Lessons from the Field" (paper prepared for the Breakthrough Institute, January 2015), 3. Cited with author's permission.

148   **a moment of atomic-age madness:** Holmes & Narver, Inc., *Project Gasbuggy Site Restoration Final Report* (United States Department of Energy, Nevada Operations Office, July 1983), 1, www.lm.doe.gov/Gasbuggy/ GSB000018.pdf.

149   **swapping water for gel would cut the per-well cost:** Michael Shellenberger, "Interview with Dan Steward, Former Mitchell Energy Vice President," *The Breakthrough Institute,* December 12, 2011, http://the breakthrough.org/archive/interview_with_dan_steward_for.

149   **almost twice the size:** Douglas Martin, "George Mitchell, a Pioneer in Hydraulic Fracturing, Dies at 94," *New York Times,* July 26, 2013.

150   **threw the federal government's weight behind this effort:** Michael Shel-

lenberger, Ted Nordhaus, Alex Trembath, and Jesse Jenkins, "Where the Shale Gas Revolution Came From: Government's Role in the Development of Hydraulic Fracturing in Shale" (paper prepared for the Breakthrough Institute, May 2012), 6, http://thebreakthrough.org/index.php/programs/energy-and-climate/where-the-shale-gas-revolution-came-from. See also Zuckerman, *Frackers*, 56; Eduardo Porter, "Behind the Drop in Oil Prices, Washington's Hand," *New York Times*, January 20, 2015; and King, Nordhaus, and Shellenberger, "Shale Gas and Innovation Policy," 7 (cited with author's permission).

151   **it created a tax credit as well:** Yergin, *The Quest*, 328.

151   **the Department of Energy spent some $24 billion:** Michael Shellenberger and Ted Nordhaus, "A Boom in Shale Gas? Credit the Feds," *Washington Post*, December 16, 2011.

151   **"what really made it happen":** Author interview with Robert A. Hefner III, February 13, 2015.

151   **Michael Giberson:** Michael Giberson, "Did the Federal Government Invent the Shale Gas Boom?," KnowledgeProblem.com, December 20, 2011, http://knowledgeproblem.com/2011/12/20/did-the-federal-government-invent-the-shale-gas-boom/.

151   **openly acknowledged the state's role:** Ted Nordhaus and Michael Shellenberger, "Lessons from the Shale Revolution," American Enterprise Institute, February 22, 2012.

151   **"did a hell of a lot of work":** Shellenberger, "Interview with Dan Steward."

152   **"If there is one key lesson":** Porter, "Behind the Drop in Oil Prices."

152   **"marvelously elegant system":** Gold, *The Boom*, 24.

152   **why the United States has so many independent energy firms:** Robert A. Hefner III, "United States of Gas."

152   **this high-tech free-for-all:** Ibid.

153   **only managed to bore about 1.5 million:** Ibid.

154   **Europe sits on about as much shale gas as the United States does:** "Frack to the Future," *The Economist*, February 2, 2013.

154   **The entire region produces no commercial shale gas:** Gregor Erbach, "Shale Gas and EU Energy Security" (European Parliament Briefing, December 2014), http://www.europarl.europa.eu/RegData/etudes/BRIE/2014/542167/EPRS_BRI(2014)542167_REV1_EN.pdf.

154   **Spencer Dale:** "BP Doesn't See Significant Shale Gas Production in Europe by 2035," Natural Gas Europe, February 18, 2015.

154   **Europe's much higher population density:** Paul Stevens, "The 'Shale Gas Revolution': Hype and Reality" (Chatham House Report, September 2010), 25, https://www.chathamhouse.org/sites/files/chathamhouse/public/Research/Energy,%20Environment%20and%20Development/r_0910stevens.pdf.

154 **"popular ignorance overrul[ing] science":** Ibid., 8.

154 **Russian imports account for about a third of Europe's total consumption:** Daniel Gross, "Russia Is Europe's Gas Station," July 24, 2014.

154 **have accused Moscow of funding:** Andrew Higgins, "Russian Money Suspected Behind Fracking Protests," *New York Times*, November 30, 2014.

155 **dividing up a bear hide:** Marek Strzelecki, "Poland Shale Boom Falters as State Targets Higher Taxes," Bloomberg, May 21, 2013.

155 **has up to 50 percent more recoverable gas:** Steven Mufson, "China Struggles to Tap Its Shale Gas," *Washington Post*, April 30, 2013.

155 **China only managed to produce:** China's total shale gas production in 2014 totaled 46 billion cubic feet; see "China 2014 Gas Output Growth Quickens," Reuters, January 13, 2015. In 2013 the United States produced 82 billion cubic feet per day; see United States Energy Information Administration, "Shale Gas Provides Largest Share of U.S. Natural Gas Production in 2013," *Today in Energy*, November 25, 2014.

155 **the same number that tiny North Dakota drilled:** Mufson, "China Struggles to Tap Its Shale Gas."

156 **created new subsidies for shale producers:** Keith Bradsher, "Natural Gas Production Falls Short in China," *New York Times*, August 21, 2014.

156 **waived import duties:** Lei Tian, Zhongmin Wang, Alan Krupnick, and Xiaoli Liu, "Stimulating Shale Gas Development in China: A Comparison with the US Experience" (Resources for the Future Discussion Paper, July 2014), 113, http://www.rff.org/files/sharepoint/WorkImages/Download/RFF-DP-14-18.pdf.

156 **is thought to hold 55 percent of the country's shale gas:** Alan Krupnick, Zhongmin Wang, and Yushuang Wang, "Environmental Risks of Shale Gas Development in China," *Energy Policy 75* (December 2014): 118.

156 **folded together in ridges:** United States Energy Information Administration, *Technically Recoverable Shale Oil and Shale Gas Resources: An Assessment of 137 Shale Formations in 41 Countries Outside the United States* (Washington, DC, 2013), xx–9, http://www.eia.gov/analysis/studies/worldshalegas/archive/2013/pdf/fullreport_2013.pdf.

156 **"a major sticking point":** Richard Anderson, "Shale Industry Faces Global Reality Check," BBC News, April 7, 2014.

156 **fracking is a thirsty process:** Ryan Holeywell, "A Dash of Saltwater Could Make Fracturing More Palatable," *Houston Chronicle*, March 21, 2014.

157 **"Nobody gets fired for partnering with Shell":** Author interview with Elizabeth Muller, February 17, 2015.

158 **But China's market remains very far:** Tian, Wang, Krupnick, and Liu, "Stimulating Shale Gas Development in China," 113–14.

158 **ten years before China produces shale energy:** Anderson, "Shale Indus-
     try Faces Global Reality Check."

158 **which the government quietly lowered:** Anthony Fensom, "China: The
     Next Shale-Gas Superpower?," *National Interest,* October 9, 2014.

158 **"You can forget about the next five to 10 years":** Anderson, "Shale Indus-
     try Faces Global Reality Check."

Chapter 8: Manufacture Your Miracle

159 **a tenth of the population was dead:** Iain Marlow, "South Korea's *Chaebol*
     Problem," *Globe and Mail,* April 24, 2015.

159 **half of all houses on the peninsula were leveled:** Daniel Tudor, *Korea: The
     Impossible Country* (North Clarendon, VT: Tuttle Publishing, 2012), 21.

159 **nine hundred factories:** Gregg A. Brazinsky, *Nation Building in South
     Korea: Koreans, Americans, and the Making of a Democracy* (Chapel Hill:
     University of North Carolina Press, 2007), 32.

160 **the average South Korean male now stands 3.5 inches taller:** Choe Sang-
     hun, "South Korea Stretches Standards for Success," *New York Times,* De-
     cember 22, 2009.

161 **he would blame his small stature:** Chong-Sik Lee, *Park Chung-Hee: From
     Poverty to Power* (Palos Verdes, CA: KHU Press, 2012), 34.

162 **three out of every five citizens were subsistence farmers:** Mark Clifford,
     Troubled Tiger: Businessmen, Bureaucrats, and Generals in South Korea (Ar-
     monk, NY: M. E. Sharpe, 1998), 43.

162 **mostly rice and fish:** Barry Eichengreen, Dwight H. Perkins, and Kwanho
     Shin, *From Miracle to Maturity: The Growth of the Korean Economy* (Cam-
     bridge, MA: Harvard University Press, 2012), 135.

162 **totaled a paltry $41 million a year:** Bruce Cumings, *Korea's Place in the
     Sun: A Modern History,* updated ed. (1997; repr., New York: W. W. Nor-
     ton, 2005), 355.

162 **Washington made its displeasure clear:** Ibid., 359.

163 **"Park was basically illegitimate":** Author interview with Marcus Noland,
     June 11, 2015. All following Noland quotations are from this interview
     unless otherwise specified.

163 **its population ate most of what it managed to grow:** Author interview
     with Dwight Perkins, June 15, 2015. All following Perkins quotations are
     from this interview unless otherwise specified

163 **"military-backed forced-pace industrialization":** Cumings, *Korea's Place
     in the Sun,* 311.

164 **a subject he'd study obsessively:** Chung-in Moon and Byung-joon Jun,
     "Modernization Strategy: Ideas and Influences," in *The Park Chung Hee*

Era: The Transformation of South Korea, ed. Byung-Kook Kim and Ezra F. Vogel (Cambridge, MA: Harvard University Press, 2011), 120.

164   **Korean wages averaged about a tenth of those in the United States:** Cumings, *Korea's Place in the Sun*, 313.

164   *puguk kangbyŏng*: Byung-Kook Kim, "Introduction: The Case for Political History," in Byung-Kook Kim and Vogel, *Park Chung Hee Era*, 3.

164   **"Confrontation between democracy and Communism":** Park Chung Hee and Shin Bum Shik, *Major Speeches by Korea's Park Chung Hee* (Seoul: Hollym Corporation, 1970), 124.

164   **"let's fight while we work":** Ibid., 243.

164   **building schools, highways, ports:** Stephan Haggard and Myung-koo Kang, "The Politics of Growth in South Korea: Miracle, Crisis, and the New Market Economy," 3, in *Oxford Handbook on the Politics of Development*, ed. Carol Lancaster and Nicolas van de Walle (Oxford: Oxford University Press, forthcoming).

164   **the technocratic competence and the can-do spirit:** Hyung-A Kim, "State Building: The Military Junta's Path to Modernity Through Administrative Reform," in Byung-Kook Kim and Vogel, *Park Chung Hee Era*, 103.

165   **Park despised these firms:** Eun Mee Kim and Gil-sung Park, "The *Chaebol*," in Kim and Vogel, *Park Chung Hee Era*, 271.

165   **In Park's mind that made them parasites:** Hyung-A Kim, "State-Building," 94.

165   **Only after the unlucky executives agreed:** Haggard and Kang, "Politics of Growth in South Korea," 5.

165   **Park "coaxed, wheedled, intimidated":** Cho Mu-hyun, "The *Chaebols*: The Rise of South Korea's Mighty Conglomerates," CNET.com, April 6, 2015.

165   **Those who did were richly rewarded:** See Eichengreen, Perkins, and Shin, *From Miracle to Maturity*, and Dani Rodrik, Gene Grossman, and Victor Norman, "Getting Interventions Right: How South Korea and Taiwan Grew Rich," *Economic Policy* 10, no. 20 (April 1995): 53–107.

166   **often getting them thirdhand from the southern United States:** Noland interview.

166   **spooked by a sudden reduction in US economic assistance:** Moon and Jun, "Modernization Strategy," 119.

166   **South Korea needed to move up the value chain:** Haggard and Kang, "Politics of Growth in South Korea," 7.

166   **the notion that refined iron ore could be a source and symbol of national strength:** Byung-Kook Kim, "The Leviathan: Economic Bureaucracy Under Park," in Byung-Kook Kim and Vogel, *Park Chung Hee Era*, 223.

166 **the Heavy and Chemical Industrialization Plan:** Eichengreen, Perkins, and Shin, *From Miracle to Maturity,* 78.

166 **"a proven track record of risk taking":** Eun Mee Kim and Park, *"Chaebol,"* 267.

166 **the "Gold Pagoda Industrial Medal":** Cumings, *Korea's Place in the Sun,* 312.

166 **Park also carefully protected his new corporate champions:** Wonhyuk Lim, "The Emergence of the *Chaebol* and the Origins of the '*Chaebol* Problem,'" in *Economic Crisis and Corporate Restructuring in Korea,* ed. Stephan Haggard, Wonhyuk Lim, and Euysung Kim (Cambridge: Cambridge University Press, 2003), 42.

167 **The move single-handedly kept the company afloat:** Rodrik, Grossman, and Norman, "Getting Interventions Right," 81–82.

167 **he even banned miniskirts and rock music:** Euny Hong, *The Birth of Korean Cool: How One Nation Is Conquering the World Through Pop Culture* (New York: Picador, 2014), 109.

167 **a poll by the newspaper *JoongAng Ilbo*:** Won-Taek Kang, "Missing Dictator in a New Democracy: Analyzing the 'Park Chung Hee Syndrome' in South Korea," *Political and Military Sociology: An Annual Review* 38 (2010): 2.

167 **Park had increased South Korea's literacy rate:** John McKay, *South Korea's Education and Skills Development: Some Lessons from Africa,* Global Best Practices, Report No. 2 (Johannesburg: South African Institute of International Affairs, 2005), 17, https://www.africaportal.org /dspace/articles/south-koreas-education-and-skills-development-some -lesson-africa.

167 **a "competent, honest, and efficient bureaucracy":** Rodrik, Grossman, and Norman, "Getting Interventions Right," 91.

168 **yogurt was a "strategic industry":** Hugo Dixon, "Do National Champions Merit Protection?," Reuters, May 5, 2014.

168 *muneo kyeongyeong*: Tudor, *Korea,* 71.

168 **the top fifty of them accounted for 94 percent:** Marlow, "South Korea's *Chaebol* Problem."

169 **just wasn't very interested in the economy:** Perkins interview.

169 **allowing the conglomerates to virtually capture:** Eichengreen, Perkins, and Shin, *From Miracle to Maturity,* 81.

170 **the first time an OECD member had asked the IMF for help:** Ibid., 275.

171 **Kim had paid a huge price for such principles:** Cumings, *Korea's Place in the Sun,* 396.

171 **a last-minute intervention by a mysterious plane:** Mary Jordan, "Now

Kim Governs After Being Jailed by the Dictators He Fought," *Washington Post,* December 19, 1997.

171 **It took a second American intervention:** Cumings, *Korea's Place in the Sun,* 366.

171 **the "collusive intimacy between business and government":** Ibid., 398.

171 **"democracy and the market economy":** Stephan Haggard, *The Political Economy of the Asian Financial Crisis* (Washington, DC: Institute for International Economics, 2000), 101.

172 **"do whatever it takes to realize politics":** "Words of Kim Dae Jung: Call for Reconciliation," *New York Times,* February 25, 1998.

172 **His election so panicked investors:** Susan L. Kang, *Human Rights and Labor Solidarity: Trade Unions in the Global Economy* (Philadelphia: University of Pennsylvania Press, 2012), 93.

172 **he'd long favored precisely such changes:** Cumings, *Korea's Place in the Sun,* 397.

172 **he went beyond them in many cases:** Eichengreen, Perkins, and Shin, *From Miracle to Maturity,* 82.

172 **To weaken the power of corrupt bureaucrats:** Haggard and Kang, "The Politics of Growth in South Korea," 14.

172 **To rekindle growth:** Ibid., 22.

172 **To promote competition:** Eichengreen, Perkins, and Shin, *From Miracle to Maturity,* 238.

173 **"one of the most significant events":** Haggard and Kang, "The Politics of Growth in South Korea," 17.

174 **"Samsuck":** Hong, *Birth of Korean Cool,* 223.

174 **grow at twice the OECD average:** Jahyeong Koo and Sherry L. Kiser, "Recovery from a Financial Crisis: The Case of South Korea," *Economic and Financial Review* (Fourth Quarter 2001): 25.

174 **to rebound from the 2008 Great Recession faster:** "What Do You Do When You Reach the Top?," *The Economist,* November 9, 2011.

174 **almost never grow by more than 4 percent a year:** Eichengreen, Perkins, and Shin, *From Miracle to Maturity,* 2.

175 **"Transitioning from agriculture to industry":** Author interview with Stephan Haggard, June 10, 2015.

175 **"companies like Samsung couldn't manufacture":** Hong, *Birth of Korean Cool,* 226.

176 **large cash gifts to the Blue House:** Haggard and Kang, "The Politics of Growth in South Korea."

176 **new Internet portals:** Hong, *Birth of Korean Cool,* 6.

176 **25 percent of the venture capital:** Andrew Woodman, "South Korea VC: State Subsidies," *Asian Venture Capital Journal,* October 31, 2012.

177 **States shouldn't even try:** Author interview with Barry Eichengreen, June 12, 2015.

177 **82 percent of the country's GDP:** "South Korea's Confused Growth Plan," *Wall Street Journal,* November 3, 2014.

177 **currently employing just 5 percent of South Korea's working population:** Jack Kim and Ju-Min Park, "South Korea's Unloved *Chaebol,*" Reuters, April 5, 2012.

177 **the most innovative country in the world:** Bloomberg Innovation Index, http://www.bloomberg.com/graphics/2015-innovative-countries/.

178 **relatively equitable:** "What Do You Do When You Reach the Top?"

CHAPTER 9: GIVE TO GET

179 **solidly middle-class country:** About half of Mexico's population now qualifies for the term. See Shannon K. O'Neil, "Six Markets to Watch: Mexico; Viva las Reformas," *Foreign Affairs,* January/February 2014.

179 **the world's most open market:** Mexico has signed forty-four free-trade agreements, more than any other in the world. See Thomas L. Friedman, "How Mexico Got Back in the Game," *New York Times,* February 23, 2013.

180 **He derided his party's old guard as "dinosaurs":** Randal C. Archibold, "In Mexico, a Candidate Stands Out Despite Attacks," *New York Times,* June 11, 2012.

180 **"in the Mexico we want, there is no room for corruption":** Dave Graham and Anahi Rama, "Enrique Pena Nieto, the New Face of Mexico's Old Rulers," Reuters, July 2, 2012.

180 **"*bombón, te quiero en mi colchón*":** Silvana Paternostro, "Beauty and the Beast," *Atlantic,* October 2011.

181 **a "political hologram":** Juan Villoro, "Falla de origen," *Reforma,* January 27, 2012.

181 **Atlacomulco Group:** Nick Miroff and William Booth, "Mexico's Leading Presidential Candidate Is Handsome, Popular and a Mystery," *Washington Post,* May 14, 2012.

182 **"the most ambitious process of economic reform seen in any country":** Author interview with Juan Pardinas, November 6, 2014. All following Pardinas quotations are from this interview unless otherwise specified.

182 **"we have come not to manage but to transform":** Author interview with Enrique Peña Nieto; see "Pact for Progress: A Conversation with Enrique Peña Nieto," *Foreign Affairs,* January/February 2014. All following Peña Nieto quotations are from this interview unless otherwise specified.

182 **hydrocarbon sales account for a full third:** Richard Fausset, "After President's First Year, Mexico Still a Mess by Many Measures," *Los Angeles Times,* December 1, 2013.

182 **"one of the most restrictive regimes in the world":** "Unfixable Pemex," *The Economist*, August 8, 2013.

182 **production had dropped by 25 percent:** Michael Crowley, "Mexico's New Mission," *Time*, February 24, 2014.

182 **lacked the wherewithal to tap its own huge shale reserves:** Elisabeth Malkin, "Mexico's State-Owned Oil Giant, Pemex, Is in Uncharted Waters," *New York Times*, October 28, 2014.

182 **80 percent of the nation's landlines and 75 percent of its broadband hookups:** "Let Mexico's Moguls Battle," *The Economist*, February 4, 2012.

182 **Less than half of the country's children were graduating from high school:** Michael Weissenstein, "Mexico Education Reform Passed by Senate, Looks to Remake Public School System," *Huffington Post*, September 4, 2013.

183 **the least effective in all of Latin America:** "The Siesta Congress," *The Economist*, January 21, 2012.

183 **"a common feeling that we needed to do something different":** Author interview with Luis Videgaray, November 5, 2014. All following Videgaray quotations are from this interview unless otherwise specified.

183 **"They said to themselves":** Author interview with Shannon O'Neil, October 30, 2014.

184 **"We had to wait sixty-one years":** Author interview with Gustavo Madero, November 4, 2014. All following Madero quotations are from this interview unless otherwise specified.

184 **"We had two avenues":** Author interview with Santiago Creel, November 6, 2014. All following Creel quotations are from this interview unless otherwise specified.

184 **"six years of confrontation":** Author interview with Jesús Zambrano, November 5, 2014. All following Zambrano quotations are from this interview unless otherwise specified.

185 **"monopolist firms, drug traffickers [and] the unions":** Juan Montes, "How Mexico Ended Political Gridlock," *Wall Street Journal*, August 15, 2013.

185 **"We had to overcome a very old maxim":** Author interview with Jesús Ortega, November 5, 2014. All following Ortega quotations are from this interview unless otherwise specified.

185 **"all three parties felt":** Author interview with Aurelio Nuño, November 4, 2014.

186 **Peña Nieto was "open to dialogue":** Graham and Rama, "Enrique Pena Nieto."

186 **Zambrano told an old friend in the PRI:** Montes, "How Mexico Ended Political Gridlock."

187 **the intimate domestic setting for the talks:** Ibid.

187 **"nothing is agreed until all is agreed":** Ibid.

189 **"substituted unelected leaders for Congress":** Author interview with Ernesto Cordero, November 3, 2014.

189 **"would have made the founding fathers turn in their graves":** Author interview with Luis Rubio, November 3, 2014.

189 **The ultimate education reform:** Fausset, "After President's First Year."

190 **generally with 80 percent legislative support:** Dave Graham, "Mexican Reform Drive Bogged Down by Opposition Strife," Reuters, April 28, 2014.

190 **they even increased tariffs on junk food:** Sarah Boseley, "Mexico to Tackle Obesity with Taxes on Junk Food and Sugary Drinks," *Guardian,* November 1, 2013.

190 **ever since President Lázaro Cárdenas nationalized the sector:** Joshua Partlow and Nick Miroff, "Mexican Senate Approves Changes to the Oil Industry," *Washington Post,* December 11, 2013.

190 **state control of the sector and the lack of competition:** Pamela K. Starr, "Mexico's Problematic Reforms," *Current History* 113, no. 760 (February 2014): 54.

191 **Peña Nieto formally announced the Pact's completion:** Enrique Peña Nieto, "Our Reform Programme Will Build a Better Future for Mexico," *Financial Times,* August 20, 2014.

192 **"Mexico is trying to do a lot of stuff":** Author interview with Pamela Starr, October 30, 2014.

192 **angry businesses decided to sit on their hands:** Rubio interview.

192 **46 percent of whom still live at or beneath the poverty level:** "Mexican Government Says Poverty Rate Rose to 46.2 Percent in 2014," Reuters, July 23, 2015.

192 **a lackluster response to Mexico's first open oil exploration auction:** Laurent Thomet, "Few Big Foreign Firms Bid in Mexico's First Oil Auction," Agence France-Presse, July 15, 2015.

192 **won't arrive for another year or two:** Elisabeth Malkin, "In Mexico Oil Market, Mood Moves from Excited to Anxious," *New York Times,* March 13, 2015.

193 **"encourage innovation":** Franklin Templeton Investments, "Mexico's Road to Reform," June 18, 2014, http://mobius.blog.franklintempleton.com/2014/06/18/mexicos-road-reform/.

193 **Foreign investment rose dramatically in 2013:** Damien Cave, "In Middle of Mexico, a Middle Class Rises," *New York Times,* November 18, 2013.

193 **Mexico's government bonds earned an "A" rating:** Erin McCarthy and Anthony Harrup, "Moody's Upgrades Mexico Bond Ratings; Government Bonds Lifted to A3, a Notch Further into Investment-Grade," *Wall Street Journal,* February 5, 2014.

193 **New gas pipelines from the United States:** "A New Mexican Revolution."

193 **homicides declined by 29 percent:** Whitney Eulich, "Mexico's Missing Students: Will Case Prove a Tipping Point?," *Christian Science Monitor,* November 6, 2014.

194 **drug-related deaths spiked in some regions:** Starr, "Mexico's Problematic Reforms," 56.

194 **kidnappings and extortion increased:** Fausset, "After President's First Year."

194 **the couple had grown concerned:** "Missing Mexico Students: Iguala Mayor 'Ordered Attack,'" BBC News, October 23, 2014.

194 **one hundred thousand people have been killed by the cartels:** "Law and Order in Mexico," *New York Times,* November 11, 2014.

194 **a $7 million mansion:** Jo Tuckman, "Mexican President Enrique Peña Nieto Faces Outcry over £4.4M Mansion," *Guardian,* November 10, 2014.

194 **Similar allegations were soon made:** Jorge Ramos, "Mexico: Three Houses, One Ostrich," *Fusion,* January 27, 2015.

195 **take a number of substantial steps to address them:** Jude Webber, "Mexico to Reform Police and Justice Systems," *Financial Times,* November 27, 2014.

195 **National Anticorruption System:** Shannon K. O'Neil, "Mexico's Fight Against Corruption," *Development Channel,* Council on Foreign Relations, May 5, 2015, http://blogs.cfr.org/development-channel/2015/05/05/mexicos-fight-against-corruption/.

195 **had been appointed by Peña Nieto himself:** Rafa Fernandez De Castro, "Government Probe Clears Mexican President and First Lady of Wrongdoing in Housing Scandal," *Fusion,* August 21, 2015.

Chapter 10: DIY Defense

199 **Bush and his top advisers had brushed off explicit warnings:** "Two Months Before 9/11, an Urgent Warning to Rice," *Washington Post,* October 1, 2006.

199 **"gave little guidance to executive branch agencies":** National Commission on Terrorist Attacks upon the United States, *The 9/11 Commission Report,* 106, http://www.9-11commission.gov/report/911Report.pdf.

200 **"I'd seen the federal government up close":** Author interview with Ray Kelly, April 4, 2014. All following Kelly quotations are from this interview unless otherwise specified.

201 **"secretary of defense, head of the CIA":** Len Levitt, "Ray Kelly: Things Falling Apart," *Huffington Post,* July 1, 2013.

201 **had cost the city some 140,000 jobs:** Lydia Polgreen, "Study Confirms 9/11 Impact on New York City Economy," *New York Times,* June 30, 2004.

201 **the city's comptroller would estimate New York's total economic losses:** Michael Cooper, "Economic Anguish of 9/11 Is Detailed by Comptroller," *New York Times,* September 5, 2002.

201 **its biggest deficit in thirty years:** Craig Horowitz, "The NYPD's War on Terror," *New York,* February 3, 2003.

201 **"didn't know what was going on in our own city":** Ibid.

201 **But the FBI and CIA gave the cops such a runaround:** Benjamin R. Barber, *If Mayors Ruled the World: Dysfunctional Nations, Rising Cities* (New Haven, CT: Yale University Press, 2013), 107.

202 **"The police could joke about the Feds":** Christopher Dickey, *Securing the City: Inside America's Best Counterterror Force—the NYPD* (New York: Simon & Schuster, 2009), 40.

202 **"When the FBI obtained information on a possible threat":** Thomas A. Reppetto, *Battleground New York City: Countering Spies, Saboteurs, and Terrorists Since 1861* (Washington, DC: Potomac Books, 2012), 237.

202 **the FBI hadn't shown the files to anyone in the NYPD:** Michael A. Sheehan, *Crush the Cell: How to Defeat Terrorism Without Terrorizing Ourselves* (New York: Three Rivers Press, 2008), 185.

202 **He sent one hundred cops:** Horowitz, "NYPD's War on Terror."

203 **Kelly's pushiness:** Ibid.

203 **the plan also worked:** Sheehan, *Crush the Cell,* 171.

203 **merely an "escort service":** Horowitz, "NYPD's War on Terror."

203 **a job other cops derisively referred to as coat holding:** Reppetto, *Battleground New York City,* 60.

203 **"It was like putting tires on a speeding car":** Dickey, *Securing the City,* 37.

204 **Their job was to serve as a sort of in-house brain trust:** Alan Feuer, "The Terror Translators," *New York Times,* September 17, 2010.

204 **Operation Nexus:** William K. Rashbaum, "Terror Makes All the World a Beat for New York Police," *New York Times,* July 15, 2002.

204 **forced the first redesign of the Freedom Tower:** William K. Rashbaum, "City to Lose Man Who Led Terror Fight," *New York Times,* May 6, 2006.

204 **It initiated the now-familiar bag checks:** Sheehan, *Crush the Cell,* 238–39.

204 **"part think tank, part detective agency":** Lydia Khalil, "Is New York a Counterterrorism Model?," Council on Foreign Relations, September 10, 2009, http://www.cfr.org/united-states/new-york-counterterrorism-model /p20174.

205 **"for 30 years, [the police] measured":** Robert Keough, "Bill Bratton on the New Crime Paradigm," *CommonWealth,* Winter 2002.

205 **had been treated as isolated events:** Paul Howard and Mark Riebling, eds., *Hard Won Lessons: Problem-Solving Principles for Local Police* (New

York: Manhattan Institute for Policy Research, May 2005), 2–3, http://www.manhattan-institute.org/pdf/scr_02.pdf.

206 **they subsequently blocked other American cities:** Michael A. Sheehan, "The Hatfields and McCoys of Counterterrorism," *New York Times*, September 26, 2009.

206 **"Do you think anybody in Washington has the balls":** William Finnegan, "The Terrorism Beat: How Is the NYPD Defending the City?" *The New Yorker*, July 25, 2005.

206 **New York was able to get an officer on the ground:** Sheehan, *Crush the Cell*, 179.

206 **a New York detective was already riding the system:** Ibid., 239.

206 **Washington gave Wyoming seven times as much funding:** Edward Wyatt, "Wyoming Insists It Needs Its Share of Terror Funds," *New York Times*, June 1, 2004.

206 **Congress actually cut antiterror grants to New York City:** Eric Lipton, "Homeland Security Grants to New York Slashed," *New York Times*, May 31, 2006.

207 **"We're still defending the city pretty much on our own dime":** Finnegan, "Terrorism Beat."

207 **the smallest "air gap between information and action":** Ibid.

207 **"I thought we discussed this already":** Sheehan, *Crush the Cell*, 231–32.

207 **"tomorrow is zero hour":** Daniel Klaidman, "Lost in Translation," *Newsweek*, October 26, 2003.

208 **Almost all aspiring agents with dual citizenship:** Tim Starks, "Need Linguists? Call the NYPD," *CQ Weekly*, November 16, 2009.

208 **90 percent of those hoping to work as translators:** Klaidman, "Lost In Translation."

208 **sixty fluent Arabic speakers:** Dickey, *Securing the City*, 140.

208 **certified in fifty-six languages:** Starks, "Need Linguists?"

208 **the FBI, the CIA, the Secret Service:** "NYPD's Foreign Language Outreach," http://www.nyc.gov/html/nypd/html/news/news_foreign_lang_outreach.shtml.

208 **"cutting-edge" security operation:** Finnegan, "Terrorism Beat."

208 **it was recently shut down:** Matt Apuzzo and Joseph Goldstein, "New York Drops Unit That Spied on Muslims," *New York Times*, April 15, 2014.

209 **"the mayors of this country":** Hunter Walker, "Mayor Bloomberg: 'I Have My Own Army,'" *Observer*, November 30, 2011.

210 **New York City had already made impressive strides:** *PlaNYC: Progress Report 2014*, 24, http://www.nyc.gov/html/planyc2030/downloads/pdf/140422_PlaNYCP-Report_FINAL_Web.pdf.

210 **"We saw that there was no possible way":** Author interview with Dan Doctoroff, May 20, 2004. All following Doctoroff quotations are from this interview unless otherwise specified.

210 **the rail extension would have met a "terminal death":** Barbara Goldberg, "NYC Subway Extension May Transform Manhattan Neighborhood," Reuters, December 18, 2014.

211 **the city lost thirty-six thousand Wall Street jobs:** Bruce Katz and Jennifer Bradley, *The Metropolitan Revolution: How Cities and Metros Are Fixing Our Broken Politics and Fragile Economy* (Washington, DC: Brookings Institution Press, 2013), 18.

211 **tens of thousands of new construction jobs:** Richard Pérez-Peña, "Cornell Alumnus Is Behind $350 Million Gift to Build Science School in City," *New York Times*, December 19, 2011.

211 **will increase the number of engineering graduate students:** Eric P. Newcomer, "Columbia Gets $15 Million to Expand a School," *New York Times*, July 30, 2012.

213 **"Unlike most new campuses":** Author interview with Seth Pinsky, March 25, 2014.

213 **these took the form of cheap leases for city buildings:** Newcomer, "Columbia Gets $15 Million to Expand a School."

215 **Bloomberg "believed you get the data":** Jonathan Lemire, "Michael Bloomberg Reshaped New York City, but Leaves Behind a Debated Legacy," Associated Press, December 14, 2013.

215 **Bloomberg "never seemed quite to get the outrage":** Barber, *If Mayors Ruled the World*, 26.

216 **New York "cannot wait for Washington to act":** Michael M. Grynbaum and Kirk Semple, "De Blasio Plans a Minimum Wage and City ID Cards," *New York Times*, February 10, 2014.

216 **"exactly the kind of challenge":** "Remarks by the President in Announcing the Clean Power Plan," White House, August 3, 2015.

Conclusion

222 **"If it works, we do it":** Author interview with Stephen R. Lewis, May 4, 2015.

References

Acemoglu, Daron, and James A. Robinson. *Why Nations Fail: The Origins of Power, Prosperity, and Poverty.* New York: Crown Business, 2012.

Acemoglu, Daron, Simon Johnson, and James A. Robinson. "An African Success Story: Botswana." Massachusetts Institute of Technology Working Paper, July 2001. http://economics.mit.edu/files/284.

Ames, Robert, Anthony Corridore, Joel N. Ephross, Edward A. Hirs III, Paul W. MacAvoy, and Richard Tavelli. "The Arithmetic of Shale Gas." Yale Graduates in Energy Study Group Report, June 15, 2012. http://marcellus coalition.org/wp-content/uploads/2012/07/The-Arithmetic-of-Shale -Gas.pdf.

Amnesty International. "*Gacaca:* A Question of Justice." December 17, 2002. https://www.amnesty.org/en/documents/afr47/007/2002/en/.

Apuzzo, Matt, and Adam Goldman. *Enemies Within: Inside the NYPD's Secret Spying Unit and bin Laden's Final Plot Against America.* New York: Touchstone, 2013.

Arnold, Catherine, Tim Conway, and Matthew Greenslade. "Cash Transfers Evidence Paper." United Kingdom Department for International Development, April 2011. http://webarchive.nationalarchives.gov.uk/+/http:/ www.dfid.gov.uk/Documents/publications1/cash-transfers-evidence paper.pdf.

Barber, Benjamin R. *If Mayors Ruled the World: Dysfunctional Nations, Rising Cities.* New Haven, CT: Yale University Press, 2013.

Barr, Michael D. *Lee Kuan Yew: The Beliefs Behind the Man.* Washington, DC: Georgetown University Press, 2000.

Bastagli, Francesca. "Poverty, Inequality and Public Cash Transfers: Lessons from Latin America." Paper presented at ERD Conference on Experiences and Lessons from Social Protection Programmes Across the Developing Word, Paris, France, June 17–18, 2010. http://eprints.lse.ac.uk/36840/1/ Poverty%20inequality%20and%20public%20cash%20transfers%20 (lsero).pdf.

Bernanke, Ben. *The Courage to Act: A Memoir of a Crisis and Its Aftermath*. New York: W. W. Norton, 2015.

Bloemraad, Irene. "Understanding 'Canadian Exceptionalism' in Immigration and Pluralism Policy." Migration Policy Institute, July 2012. http://www .migrationpolicy.org/research/TCM-canadian-exceptionalism.

Board of Governors of the Federal Reserve System. *Report on the Economic Well-Being of U.S. Households in 2014*. Washington, DC: May 2015. http:// www.federalreserve.gov/econresdata/2014-report-economic-well-being -us-households-201505.pdf.

Braconier, Henrik, Giuseppe Nicoletti, and Ben Westmore. "Policy Challenges for the Next 50 Years." Paris: OECD Publishing, 2014. http://www.oecd .org/economy/Policy-challenges-for-the-next-fifty-years.pdf.

Brazinsky, Gregg A. *Nation Building in South Korea: Koreans, Americans, and the Making of a Democracy*. Chapel Hill: University of North Carolina Press, 2007.

Brounéus, Karen. "The Trauma of Truth Telling: Effects of Witnessing in the Rwandan *Gacaca* Courts on Psychological Health." *Journal of Conflict Resolution* 54, no. 3 (2010): 408–37.

Burgis, Tom. *The Looting Machine: Warlords, Oligarchs, Corporations, Smugglers, and the Theft of Africa's Wealth*. New York: Public Affairs, 2015.

Cameron, Elspeth. "Introduction." In Cameron, *Multiculturalism and Immigration in Canada*, xv–xxiv.

———, ed. *Multiculturalism and Immigration in Canada: An Introductory Reader*. Toronto: Canadian Scholars' Press, 2004.

Campello, Tereza, and Marcello Côrtes Neri, eds. "Bolsa Família Program: A Decade of Social Inclusion in Brazil." Institute for Applied Economic Research, 2014, 24. http://www.ipea.gov.br/portal/images/stories/ PDFs/140321_pbf_sumex_ingles.pdf.

Carlsson, Jerker, Gloria Somolekae, and Nicolas Van de Walle. *Foreign Aid in Africa: Learning from Country Experiences*. Uppsala, Sweden: Nordic Africa Institute, 1997.

Červenka, Zdenek. *Republic of Botswana: A Brief Outline of Its Geographical Setting, History, Economy and Policies*. Uppsala, Sweden: Scandinavian Institute of African Studies, 1970.

Chang, Sea-jin. *Financial Crisis and Transformation of Korean Business Groups: The Rise and Fall of Chaebol*. Cambridge: Cambridge University Press, 2003.

Chung, Young-Iob. *South Korea in the Fast Lane: Economic Development and Capital Formation*. Oxford: Oxford University Press, 2007.

Clark, Phil. *The Gacaca Courts, Post-Genocide Justice and Reconciliation in Rwanda: Justice Without Lawyers*. Cambridge: Cambridge University Press, 2010.

———. "The Rules (and Politics) of Engagement: The *Gacaca* Courts and Post-Genocide Justice, Healing and Reconciliation in Rwanda." In *After Geno-*

cide: Transitional Justice, Post-Conflict Reconstruction and Reconciliation in Rwanda and Beyond, edited by Phil Clark and Zachary D. Kaufman, 297-319. New York: Columbia University Press, 2009.

Clifford, Mark L. *Troubled Tiger: Businessmen, Bureaucrats, and Generals in South Korea.* Armonk, NY: M. E. Sharpe, 1998.

Comaroff, John L., and Simon Roberts. *Rules and Processes: The Cultural Logic of Dispute in an African Context.* Chicago: University of Chicago Press, 1981.

Cook, Amelia, and Jeremy Sarkin. "Is Botswana the Miracle of Africa? Democracy, the Rule of Law, and Human Rights Versus Economic Development." *Transnational Law and Contemporary Problems* 19, no. 453 (2010): 453-89.

Crisafulli, Patricia, and Andrea Redmond. *Rwanda, Inc.: How a Devastated Nation Became an Economic Model for the Developing World.* New York: Palgrave Macmillan, 2012.

Cumings, Bruce. *Korea's Place in the Sun: A Modern History.* Reprint, New York: W. W. Norton, 2005.

Day, Richard J. F. *Multiculturalism and the History of Canadian Diversity.* Toronto: University of Toronto Press, 2000.

De Brauw, Alan, Daniel O. Gilligan, John Hoddinott, and Shalini Roy. "The Impact of Bolsa Família on Schooling." International Food Policy Research Institute Discussion Paper, January 2014. http://papers.ssrn.com/sol3/papers.cfm?abstract_id=2405714&download=yes.

Denbow, James, and Phenyo C. Thebe. *Culture and Customs of Botswana.* Westport, CT: Greenwood Press, 2006.

Des Forges, Alison. *Leave None to Tell the Story: Genocide in Rwanda.* New York: Human Rights Watch, 1999.

Díaz Langou, Gala, and Paula Forteza. "Validating One of the World's Largest Conditional Cash Transfer Programmes: A Case Study on How an Impact Evaluation of Brazil's Bolsa Família Programme Helped Silence Its Critics and Improve Policy." International Initiative for Impact Evaluation Working Paper, August 2012. http://www.3ieimpact.org/media/filer_public/2012/11/30/wp-_16_brazil_case_study_-_final.pdf.

Dickey, Christopher. *Securing the City: Inside America's Best Counterterror Force— the NYPD.* New York: Simon & Schuster, 2009.

Dizard, Jake, Christopher Walker, and Vanessa Tucker, eds. *Countries at the Crossroads: An Analysis of Democratic Governance, 2011.* New York: Freedom House; Lanham, MD: Rowman & Littlefield, 2011.

Dunn, Christopher. "Intergenerational Earnings Mobility in Brazil and Its Determinants." Unpublished paper, University of Michigan, September 2003.

Easterly, William. *The Tyranny of Experts: Economists, Dictators, and the Forgotten Rights of the Poor.* New York: Basic Books, 2013.

Economist Intelligence Unit. *Democracy Index 2014: Democracy and Its Dis-*

contents. *The Economist* 2015. http://www.sudestada.com.uy/Content/Articles/421a313a-d58f-462e-9b24-2504a37f6b56/Democracy-index-2014.pdf.

Eichengreen, Barry J. *The Korean Economy: From a Miraculous Past to a Sustainable Future.* Cambridge, MA: Harvard University Press, 2015.

Eichengreen, Barry J., Dwight H. Perkins, and Kwanho Shin. *From Miracle to Maturity: The Growth of the Korean Economy.* Cambridge, MA: Harvard University Press, 2012.

El-Gamal, Mahmoud A., and Amy Myers Jaffe. *Oil, Dollars, Debt, and Crises: The Global Curse of Black Gold.* Cambridge: Cambridge University Press, 2010.

Emmerson, Donald K. "Minding the Gap Between Democracy and Governance." In *Democracy in East Asia: A New Century,* edited by Larry Diamond, Marc F. Plattner, and Yun-han Chu, 227–36. Baltimore: Johns Hopkins University Press, 2013.

English, John. *Citizen of the World: The Life of Pierre Elliott Trudeau.* Vol. 1, *1919–1968.* Toronto: Alfred A. Knopf Canada, 2006.

———. *Just Watch Me: The Life of Pierre Elliott Trudeau, 1968–2000.* Toronto: Alfred A. Knopf Canada, 2009.

Erbach, Gregor. "Shale Gas and EU Energy Security." European Parliament Briefing, December 2014. http://www.europarl.europa.eu/RegData/etudes/BRIE/2014/542167/EPRS_BRI(2014)542167_REV1_EN.pdf.

Feldstein, Martin. "Oil Dependence and National Security: A Market-Based System for Reducing U.S. Vulnerability." Paper, National Bureau of Economic Research, October 2001. http://www.nber.org/feldstein/oil.html.

Fiszbein, Ariel, Norbert Schady, Francisco H. G. Ferreira, Margaret Grosh, Nial Kelleher, Pedro Olinto, and Emmanuel Skoufias. *Conditional Cash Transfers: Reducing Present and Future Poverty.* Washington, DC: World Bank, 2009.

Font, Mauricio A. *Transforming Brazil: A Reform Era in Perspective.* Lanham, MD: Rowman & Littlefield, 2003.

Fried, Brian J. "Distributive Politics and Conditional Cash Transfers: The Case of Brazil's Bolsa Família." *World Development* 40, no. 5 (2012): 1042–53.

Gillespie, Angus Kress. *Crossing Under the Hudson: The Story of the Holland and Lincoln Tunnels.* New Brunswick, NJ: Rivergate Books, 2011.

Gold, Russell. *The Boom: How Fracking Ignited the American Energy Revolution and Changed the World.* New York: Simon & Schuster, 2014.

Goldman Sachs Financial Workbench. *Emerging Markets Strategy: The Lulameter.* Goldman Sachs, June 2002. http://moya.bus.miami.edu/~sandrade/Lulameter_GS.pdf.

Gordon, Alastair. *Naked Airport: A Cultural History of the World's Most Revolutionary Structure.* Chicago: University of Chicago Press, 2004.

Gourevitch, Philip. *We Wish to Inform You That Tomorrow We Will Be Killed with Our Families*. New York: Farrar, Straus and Giroux, 1998.

Grant, Sandy. *Botswana: An Historical Anthology*. Cambridgeshire, UK: Melrose Books, 2012.

Gupta, L. "1998 Rwanda: Follow-Up Survey of Rwandan Children's Reactions to War Related Violence from the 1994 Genocide." UNICEF, 1998. http://www.unicef.org/evaldatabase/index_14242.html.

Hadiwinata, Bob S. *The Politics of NGOs in Indonesia: Developing Democracy and Managing a Movement*. London: RoutledgeCurzon, 2003.

Haggard, Stephan. *The Political Economy of the Asian Financial Crisis*. Washington, DC: Institute for International Economics, 2000.

Haggard, Stephan, and Myung-koo Kang. "The Politics of Growth in South Korea: Miracle, Crisis, and the New Market Economy." In *Oxford Handbook on the Politics of Development*, edited by Carol Lancaster and Nicolas van de Walle, Oxford: Oxford University Press, forthcoming.

Han, Yong-Sup. "The May Sixteenth Military Coup." In Byung-Kook Kim and Vogel, *Park Chung Hee Era*, 35–57.

Hanlon, Joseph, Armando Barrientos, and David Hulme. *Just Give Money to the Poor: The Development Revolution from the Global South*. Sterling, VA: Kumarian Press, 2010.

Harrison, Lawrence E. *The Central Liberal Truth: How Politics Can Change a Culture and Save It from Itself*. Oxford: Oxford University Press, 2008.

Harvey, Charles. "Banking Policy in Botswana: Orthodox but Untypical." Institute of Development Studies Working Paper, January 1996. http://www.ids.ac.uk/publication/banking-policy-in-botswana-orthodox-but-untypical.

Harvey, Charles, and Stephen R. Lewis Jr. *Policy Choice and Development Performance in Botswana*. New York: St. Martin's Press, 1990.

Hatzfeld, Jean. *The Antelope's Strategy: Living in Rwanda After the Genocide*. New York: Picador, 2010.

Hawkens, Freda. "Immigration Policy in the Late 1960s." In Cameron, *Multiculturalism and Immigration in Canada*, 59–64.

Hefner, Robert W. *Civil Islam: Muslims and Democratization in Indonesia*. Princeton, NJ: Princeton University Press, 2000.

———. "Shari'a Politics and Indonesian Democracy." *Review of Faith and International Affairs* 10, no. 4 (2012): 61–69.

Hinojosa-Ojeda, Raúl. "Raising the Floor for American Workers: The Economic Benefits of Comprehensive Immigration Reform." Center for American Progress and the Immigration Policy Center, January 2010. https://cdn.americanprogress.org/wp-content/uploads/2012/09/immigrationeconreport3.pdf.

Hirsch, Robert L., Roger Bezdek, and Robert Wendling. "Peaking of World Oil

Production: Impacts, Mitigation, and Risk Management." Paper sponsored by the National Energy Technology Laboratory, February 2005.

Holm, John D. "Botswana: A Paternalistic Democracy." *World Affairs* 150, no. 1 (Summer 1987): 21–30.

Holmes & Narver, Inc. *Project Gasbuggy Site Restoration Final Report*. United States Department of Energy, Nevada Operations Office, July 1983.

Hong, Euny. *The Birth of Korean Cool: How One Nation Is Conquering the World Through Pop Culture*. New York: Picador, 2014.

Howard, Paul, and Mark Riebling, eds. *Hard Won Lessons: Problem-Solving Principles for Local Police*. New York: Manhattan Institute for Policy Research, May 2005. http://www.manhattan-institute.org/pdf/scr_02.pdf.

Hughes, John. *Islamic Extremism and the War of Ideas: Lessons from Indonesia*. Stanford, CA: Hoover Institution Press, 2010.

Human Rights Watch. *Justice Compromised: The Legacy of Rwanda's Community-Based Gacaca Courts*. New York: Human Rights Watch, 2011.

Humphreys, Macartan, Jeffrey D. Sachs, and Jospeh E. Stilgitz, eds. *Escaping the Resource Curse*. New York: Columbia University Press, 2007.

Hunter, Wendy, and Timothy J. Power. "Rewarding Lula: Executive Power, Social Policy, and the Brazilian Elections of 2006." *Latin American Politics and Society* 49, no. 1 (Spring 2007): 1–30.

Hunter, Wendy, and Natasha Borges Sugiyama. "Assessing the Bolsa Família: Successes, Shortcomings, and Unknowns." Paper presented at Democratic Brazil Emergent, Brazilian Studies Programme, University of Oxford and the Brazil Institute, King's College London, February 21–22, 2013.

———. "Transforming Subjects into Citizens: Insights from Brazil's Bolsa Família." *Perspectives on Politics* 12, no. 4 (December 2014): 1–17.

Iimi, Atsushi. "Did Botswana Escape from the Resource Curse?" International Monetary Fund Working Paper, June 2006. https://www.imf.org/external/pubs/ft/wp/2006/wp06138.pdf.

Institute for Policy Analysis of Conflict. *Weak, Therefore Violent: The Mujahidin of Western Indonesia*. IPAC, 2013. http://file.understandingconflict.org/file/2013/11/IPAC_Weak_Therefore_Violent.pdf.

International Business Publications. *Indonesia Country Study Guide*. Vol. 1, *Strategic Information and Developments*. Washington, DC: International Business Publications, 2013.

International Crisis Group. "How Indonesia Extremists Regroup." Asia Report, July 16, 2012. http://www.crisisgroup.org/~/media/Files/asia/south-east-asia/indonesia/228-how-indonesian-extremists-regroup.pdf.

Jefferis, Keith. "Botswana and Diamond-Dependent Development." In *Botswana: Politics and Society*, edited by W. A. Edge and M. H. Lekorwe, 300–318. Pretoria: J. L. van Schaik, 1998.

———. "Macroeconomic Management in a Mineral-Rich Economy." Inter-

national Growth Center Policy Note 14/0105, March 2014. http://www
.theigc.org/wp-content/uploads/2014/09/Jefferis-2013-Policy-Brief.pdf.

Jones, Seth G. *A Persistent Threat: The Evolution of al Qa'ida and Other Salafi Jihadists*. Santa Monica, CA: Rand Corporation, 2014.

Jones, Sidney. "Indonesian Government Approaches to Radical Islam Since 1998." In Künkler and Stepan, *Democracy and Islam in Indonesia*, 109–25.

Kallen, Evelyn. "Multiculturalism: Ideology, Policy and Reality." In Cameron, *Multiculturalism and Immigration in Canada*, 78–85.

Kang, Susan L. *Human Rights and Labor Solidarity: Trade Unions in the Global Economy*. Philadelphia: University of Pennsylvania Press, 2012.

Kang, Won-Taek. "Missing Dictator in a New Democracy: Analyzing the 'Park Chung Hee Syndrome' in South Korea." *Political and Military Sociology: An Annual Review* 38 (2010): 1–25.

Katz, Bruce, and Jennifer Bradley. *The Metropolitan Revolution: How Cities and Metros Are Fixing Our Broken Politics and Fragile Economy*. Washington, DC: Brookings Institution Press, 2013.

Kelley, Ninette, and Michael Trebilcock. *The Making of the Mosaic: A History of Canadian Immigration Policy*. 2nd ed. Toronto: University of Toronto Press, 2010.

Kharas, Homi, and Geoffrey Gertz. "The New Global Middle Class: A Cross-Over from West to East." In *China's Emerging Middle Class: Beyond Economic Transformation*, edited by Cheng Li, 32–51. Washington, DC: Brookings Institution Press, 2010.

Kim, Byung-Kook. "Introduction: The Case for Political History." In Kim and Vogel, *Park Chung Hee Era*, 1–31.

———. "The Leviathan: Economic Bureaucracy under Park." In Kim and Vogel, *Park Chung Hee Era*, 200–232.

Kim, Byung-Kook, and Ezra F. Vogel, eds. *The Park Chung Hee Era: The Transformation of South Korea*. Cambridge, MA: Harvard University Press, 2011.

Kim, Eun Mee, and Gil-Sung Park. "The *Chaebol*." In Kim and Vogel, *Park Chung Hee Era*, 265–94.

Kim, Hyung-A. "State Building: The Military Junta's Path to Modernity Through Administrative Reform." In Kim and Vogel, *Park Chung Hee Era*, 85–112.

Kinzer, Stephen. *A Thousand Hills: Rwanda's Rebirth and the Man Who Dreamed It*. New York: John Wiley & Sons, 2009.

Klitgaard, Robert E. *Controlling Corruption*. Berkeley: University of California Press, 1988.

———. *Tropical Gangsters*. New York: Basic Books, 1990.

Knowles, Valerie. *Strangers at Our Gates: Canadian Immigration and Immigration Policy, 1540–2006*. Toronto: Dundurn Press, 2007.

Koo, Jahyeong, and Sherry L. Kiser. "Recovery from a Financial Crisis: The Case of South Korea." *Economic and Financial Review* (Fourth Quarter 2001): 24–36.

Krupnick, Alan, Zhongmin Wang, and Yushuang Wang. "Environmental Risks of Shale Gas Development in China." *Energy Policy* 75 (2014): 117–25.

Künkler, Mirjam, and Alfred C. Stepan, eds. *Democracy and Islam in Indonesia.* New York: Columbia University Press, 2013.

———. "Indonesian Democratization in Theoretical Perspective." In Künkler and Stepan, *Democracy and Islam in Indonesia,* 3–23.

Larson, Catherine Claire. *As We Forgive: Stories of Reconciliation from Rwanda.* Grand Rapids, MI: Zondervan, 2009.

Lavinas, Lena. "21st Century Welfare." *New Left Review* 84, no. 6 (November/December 2013): 5–40.

Lee, Chong-Sik. *Park Chung-Hee: From Poverty to Power.* Palos Verdes, CA: KHU Press, 2012.

Lee, Jeff. "The Failure of Political Islam in Indonesia: A Historical Narrative." *Stanford Journal of East Asian Affairs* 4, no. 1 (Winter 2004): 85–104.

Lee, Kuan Yew. *From Third World to First: The Singapore Story, 1965–2000.* New York: HarperCollins, 2000.

———. *The Singapore Story: Memoirs of Lee Kuan Yew.* Singapore: Times Editions, 1998.

———. *The Wit and Wisdom of Lee Kuan Yew.* Singapore: Editions Didier Millet, 2013.

Leith, J. Clark. *Why Botswana Prospered.* Montreal: McGill-Queen's University Press, 2005.

Li, Peter S. *Destination Canada: Immigration Debates and Issues.* Don Mills, ON: Oxford University Press, 2003.

Lim, Wonhyuk. "The Emergence of the *Chaebol* and the Origins of the '*Chaebol* Problem.'" In *Economic Crisis and Corporate Restructuring in Korea,* edited by Stephan Haggard, Wonhyuk Lim, and Euysung Kim, 35–52. Cambridge: Cambridge University Press, 2003.

Lindert, Kathy, and Vanina Vincensini. "Social Policy, Perceptions and the Press: An Analysis of the Media's Treatment of Conditional Cash Transfers in Brazil." World Bank Social Protection Discussion Paper, December 2010. http://siteresources.worldbank.org/SOCIALPROTECTION/Resources/SP-Discussion-papers/Safety-Nets-DP/1008.pdf.

Lindert, Kathy, Anja Linder, Jason Hobbs, and Bénédicte de la Brière. "The Nuts and Bolts of Brazil's Bolsa Família Program: Implementing Conditional Cash Transfers in a Decentralized Context." World Bank Special Protection Discussion Paper, May 2007. http://siteresources.worldbank.org/INTLACREGTOPLABSOCPRO/Resources/BRBolsaFamilia DiscussionPaper.pdf.

Masire, Quett Ketumile Joni. *Very Brave or Very Foolish? Memoirs of an African Democrat*. Gaborone: Macmillan Botswana, 2006.

McKay, John. *South Korea's Education and Skills Development: Some Lessons from Africa*, Global Best Practices, Report No. 2. Johannesburg: South African Institute of International Affairs, 2005, 17. http://dspace.africaportal .org/jspui/bitstream/123456789/30299/1/REPORT%202%20(2005)%20 -%20SOUTH%20KOREA'S%20EDUCATION%20SKILLS% 20DEVELOPMENT%20-%20SOME%20LESSONS%20FOR%20 AFRICA.pdf?1.

McKinsey Global Institute. *Reverse the Curse: Maximizing the Potential of Resource-Driven Economies*. McKinsey & Company, December 2013. http://www.mckinsey.com/insights/energy_resources_materials/reverse_ the_curse_maximizing_the_potential_of_resource_driven_economies.

Meagher, Patrick. "Anti-Corruption Agencies: A Review of Experience." Paper Prepared for the World Bank. IRIS Center, University of Maryland, August 2002. http://www1.worldbank.org/publicsector/anticorrupt/feb 06course/summaryWBPaperACagencies.pdf.

Meijia, Paul Ximena, and Vincent Castel. *Could Oil Shine Like Diamonds? How Botswana Avoided the Resource Curse and Its Implications for a New Libya*. African Development Bank, 2012. http://www.afdb.org/en/news-and -events/article/could-oil-shine-like-diamonds-how-botswana-avoided -the-resource-curse-and-its-implications-for-a-new-libya-9979/.

Mo, Jongryn, and Barry R. Weingast. *Korean Political and Economic Development: Crisis, Security, and Institutional Rebalancing*. Cambridge, MA: Harvard University Press, 2013.

Molyneux, Maxine. "Mothers at the Service of the New Poverty Agenda: Progresa/Oportunidades, Mexico's Conditional Transfer Programme." *Social Policy and Administration* 40, no. 4 (August 2006): 425–49.

Moon, Chung-in, and Byung-joon Jun. "Modernization Strategy: Ideas and Influences." In Kim and Vogel, *Park Chung Hee Era*, 115–39.

Mujani, Saiful, and R. William Liddle. "Muslim Indonesia's Secular Democracy." *Asian Survey* 49, no. 4 (July/August 2009): 573–90.

Mungazi, Dickson A. *We Shall Not Fail: Values in the National Leadership of Seretse Khama, Nelson Mandela, and Julius Nyerere*. Trenton, NJ: Africa World Press, 2005.

Mushabac, Jane, and Angela Wigan. *A Short and Remarkable History of New York City*. New York: Fordham University Press, 1999.

National Commission on Terrorist Attacks upon the United States. *The 9/11 Commission Report*. July 22, 2004. http://www.9-11commission.gov/ report/911Report.pdf.

Ng, Irene. *The Singapore Lion: A Biography of S. Rajaratnam*. Singapore: Institute of Southeast Asian Studies, 2010.

Noland, Marcus. "Post-Conflict Planning and Reconstruction: Lessons from the American Experience in Korea." East-West Center Working Paper, June 2010. http://www.eastwestcenter.org/system/tdf/private/econwp112 .pdf?file=1&type=node&id=32422.

Nyati-Ramahobo, Lydia. "The Language Situation in Botswana." In *Language Planning and Policy in Africa*. Vol. 1, *Botswana, Malawi, Mozambique, and South Africa*, edited by Richard B. Baldauf and Robert B. Kaplan, 21–78. Clevedon: Multilingual Matters, 2004.

Nyirubugara, Olivier. *Complexities and Dangers of Remembering and Forgetting in Rwanda*. Vol. 1, *Memory Traps*. Leiden, Netherlands: Sidestone Press, 2013.

Oehlers, Alfred. "Corruption: The Peculiarities of Singapore." In *Corruption and Good Governance in Asia*, edited by Nicholas Tarling, 149–64. London: Routledge, 2005.

Onoma, Ato Kwamena. *The Politics of Property Rights Institutions in Africa*. Cambridge: Cambridge University Press, 2010.

Orrú, Marco. "Dirigiste Capitalism in France and South Korea." In *The Economic Organization of East Asian Capitalism*, edited by Marco Orrú, Nicole Woolsey Biggart, and Gary G. Hamilton, 368–82. Thousand Oaks, CA: Sage, 1997.

Parent, Geneviève. "Reconciliation and Justice After Genocide: A Theoretical Exploration." *Genocide Studies and Prevention: An International Journal* 5, no. 3 (2010): 277–92.

Park, Chung Hee, and Shin Bum Shik. *Major Speeches by Korea's Park Chung Hee*. Seoul: Hollym Corporation, 1970.

Pegg, Scott. "Has Botswana Beaten the Resource Curse?" In *Mineral Rents and the Financing of Social Policy*, edited by Katja Hujo, 257–84. Basingstoke, UK: Palgrave Macmillan, 2012.

Pinker, Steven. *The Better Angels of Our Nature: Why Violence Has Declined*. New York: Viking, 2011.

Pisani, Elizabeth. *Indonesia, Etc.: Exploring the Improbable Nation*. New York: W. W. Norton, 2014.

Porter, Michael D., Gentry White, and Lorraine Mazerolle. "Innovative Methods for Terrorism and Counterterrorism Data." In *Evidence-Based Counterterrorism Policy*, edited by Cynthia Lum and Leslie W. Kennedy, 91–112. New York: Springer, 2011.

Pozen, Joanna, Richard Neugebauer, and Joseph Ntaganira. "Assessing the Rwanda Experiment: Popular Perceptions of *Gacaca* in Its Final Phase." *International Journal of Transitional Justice* 8, no. 1 (2014): 1–22.

Proctor, J. H. "The House of Chiefs and the Political Development of Botswana." *Journal of Modern African Studies* 6, no. 1 (1968): 59–79.

Quah, Jon S. T. *Combating Corruption Singapore-Style*. Maryland Series in Contemporary Asian Studies, no. 2. Baltimore: University of Maryland Francis King Carey School of Law, 2007.

———. "Curbing Corruption in a One-Party Dominant System: Learning from Singapore's Experience." In *Preventing Corruption in Asia: Institutional Design and Policy Capacity,* edited by Ting Gong and Stephen K. Ma, 131–47. London: Routledge, 2009.

———. "Different Paths to Curbing Corruption: A Comparative Analysis." In *Different Paths to Curbing Corruption: Lessons from Denmark, Finland, Hong Kong, New Zealand and Singapore,* edited by Jon S. T. Quah, 1–22. London: Emerald Publishing, 2013.

Ranstorp, Magnus. "Preventing Violent Radicalization and Terrorism: The Case of Indonesia." Center for Asymmetric Threat Studies, Swedish National Defence College, 2009. https://www.fhs.se/Documents/Externwebben/forskning/centrumbildningar/CATS/publikationer/Preventing%20Violent%20Radicalization%20and%20Terrorism%20-%20The%20Case%20of%20Indonesia.pdf.

Redfern, John. *Ruth and Seretse: "A Disreputable Transaction."* London: Camelot Press, 1995.

Reitz, Jeffrey G. "Economic Opportunity, Multiculturalism, and the Roots of Popular Support for High Immigration in Canada." In *Anti-immigrant Sentiments, Actions and Policies in the North American Region and the European Union,* edited by Mónica Verea. Mexico City: Center for Research on North America, Universidad Nacional Autónoma de México, 2012.

———. "Pro-immigration Canada: Social and Economic Roots of Popular Views." Institute for Research on Public Policy Study, paper no. 20. October 2011. http://oppenheimer.mcgill.ca/IMG/pdf/IRPP_Study_no20.pdf.

Reppetto, Thomas A. *Battleground New York City: Countering Spies, Saboteurs, and Terrorists Since 1861.* Washington, DC: Potomac Books, 2012.

Rettig, Max. "*Gacaca*: Truth, Justice, and Reconciliation in Postconflict Rwanda?" *African Studies Review* 51, no. 3 (December 2008): 25–50.

Riccio, James, Nadine Dechausay, Cynthia Miller, Stephen Nuñez, Nandita Verma, and Edith Yang. "Conditional Cash Transfers in New York City: The Continuing Story of the Opportunity NYC–Family Rewards Demonstration." MDRC, September 2013. http://files.eric.ed.gov/fulltext/ED545453.pdf.

Rodrik, Dani, Gene Grossman, and Victor Norman. "Getting Interventions Right: How South Korea and Taiwan Grew Rich." *Economic Policy* 10, no. 20 (April 1995): 53–107.

Ross, Michael L. *The Oil Curse: How Petroleum Wealth Shapes the Development of Nations.* Princeton, NJ: Princeton University Press, 2012.

Rotberg, Robert I., ed. *Corruption, Global Security, and World Order.* Washington, DC: Brookings Institution Press, 2009.

———. "How Corruption Compromises World Peace and Stability." In Rotberg, *Corruption, Global Security, and World Order,* 1–26.

———. "Leadership Alters Corrupt Behavior." In Rotberg, *Corruption, Global Security, and World Order,* 341–58.

———. *Transformative Political Leadership: Making a Difference in the Developing World.* Chicago: University of Chicago Press, 2012.

Sadat, Leila Nadya. "The Legacy of the International Criminal Tribunal for Rwanda." Whitney R. Harris World Law Institute Occasional Paper, July 2012. http://law.wustl.edu/harris/documents/ICTRLecture-Legacy Ad%20HocTribunals9.12.12.pdf.

Schapera, Isaac. "The Political Organization of the Ngwato of Bechuanaland Protectorate." In *African Political Systems,* edited by E. E. Evans-Pritchard and Meyer Fortes, 56–82. Oxford: Oxford University Press, 1940.

Scher, Daniel, and Christine MacAulay. "The Promise of Imihigo: Decentralized Service Delivery in Rwanda, 2006–2010." Innovations for Successful Societies, Princeton University, 2010. http://successfulsocieties.princeton .edu/sites/successfulsocieties/files/Policy_Note_ID133.pdf.

Schuck, Peter H. *Why Government Fails So Often: And How It Can Do Better.* Princeton, NJ: Princeton University Press, 2014.

Schwartz, Mildred A. *Public Opinion and Canadian Identity.* Scarborough, ON: Fitzhenry and Whiteside, 1967.

Scott, Robyn. *Twenty Chickens for a Saddle: The Story of an African Childhood.* New York: Penguin Press, 2008.

Sebastian, Leonard C. *Realpolitik Ideology: Indonesia's Use of Military Force.* Singapore: Institute of Southeast Asian Studies, 2006.

Sheehan, Michael A. *Crush the Cell: How to Defeat Terrorism Without Terrorizing Ourselves.* New York: Three Rivers Press, 2008.

Soares, Sergi, Rafael Guerreiro Osório, Fábio Veras Soares, Marcelo Madeiros, and Eduardo Zepeda. "Conditional Cash Transfers in Brazil, Chile, and Mexico: Impacts upon Inequality." International Poverty Center Working Paper, April 2007. http://www.ipc-undp.org/pub/IPCWorkingPaper35 .pdf.

Starr, Pamela K. "Mexico's Problematic Reforms." *Current History* 113, no. 760 (February 2014): 51–56.

Stevens, Paul. "The 'Shale Gas Revolution': Hype and Reality." Chatham House Report, September 2010. https://www.chathamhouse.org/sites/files/ chathamhouse/public/Research/Energy,%20Environment%20and%20 Development/r_0910stevens.pdf.

Steward, John. "Only Healing Heals: Concepts and Methods of Psycho-Social Healing in Post-Genocide Rwanda." In *After Genocide: Transitional Justice, Post-Conflict Reconstruction and Reconciliation in Rwanda and Beyond,* edited by Phil Clark and Zachary D. Kaufman, 171–90. New York: Columbia University Press, 2009.

Stiglitz, Joseph E. *Globalization and Its Discontents*. New York: W. W. Norton, 2002.

Straus, Scott, and Lars Waldorf, eds. *Remaking Rwanda: State Building and Human Rights After Mass Violence*. Madison: University of Wisconsin Press, 2011.

Sugiyama, Natasha Borges, and Wendy Hunter. "Whither Clientelism? Good Governance and Brazil's Bolsa Família Program." *Comparative Politics* 46, no. 1 (October 2013): 43–62.

Svensson, Jakob. "Eight Questions About Corruption." *Journal of Economic Perspectives* 19, no. 3 (Summer 2005): 19–42.

Tian, Lei, Zhongmin Wang, Alan Krupnick, and Xiaoli Liu. "Stimulating Shale Gas Development in China: A Comparison with the US Experience." Resources for the Future Discussion Paper, July 2014. http://www.rff.org/files/sharepoint/WorkImages/Download/RFF-DP-14-18.pdf.

Tlou, Thomas, Neil Parsons, and Willie Henderson. *Seretse Khama, 1921–80*. Braamfontein: Macmillan South Africa, 1995.

Triadafilopoulos, Triadafilos. "Dismantling White Canada: Race, Rights, and the Origins of the Points System." In *Wanted and Welcome?: Policies for Highly Skilled Immigrants in Comparative Perspective*, edited by Triadafilos Triadafilopoulos. New York: Springer Science and Business Media, 2013.

Trudeau, Pierre Elliott. *Memoirs*. Toronto: McClelland & Stewart, 1993.

Tudor, Daniel. *Korea: The Impossible Country*. North Clarendon, VT: Tuttle Publishing, 2012.

Turnbull, C. M. *A History of Singapore, 1819–1988*. Oxford: Oxford University Press, 1989.

Twagilimana, Aimable. *Historical Dictionary of Rwanda*. New York: Rowman & Littlefield, 1997.

United States Department of State. *Country Reports on Terrorism 2013*. http://www.state.gov/j/ct/rls/crt/2013.

United States Energy Information Administration. *Annual Energy Outlook 2014: With Projections to 2040*. http://www.eia.gov/forecasts/aeo/pdf/0383(2014).pdf.

———. *Technically Recoverable Shale Oil and Shale Gas Resources: An Assessment of 137 Shale Formations in 41 Countries Outside the United States*. Washington, DC, 2013. http://www.eia.gov/analysis/studies/worldshalegas/archive/2013/pdf/fullreport_2013.pdf.

Uvin, Peter. "The Introduction of a Modernized *Gacaca* for Judging Suspects of Participation in the Genocide and the Massacres of 1994 in Rwanda." Discussion paper prepared for the Belgian Secretary of State for Development Cooperation, 2000. https://www.researchgate.net/publication/260399376_The_Introduction_of_a_Modernized_Gacaca_for_Judging_Suspects_of_Participation_in_the_Genocide_and_the_Massacres_of_1994_in_Rwanda_A_Discussion_Paper.

Vasil, Raj. *Governing Singapore: A History of National Development and Democracy.* St. Leonards, NSW, Australia: Allen & Unwin, 2000.

Vogel, Ezra F. "Nation Rebuilders: Mustafa Kemal Atatürk, Lee Kuan Yew, Deng Xiaoping, and Park Chung Hee." In Byung-Kook Kim and Vogel, *Park Chung Hee Era,* 513–41.

Waters, Mary C., and Marisa Gerstein Pineau, eds. *The Integration of Immigrants into American Society.* Washington, DC: National Academies Press, 2015.

Waugh, Colin M. *Paul Kagame and Rwanda: Power, Genocide and the Rwandan Patriotic Front.* Jefferson, NC: McFarland & Company, 2004.

Williams, Susan. *Colour Bar: The Triumph of Seretse Khama and His Nation.* New York: Penguin, 2007.

World Bank. *World Development Report 2011: Conflict, Security, and Development.* Washington, DC: World Bank, 2011.

Yergin, Daniel. *The Quest: Energy, Security, and the Remaking of the Modern World.* New York: Penguin Press, 2011.

Zonis, Marvin, Dan Lefkovitz, and Sam Wilkin. *The Kimchi Matters: Global Business and Local Politics in a Crisis-Driven World.* Chicago: Agate Publishing, 2003.

Zuckerman, Gregory. *The Frackers: The Outrageous Inside Story of the New Billionaire Wildcatters.* New York: Portfolio, 2013.

ACKNOWLEDGMENTS

This is my first book, which means that I started it with some ludicrously misguided notions about what the experience would be like. One of the biggest was assuming that it would be a solitary endeavor. How wrong that turned out to be.

The truth is that producing a book like this one involves a huge number of people. I'm incredibly grateful to all of them. In many cases, I never could have pulled this off without their help. In a few others, I suppose I could have, but neither I nor the book would have emerged as well as we did. Assuming that the end result is actually any good, they deserve most of the credit for it.

I want to start by thanking one of the first non-blood relatives I told about this project: Andrew Wylie. To my amazement, the world's most powerful literary agent offered to represent me on the spot. All these months later, I continue to find Andrew's confidence in me slightly mystifying. But whatever his reasoning, he's become a zealous champion of mine, and I feel very lucky to have him and his staff, especially James Pullen, on my side.

I'm also grateful to Andrew for connecting me with Tim Duggan, who became my editor at Crown. As a longtime editor myself, I'd always rather be the one wielding the red pen. But Tim made the role-reversal as painless as possible, and his smart suggestions improved my draft significantly. He also knew just when my self-confidence needed bolstering. He and everyone else at Crown were a delight to work with—especially Sarah Pekdemir, Penny Simon, William Wolfslau, and Norman Watkins. So was Andy Young, my sharp-eyed fact-checker.

A long list of friends and colleagues helped me navigate the writing process and shape my ideas along the way. They read drafts, offered counsel, listened to me kvetch, and kept me going when I doubted myself. So thank you to Eric Block, Steven Cook, Avi Gesser, Paul Golob, Laurie Hays, Daniel Kurtz-Phelan, Adam Kushner, Anja Manuel, Tyler Maroney, Adam Segal, Geoff Shandler, Ruchir Sharma, Peter Van Praagh, Joshua Wallack, and Jonathan Weisstub. Thanks especially to my fidus Achates, Alexander Hardy, who played the role of amateur psychologist (despite his surgical training) and gave me advice (inevitably hilarious, often helpful, occasionally irresponsible) on everything from titles to typography.

I owe a big debt to John Delury, Philip Gourevitch, Keith Jefferis, Joshua Kurlantzick, Shannon O'Neil, Seth Pinsky, Jon S. T. Quah, Jeffrey Reitz, Michael Shellenberger, Julia Sweig, and Valerie Wirtschafter for reading individual chapters and correcting my worst mistakes. And I owe even more to three good friends and colleagues who also happen to be crack professional editors. Stuart Reid, Carla Robbins, and Justin Vogt foolishly agreed to pore over every word in this book. Then they actually did it, and the result is much better for it.

At various points, Nikita Lalwani, Anna Kordunsky, and Jordan Schneider contributed research, as did my assistant Christine Clark, who worked tirelessly to help me sort through the literature, nail down statistics, and track down sources; she has made me look far more knowledgeable than I actually am. As you'd expect, this book involved a lot of reporting, and I'm grateful to Flavia Antunes, Rosanna Fuentes Berain, Ambassador Robert Blake, Joe Cochrane, Aaron Connelly, Alex Feldman, Nisid Hajari, Ana Paula Odorica Mariscal, Alexandre Menezes, Ambassador Earl Miller, and Maurice Tempelsman for connecting me to the right people in the dozen countries I visited in the course of that work. Let me also thank Lucy Congers (Mexico) and Rusma (Indonesia) for acting as translators.

Back in New York, Joanna and Daniel Rose provided me with an extraordinary asset most urban writers can only dream of: a quiet writing office. It proved an invaluable gift for which I'm deeply indebted to them.

Of course, all the time I spent in that office was time I didn't spend at my day job. Yet my wonderful colleagues at *Foreign Affairs* and the Council on Foreign Relations never—well, rarely—complained. I know my absence made life harder for them in some ways (though probably easier in others). So for their forbearance, support, and advice, I want to thank Richard Haass, Jim Lindsay, Jan Mowder Hughes, Andrew Palladino, Jake Meth, Iva Zoric, and Irina Faskianos. And special thanks to Katie Allawala, Stuart Reid, Justin Vogt, Ann Tappert, Sarah Foster, and everyone else at the magazine for stepping up and stepping in while I was obsessing over *The Fix*.

Finally, I need to thank the people who made me the kind of person who could write this book in the first place.

I've been incredibly lucky in my career to enjoy the mentorship of several brilliant writers, editors, and thinkers. Two deserve mention here. Fareed Zakaria has hired me twice: first as a junior editor at *Foreign Affairs* (when I knew next to nothing about journalism *or* foreign affairs) and then at *Newsweek*. In the years since, he has provided endless assistance, advice, and friendship. I don't know where I'd be without all that, but I know I wouldn't be here. Gideon Rose, meanwhile, has been the best boss I can imagine. He has been unbelievably generous and patient with me, in some ways I deserved but many that I didn't. And he has shaped the way I think about politics and international affairs more than any other individual.

Except for my family, that is—who also gave me the confidence to believe that my work was worth sharing. Thank you to my brothers, Noah and Andrew, and their wives, Julie and Tina. As for my parents, Bill and Rochelle, the words "thank you" don't begin to do justice to the debt I owe you, or to the gratitude I feel. But they're the best I have to offer. Know that I'm incredibly proud to be your son and to be able to share this book with you, and know that *I* know that without your decades of love, your teaching, your hard work, and your inestimable support there would be no book (of course, there'd be no me either).

Finally, I want to thank the four people to whom I dedicate *The Fix*.

Gerome and Novi: you were amazingly patient with me during the time it took me to write this, even though it meant I was home less and distracted more when I was there. Your love and good cheer and exuberant humor and irrational faith in me always kept me going—and made me work as efficiently as I could, so that I could get back to you guys as soon as possible.

Leo: you're still too young to understand these words. But as you'll someday learn, you and this book are twins of a sort. Your mom and I first found out about you the same week that I signed my contract with Crown, and you and the book grew and took shape simultaneously— though you beat it into the world by arriving in between chapters 6 and 7. What I thought would be impossible timing turned out to be perfect timing. For you have brought me improbable amounts of joy and strength, to a degree I never dared hope for. In many ways, this book is your book.

And last, my sweet Alexis: I struggle to know how to thank you, for you've given me the most of all. You are my first reader, my best friend, my closest confidante. You made this book possible. You made this book better. I don't know how I'll ever repay you for it and for everything else. But I'm going to do my damnedest.

Index